Survival Communications
in California: Northern Region

CALIFORNIA REPUBLIC

John E. Parnell, KK4HWX

13 ISBN 978-1-62512-208-7

Cover design by:
Lynda Colón
FREELANCE GRAPHIC DESIGN &
MARKETING COMMUNICATIONS
www.hirelynda.webs.com

I do wish to acknowledge the hard work of **Angie Shirley** in putting together the database required for this book. Without her efforts, this book could not have been done.

Titles available in this series:

Survival Communications in Alabama
Survival Communications in Alaska
Survival Communications in Arizona
Survival Communications in Arkansas
Survival Communications in California
Survival Communications in Colorado
Survival Communications in Connecticut
Survival Communications in Delaware
Survival Communications in Florida
Survival Communications in Georgia
Survival Communications in Hawaii
Survival Communications in Idaho
Survival Communications in Illinois
Survival Communications in Indiana
Survival Communications in Iowa
Survival Communications in Kansas
Survival Communications in Kentucky
Survival Communications in Louisiana
Survival Communications in Maine
Survival Communications in Maryland
Survival Communications in Massachusetts
Survival Communications in Michigan
Survival Communications in Minnesota
Survival Communications in Mississippi
Survival Communications in Missouri

Survival Communications in Montana
Survival Communications in Nebraska
Survival Communications in Nevada
Survival Communications in New Hampshire
Survival Communications in New Jersey
Survival Communications in New Mexico
Survival Communications in New York
Survival Communications in North Carolina
Survival Communications in North Dakota
Survival Communications in Ohio
Survival Communications in Oklahoma
Survival Communications in Oregon
Survival Communications in Pennsylvania
Survival Communications in Rhode Island
Survival Communications in South Carolina
Survival Communications in South Dakota
Survival Communications in Tennessee
Survival Communications in Texas
Survival Communications in Utah
Survival Communications in Vermont
Survival Communications in Virginia
Survival Communications in Washington
Survival Communications in West Virginia
Survival Communications in Wisconsin
Survival Communications in Wyoming

The above titles are available from your favorite online or brick-and-mortar bookstore or directly from the publisher at Tutor Turtle Press LLC, 1027 S. Pendleton St. – Suite B-10, Easley, SC 29642.

TABLE OF CONTENTS

Appendix A – California Ham Radio Clubs

ARRL Affiliated Amateur and Ham Radio Clubs – By City

Appendix B – California: Central Region Ham Licensees by City

Survival Communications in California

Perhaps you have prepared for WTSHTF or TEOTWAWKI with respect to food, water, self-defense and shelter. But what about communication?

Whenever there is a disaster (hurricane, earthquake, economic collapse, nuclear war, EMF, solar eruption, etc.), the normal means of communication that we're all reliant upon (cell phone, land line phone, the Internet, etc.) will probably be, at best, sporadic and at worst, non-existent.

As this author sees it, short of smoke signals and mirrors, there are three options for communication in "trying times": (1) GMRS or FRS radios; (2) CB radios; and (3) ham or amateur radio. Let's consider each of these options to come up with the most acceptable one.

GMRS (General Mobile Radio Service) / FRS (Family Radio Service)

GMRS (General Mobile Radio Service) / FRS (Family Radio Service) radios work optimally over short distances where there is minimal interference. Originally designed to be used as pagers, particularly inside a building or other such confined area, these radios are low-cost and convenient to carry. Unfortunately their small size and light weight comes with a trade-off – short range and short battery life. These radios are supposed to be able to communicate for up to 25-30 miles. Right. That's on level terrain, without buildings or trees getting in the way. While battery life technology is constantly improving, you will need spare batteries to keep communicating or someway of recharging the ones in the radio. In this author's opinion, GMRS/FRS radios are not first choice when concerned with medium or long range communication.

CB (Citizens Band)

CB (Citizens Band) radios operate in a frequency range originally reserved for ham or amateur radio operation. Because of the overwhelming number of people wishing quick, low-cost, regulation-free communication, the FCC (Federal Communication Commission) split off a portion of the frequency spectrum and allowed anyone to purchase a CB radio and start communicating. No test. No license. Just personal/business communication. Today, CB radios are readily available in such outlets as eBay and Craigslist. This author has seen them at yard/garage/tag sales and at flea markets.

CB radios come in a variety of "flavors." Fixed units, sometimes referred to as base units are intended for home use. For the most part, they derive their power from the utility company. In the event of loss of electricity, most base units can also be connected to a 12-volt battery, like that in your car/truck. If you choose to obtain a fixed unit, make sure you know how to connect the unit to the battery – ahead of time. Trying to figure this out when you're under extra stress is not a good situation.

A second type of CB radio is designed to be mobile, that is, installed in your car/truck. It gets its power from the vehicle's battery. You can either attach an antenna permanently to the vehicle or have a removable, magnetic type antenna.

The third type of CB radio is designed for handheld use. They are small and light. Most weigh less than a pound and operate on batteries. Yes, using batteries in a CB poses the same limitations as those by the GMRS/FRS radios, but have the added advantage that most handheld units come with a cigarette lighter adapter. Comes in handy when you are on the move and wish to be able to communicate both from a vehicle and also when you have to abandon it.

While they have a greater range than GMRS/FRS radios, CB radios are, legally, limited to operate on 40 channels, with a power rating of four (4) watts or less. Yes, it is possible to alter CB radios to get around these limitations, but not legally,

Ham/Amateur Radio

Ham/Amateur radio is very appealing. With a ham radio, you are not limited to less than 50 miles, but can communicate with anyone in the world (who also has access to a ham radio, of course).

Standardized Amateur Radio Prepper Communications Plan

In the event of a nationwide catastrophic disaster, the nationwide network of Amateur Radio licensed preppers will need a set of standardized meeting frequencies to share information and coordinate activities between various prepper groups. This Standardized Amateur Radio Communications Plan establishes a set of frequencies on the 80 meter, 40 meter, 20 meter, and 2 meter Amateur Radio bands for use during these types of catastrophic disasters.

Routine nets will not be held on all of these frequencies, but preppers are encouraged to use them when coordinating with other preppers on a routine basis. Routine nets may be conducted by The American Preparedness Radio Net (TAPRN) on these or other frequencies as they see fit. However, TAPRN will promote the use of these standardized frequencies by all Amateur Radio licensed preppers during times of catastrophic disaster. The promotion of this Standardized Amateur Radio Communications Plan is encouraged by all means within the prepper community, including via Amateur Radio, Twitter, Facebook, and various blogs.

Standardized Frequencies and Modes
80 Meters – 3.818 MHz LSB (TAPRN Net: Sundays at 9 PM ET) 40 Meters – 7.242 MHz LSB 40 Meters Morse Code / Digital – 7.073 MHz USB (TAPRN: Sundays at 7:30 PM ET on CONTESTIA 4/250) 20 Meters – 14.242 MHz USB 2 Meters – 146.420 MHz FM

Nets and Network Etiquette

In times of nationwide catastrophic disaster, the ability of any one prepper to initiate and sustain themselves as a net control may be limited by the availability of power and other resource shortages. However, all licensed preppers are encouraged to maintain a listening watch on these frequencies as often as possible during a catastrophic disaster. Preppers may routinely announce themselves in the following manner:

• This is [Your Callsign Phonetically] in [Your State], maintaining a listening watch on [Standard Frequency] for any preppers on frequency seeking information or looking to provide information. Please call [Your Callsign Phonetically]. Preppers exchanging information that may require follow up should agree upon a designated time to return to the frequency and provide further information. If other stations are utilizing the frequency at the designated time you return, maintain watch and proceed with your communications when those stations are finished. If your communications are urgent and the stations on frequency are not passing information of a critical nature, interrupt with the word "Break" and request use of the frequency.

For More Information

Catastrophe Network: http://www.catastrophenetwork.org or @CatastropheNet on Twitter The American Preparedness Radio Network: http://www.taprn.com or @TAPRN on Twitter

© 2011 Catastrophe Network, Please Distribute Freely

In order to use a ham radio, legally, one must be licensed to do so by the FCC (other countries have analogous governmental bodies to regulate ham radio). To obtain a license is quite easy – take a test and pay your license fee. There are currently three classes of license – Technician, General, and Amateur Extra. With each of these licenses come specific abilities.

Technician class is the beginning level. The exam consists of 35 multiple choice questions randomly drawn from a pool of 395 questions. The question pool is readily available online for free downloading (http://www.ncvec.org/downloads/Revised%20Element%202.Pdf) or in such publications at *Ham Radio License Manual Revised 2nd Edition* (ISBN 978-0-87259-097-7). The current Technician pool of questions is to be used from July 1, 2010 to June 30, 2014. Be sure the question pool you are studying from is current. You will need to score at least 26 correct to pass. (Do not worry, Morse Code is no longer on the test, although many ham operators use it anyway.) You do not need to take a formal class in order to qualify to take the exam. You can learn the material on your own. Most people spend 10-15 hours studying and then successfully take the exam. The cost of taking the exam is under $20. The exam is given in MANY locations throughout the US. Usually the exam is given by area ham clubs. You do not have to belong to the club to take the exam. Check Appendix A for a listing of clubs in California.

Topics for the Technician License in Amateur Radio

The Technician license exam covers such topics as basic regulations, operating practices, and electronic theory, with a focus on VHF and UHF applications. Below is the syllabus for the Technician Class.

Subelement T1 – FCC Rules, descriptions and definitions for the amateur radio service, operator and station license responsibilities

[6 Exam Questions – 6 Groups]

T1A – Amateur Radio services; purpose of the amateur service, amateur-satellite service, operator/primary station license grant, where FCC rules are codified, basis and purpose of FCC rules, meanings of basic terms used in FCC rules

T1B – Authorized frequencies; frequency allocations, ITU regions, emission type, restricted sub-bands, spectrum sharing, transmissions near band edges

T1C – Operator classes and station call signs; operator classes, sequential, special event, and vanity call sign systems, international communications, reciprocal operation, station license licensee, places where the amateur service is regulated by the FCC, name and address on ULS, license term, renewal, grace period

T1D – Authorized and prohibited transmissions

T1E – Control operator and control types; control operator required, eligibility, designation of control operator, privileges and duties, control point, local, automatic and remote control, location of control operator

T1F – Station identification and operation standards; special operations for repeaters and auxiliary stations, third party communications, club stations, station security, FCC inspection

---

Subelement T2 – Operating Procedures

[3 Exam Questions – 3 Groups]

T2A – Station operation; choosing an operating frequency, calling another station, test transmissions, use of minimum power, frequency use, band plans

T2B – VHF/UHF operating practices; SSB phone, FM repeater, simplex, frequency offsets, splits and shifts, CTCSS, DTMF, tone squelch, carrier squelch, phonetics

T2C – Public service; emergency and non-emergency operations, message traffic handling

---

Subelement T3 – Radio wave characteristics, radio and electromagnetic properties, propagation modes

[3 Exam Questions – 3 Groups]

T3A – Radio wave characteristics; how a radio signal travels; distinctions of HF, VHF and UHF; fading, multipath; wavelength vs. penetration; antenna orientation

T3B – Radio and electromagnetic wave properties; the electromagnetic spectrum, wavelength vs. frequency, velocity of electromagnetic waves

T3C – Propagation modes; line of sight, sporadic E, meteor, aurora scatter, tropospheric ducting, F layer skip, radio horizon

Subelement T4 - Amateur radio practices and station setup

[2 Exam Questions – 2 Groups]

T4A – Station setup; microphone, speaker, headphones, filters, power source, connecting a computer, RF grounding

T4B – Operating controls; tuning, use of filters, squelch, AGC, repeater offset, memory channels

Subelement T5 – Electrical principles, math for electronics, electronic principles, Ohm's Law

[4 Exam Questions – 4 Groups]

T5A – Electrical principles; current and voltage, conductors and insulators, alternating and direct current

T5B – Math for electronics; decibels, electronic units and the metric system

T5C – Electronic principles; capacitance, inductance, current flow in circuits, alternating current, definition of RF, power calculations

T5D – Ohm's Law

Subelement T6 – Electrical components, semiconductors, circuit diagrams, component functions

[4 Exam Groups – 4 Questions]

T6A – Electrical components; fixed and variable resistors, capacitors, and inductors; fuses, switches, batteries

T6B – Semiconductors; basic principles of diodes and transistors

T6C – Circuit diagrams; schematic symbols

T6D – Component functions

Subelement T7 – Station equipment, common transmitter and receiver problems, antenna measurements and troubleshooting, basic repair and testing

[4 Exam Questions – 4 Groups]

T7A – Station radios; receivers, transmitters, transceivers

T7B – Common transmitter and receiver problems; symptoms of overload and overdrive, distortion, interference, over and under modulation, RF feedback, off frequency signals; fading and noise; problems with digital communications interfaces

T7C – Antenna measurements and troubleshooting; measuring SWR, dummy loads, feedline failure modes

T7D – Basic repair and testing; soldering, use of a voltmeter, ammeter, and ohmmeter

Subelement T8 – Modulation modes, amateur satellite operation, operating activities, non-voice communications

[4 Exam Questions – 4 Groups]

T8A – Modulation modes; bandwidth of various signals

T8B – Amateur satellite operation; Doppler shift, basic orbits, operating protocols

T8C – Operating activities; radio direction finding, radio control, contests, special event stations, basic linking over Internet

T8D – Non-voice communications; image data, digital modes, CW, packet, PSK31

Subelement T9 – Antennas, feedlines

[2 Exam Groups – 2 Questions]

T9A – Antennas; vertical and horizontal, concept of gain, common portable and mobile antennas, relationships between antenna length and frequency

T9B – Feedlines; types, losses vs. frequency, SWR concepts, matching, weather protection, connectors

Subelement T0 – AC power circuits, antenna installation, RF hazards

[3 Exam Questions – 3 Groups]

T0A – AC power circuits; hazardous voltages, fuses and circuit breakers, grounding, lightning protection, battery safety, electrical code compliance

T0B – Antenna installation; tower safety, overhead power lines

T0C – RF hazards; radiation exposure, proximity to antennas, recognized safe power levels, exposure to others

Once your name and call sign are available in the FCC database, you have the privilege of operating on all VHF (2 m) and UHF (70 cm) frequencies above 30 megahertz (MHz) and HF frequencies 80, 40, and 15 meter, and on the 10 meter band using Morse code (CW), voice, and digital mode. For a Technician license in California, your call sign will consist of a two-letter prefix beginning with K or W, the number six (6), and a three-letter suffix. The single digit number in the call sign is determined according to which area of the US you obtain your first license. Even though you may move to another state, you keep this number in your call sign. This is also true should you upgrade to a higher license and get a new call sign. The numeral portion of your call sign stays the same.

Call Sign Numbers

Below is a chart showing the various numbers and the state(s) in which you would obtain the number.

Call Sign Number	State(s)
0	CO, IA, KS, MN, MO, NE, ND, SD
1	CT, ME, MA, NH, RI, VT
2	NJ, NY
3	DE, DC, MD, PA
4	AL, FL, GA, KY, NC, SC, TN, VA
5	AR, LA, MS, NM, OK, TX
6	CA
7	AZ, ID, MT, NV, OR, WA, UT, WY
8	MI, OH, WV
9	IL, IN, WI

Residents of Alaska may have any of the following call sign prefixes assigned to them: AL0-7, KL0-7, NL0-7, or WL0-7. Likewise, residents of Hawaii may have the prefix AH6-7, KH6-7, NH6-7, or WH6-7 assigned.

Once you obtain your Technician license, do not stop there. Go and get your General license.

General is the second of three ham license classes. Like the Technician license, to get a General license, you merely have to take a 35-question multiple choice exam and pay your license fee. Passing is still at least 26 correct answers and the fee is the same (less than $20). Again the question pool is available for free online (http://www.ncvec.org/page.php?id=358). It is also available in such print publications as *The ARRL General Class License Manual 7th Edition* (ISBN 978-0-87259-811-9). The current General pool of questions is to be used from July 1, 2011 to June 30, 2015. Be sure the question pool you are using is current. Being a bit more comprehensive than the Technician license, the General license usually requires 15-20 hours of study to learn the material. Check Appendix A for a listing of clubs in California where you might take your exam. Once your name and NEW call sign is listed in the FCC database, you're good to go. For a General license in California, your call sign will consist of a one-letter prefix beginning with K, N or W, the number six (6), and a three-letter suffix.

Topics for the General License in Amateur Radio

The General license exam covers regulations, operating practices and electronic theory. Below is the syllabus for the General Class.

Subelement G1 – Commission's Rules
(5 Exam Questions – 5 Groups) G1A – General Class control operator frequency privileges; primary and secondary allocations G1B – Antenna structure limitations; good engineering and good amateur practice, beacon operation; restricted operation; retransmitting radio signals G1C – Transmitter power regulations; data emission standards G1D – Volunteer Examiners and Volunteer Examiner Coordinators; temporary identification G1E – Control categories; repeater regulations; harmful interference; third party rules; ITU regions

Subelement G2 – Operating procedures
(5 Exam Questions – 5 Groups) G2A – Phone operating procedures; USB/LSB utilization conventions; procedural signals; breaking into a OSO in progress; VOX operation G2B – Operating courtesy; band plans, emergencies, including drills and emergency communications G2C – CW operating procedures and procedural signals; Q signals and common abbreviations; full break in G2D – Amateur Auxiliary; minimizing interference; HF operations

G2E – Digital operating; procedures, procedural signals and common abbreviations

Subelement G3 – Radio wave propagation

(3 Exam Questions – 3 Groups)

G3A – Sunspots and solar radiation; ionospheric disturbances; propagation forecasting and indices

G3B – Maximum Usable Frequency; Lowest Usable Frequency; propagation

G3C – Ionospheric layers; critical angle and frequency; HF scatter; Near Vertical Incidence Sky waves

Subelement G4 – Amateur radio practices

(5 Exam Questions – 5 Groups)

G4A – Station Operation and setup

G4B – Test and monitoring equipment; two-tone test

G4C – Interference with consumer electronics; grounding; DSP

G4D – Speech processors; S meters; sideband operation near band edges

G4E – HF mobile radio installations; emergency and battery powered operation

Subelement G5 – Electrical principles

(3 Exam Questions – 3 Groups)

G5A – Reactance; inductance; capacitance; impedance; impedance matching

G5B – The Decibel; current and voltage dividers; electrical power calculations; sine wave root-mean-square (RMS) values; PEP calculations

G5C – Resistors; capacitors and inductors in series and parallel; transformers

Subelement G6 – Circuit components

(3 Exam Questions – 3 Groups)

G6A – Resistors; capacitors; inductors

G6B – Rectifiers; solid state diodes and transistors; vacuum tubes; batteries

G6C – Analog and digital integrated circuits (ICs); microprocessors; memory; I/O devices; microwave ICs (MMICs); display devices

Subelement G7 – Practical circuits

(3 Exam Questions – 3 Groups)

G7A – Power supplies; schematic symbols

G7B – Digital circuits; amplifiers and oscillators

G7C – Receivers and transmitters; filters, oscillators

Subelement G8 – Signals and emissions

(2 Exam Questions – 2 Groups)

G8A – Carriers and modulation; AM; FM; single and double sideband; modulation envelope; overmodulation

G8B – Frequency mixing; multiplication; HF data communications; bandwidths of various modes; deviation

Subelement G9 – Antennas and feed lines

(4 Exam Questions – 4 Groups)

G9A – Antenna feed lines; characteristic impedance and attenuation; SWR calculation, measurement and effects; matching networks

G9B – Basic antennas

G9C – Directional antennas

G9D – Specialized antennas

Subelement G0 – Electrical and RF safety

(2 Exam Questions – 2 Groups)

G0A – RF safety principles, rules and guidelines; routine station elevation

G0B – Safety in the ham shack; electrical shock and treatment, safety grounding, fusing, interlocks, wiring, antenna and tower safety

With a General license, you can use all VHF and UHF frequencies and most of the HF frequencies. You would have access to the 160, 30, 17, 12, and 10 meter bands and access to major parts of the 80, 40, 20, and 15 meter bands. Of course, this is in addition to all bands available to Technician license holders.

Amateur Extra is the third of three ham license classes. Like the Technician and General classes, you merely have to pass a test and pay your fee to get your Amateur Extra license. This class of license is more comprehensive than the lower license classes. The exam is longer – 50 questions – and the minimum passing score is higher – 37. However, once you get your Amateur Extra license, all ham frequencies, VHF, UHF and HF are available for your enjoyment. The Extra exam covers regulations, specialized operating practices, advanced electronics theory, and radio equipment design.

Like for the other license classes, the question pool for the Amateur Extra license is available online for downloading (http://www.ncvec.org/downloads/REVISED%202012-2016%20Extra%20Class%20Pool.doc). It is also available in print form in such publications as *The ARRL Extra Class License Manual Revised 9th Edition* (ISBN 978-0-87259-887-4).

Topics for the Extra License in Amateur Radio

Below is the syllabus for the Amateur Extra Class for July 1, 2012 to June 30, 2016.

Subelement E1 – Commission's Rules

[6 Exam Questions – 6 Groups]

E1A – Operating Standards: frequency privileges; emission standards; automatic message forwarding; frequency sharing; stations aboard ships or aircraft

E1B – Station restrictions and special operations: restrictions on station location; general operating restrictions, spurious emissions, control operator reimbursement; antenna structure restrictions; RACES operations

E1C – Station control: definitions and restrictions pertaining to local, automatic and remote control operation; control operator responsibilities for remote and automatically controlled stations

E1D – Amateur Satellite service: definitions and purpose; license requirements for space stations; available frequencies and bands; telecommand and telemetry operations; restrictions, and special provisions; notification requirements

E1E – Volunteer examiner program: definitions, qualifications, preparation and administration of exams; accreditation; question pools; documentation requirements

E1F – Miscellaneous rules: external RF power amplifiers; national quiet zone; business communications; compensated communications; spread spectrum; auxiliary stations; reciprocal operating privileges; IARP and CEPT licenses; third party communications with foreign countries; special temporary authority

Subelement E2 – Operating procedures

[5 Exam Questions – 5 Groups]

E2A – Amateur radio in space: amateur satellites; orbital mechanics; frequencies and modes; satellite hardware; satellite operations

E2B – Television practices: fast scan television standards and techniques; slow scan television standards and techniques

E2C – Operating methods: contest and DX operating; spread-spectrum transmissions; selecting an operating frequency

E2D – Operating methods: VHF and UHF digital modes; APRS

E2E – Operating methods: operating HF digital modes; error correction

Subelement E3 – Radio wave propagation

[3 Exam Questions – 3 Groups]

E3A – Propagation and technique, Earth-Moon-Earth communications; meteor scatter

E3B – Propagation and technique, trans-equatorial; long path; gray-line; multi-path propagation

E3C – Propagation and technique, Aurora propagation; selective fading; radio-path horizon; take-off angle over flat or sloping terrain; effects of ground on propagation; less common propagation modes

Subelement E4 – Amateur practices

[5 Exam Questions – 5 Groups]

E4A – Test equipment: analog and digital instruments; spectrum and network analyzers, antenna analyzers; oscilloscopes; testing transistors; RF measurements

E4B – Measurement technique and limitations: instrument accuracy and performance limitations; probes; techniques to minimize errors; measurement of "Q"; instrument calibration

E4C – Receiver performance characteristics, phase noise, capture effect, noise floor, image rejection, MDS, signal-to-noise-ratio; selectivity

E4D – Receiver performance characteristics, blocking dynamic range, intermodulation and cross-modulation interference; 3rd order intercept; desensitization; preselection

E4E – Noise suppression: system noise; electrical appliance noise; line noise; locating noise sources; DSP noise reduction; noise blankers

Subelement E5 – Electrical principles

[4 Exam Questions – 4 Groups]

E5A – Resonance and Q: characteristics of resonant circuits: series and parallel resonance; Q; half-power bandwidth; phase relationships in reactive circuits

E5B – Time constants and phase relationships: RLC time constants: definition; time constants in RL and RC circuits; phase angle between voltage and current; phase angles of series and parallel circuits

E5C – Impedance plots and coordinate systems: plotting impedances in polar coordinates; rectangular coordinates

E5D – AC and RF energy in real circuits: skin effect; electrostatic and electromagnetic fields; reactive power; power factor; coordinate systems

Subelement E6 – Circuit components

[6 Exam Questions – 6 Groups]

E6A – Semiconductor materials and devices: semiconductor materials germanium, silicon, P-type, N-type; transistor types: NPN, PNP, junction, field-effect transistors: enhancement mode; depletion mode; MOS; CMOS; N-channel; P-channel

E6B – Semiconductor diodes

E6C – Integrated circuits: TTL digital integrated circuits; CMOS digital integrated circuits; gates

E6D – Optical devices and toroids: cathode-ray tube devices; charge-coupled devices (CCDs); liquid crystal displays (LCDs); toroids: permeability, core material, selecting, winding

E6E – Piezoelectric crystals and MMICs: quartz crystals; crystal oscillators and filters; monolithic amplifiers

E6F – Optical components and power systems: photoconductive principles and effects, photovoltaic systems, optical couplers, optical sensors, and optoisolators

Subelement E7 – Practical circuits

[8 Exam Questions – 8 Groups]

E7A – Digital circuits: digital circuit principles and logic circuits: classes of logic elements; positive and negative logic; frequency dividers; truth tables

E7B – Amplifiers: Class of operation; vacuum tube and solid-state circuits; distortion and intermodulation; spurious and parasitic suppression; microwave amplifiers

E7C – Filters and matching networks: filters and impedance matching networks: types of networks; types of filters; filter applications; filter characteristics; impedance matching; DSP filtering

E7D – Power supplies and voltage regulators

E7E – Modulation and demodulation: reactance, phase and balanced modulators; detectors; mixer stages; DSP modulation and demodulation; software defined radio systems

E7F – Frequency markers and counters: frequency divider circuits; frequency marker generators; frequency counters

E7G – Active filters and op-amps: active audio filters; characteristics; basic circuit design; operational amplifiers

E7H – Oscillators and signal sources: types of oscillators; synthesizers and phase-locked loops; direct digital synthesizers

Subelement E8 – Signals and emissions

[4 Exam Questions – 4 Groups]

E8A – AC waveforms: sine, square, sawtooth and irregular waveforms; AC measurements; average and PEP of RF signals; pulse and digital signal waveforms

E8B – Modulation and demodulation: modulation methods; modulation index and deviation ratio; pulse modulation; frequency and time division multiplexing

E8C – Digital signals: digital communications modes; CW; information rate vs. bandwidth; spread-spectrum communications; modulation methods

E8D – Waves, measurements, and RF grounding: peak-to-peak values, polarization; RF grounding

Subelement E9 – Antennas and transmission lines

[8 Exam Questions – 8 Groups]

E9A – Isotropic and gain antennas: definition; used as a standard for comparison; radiation pattern; basic antenna parameters: radiation resistance and reactance, gain, beamwidth, efficiency

E9B – Antenna patterns: E and H plane patterns; gain as a function of pattern; antenna design; Yagi antennas

E9C – Wire and phased vertical antennas: beverage antennas; terminated and resonant rhombic antennas; elevation above real ground; ground effects as related to polarization; take-off angles

E9D – Directional antennas: gain; satellite antennas; antenna beamwidth; losses; SWR bandwidth; antenna efficiency; shortened and mobile antennas; grounding

E9E – Matching: matching antennas to feed lines; power dividers

E9F – Transmission lines: characteristics of open and shorted feed lines: 1/8 wavelength; 1/4 wavelength; 1/2 wavelength; feed lines: coax versus open-wire; velocity factor; electrical length; transformation characteristics of line terminated in impedance not equal to characteristic impedance

E9G – The Smith chart

E9H – Effective radiated power; system gains and losses; radio direction finding antennas

Subelement E0 – Safety

[1 exam question – 1 group]

E0A – Safety: amateur radio safety practices; RF radiation hazards; hazardous materials

Once your new call sign is listed in the FCC database, you are good to go. For an Amateur Extra license in California, your call sign will consist of a prefix of K, N or W, the number six (6), and a two-letter suffix, or a two-letter prefix beginning with A, N, K or W, the number six (6), and a one-letter suffix, or a two-letter prefix beginning with A, the number six (6), and a two-letter suffix.

Ham radio equipment can be expensive or you can do it "on the cheap." The cost will run from a couple hundred dollars to well in the thousands, depending on what you have available. eBay, and Craigslist are good places to start looking. Most ham clubs do some sort of hamfest annually wherein club members or others are willing to part with older equipment. See Appendix A for a list of clubs in California.

Another excellent source of equipment, as well as advice on setting the equipment up and how to use it properly, is current ham operators. In Appendix B, the author has listed all the FCC licensed ham operators in California, listed by city, and then sorted by street and house number on the street. Who knows, maybe someone who lives close to you is a ham operator. Be a good neighbor, stop by and have a chat with him/her.

Like CB radios, ham radios come in three formats – base, mobile, and handheld. They can use the electric company for power, or operate off a car battery. In the opinion of this author, in spite of the slightly higher cost of the equipment and having to take a test to legally use the equipment, ham radio is the way to go when concerned about communication during times of crisis.

Canadian Call Sign Prefixes

Because of our proximity to Canada, many times ham contact is made with our northern neighbors. Below is a chart showing the origin of Canadian call sign prefixes.

Call Sign Prefix	Provence or Territory
CY0	Sable Island
CY9	St. Paul Island
VA1, VE1	New Brunswick, Nova Scotia
VA2, VE2	Quebec
VA3, VE3	Ontario
VA4, VE4	Manitoba
VA5, VE5	Saskatchewan
VA6, VE6	Alberta
VA7, VE7	British Columbia
VE8	North West Territories
VE9	New Brunswick
VO1	Newfoundland
VO2	Labrador
VY0	Nunavut
VY1	Yukon
VY2	Prince Edward Island

Common Radio Bands in the United States

Certain radio bands are more popular with ham radio enthusiasts than others. Below is a chart showing these bands and when they are most popular.

	Band (meter)	Frequency (MHz)	Use
HF	160	1.8 – 2.0	Night
	80	3.5 – 4.0	Night and Local Day
	40	7.0 – 7.3	Night and Local Day
	30	10.1 – 10.15	CW and Digital
	20	14.0 – 14.350	World Wide Day and Night
	17	18.068 – 18.168	World Wide Day and Night
	15	21.0 – 21.450	Primarily Daytime
	12	24.890 – 24.990	Primarily Daytime
	10	28.0 – 29.70	Daytime during Sunspot highs
VHF	6	50 – 54	Local to World Wide
	2	144 – 148	Local to Medium Distance
UHF	70 cm	430 – 440	Local

Common Amateur Radio Bands in Canada

160 Meter Band - Maximum bandwidth 6 kHz
1.800 - 1.820 MHz - CW
1.820 - 1.830 MHz - Digital Modes
1 830 - 1.840 MHz - DX Window
1.840 - 2.000 MHz - SSB and other wide band modes

80 Meter Band - Maximum bandwidth 6 kHz
3.500 - 3.580 MHz - CW
3.580 - 3.620 MHz - Digital Modes
3.620 - 3.635 MHz - Packet/Digital Secondary
3.635 - 3.725 MHz - CW
3.725 - 3.790 MHz - SSB and other side band modes*
3.790 - 3.800 MHz - SSB DX Window
3.800 - 4.000 MHz - SSB and other wide band modes

40 Meter Band - Maximum bandwidth 6 kHz
7.000 - 7.035 MHz - CW
7.035 - 7.050 MHz - Digital Modes
7.040 - 7.050 MHz - International packet
7.050 - 7.100 MHz - SSB
7.100 - 7.120 MHz - Packet within Region 2
7.120 - 7.150 MHz - CW
7.150 - 7.300 MHz - SSB and other wide band modes

30 Meter Band - Maximum bandwidth 1 kHz

10.100 - 10.130 MHz - CW only
10.130 - 10.140 MHz - Digital Modes
10.140 - 10.150 MHz - Packet

20 Meter Band - Maximum bandwidth 6 kHz

14.000 - 14.070 MHz - CW only
14.070 - 14.095 MHz - Digital Mode
14.095 - 14.099 MHz - Packet
14.100 MHz - Beacons
14.101 - 14.112 MHz - CW, SSB, packet shared
14.112 - 14.350 MHz - SSB
14.225 - 14.235 MHz - SSTV ·

17 Meter Band - Maximum bandwidth 6 kHz

18.068 - 18.100 MHz - CW
18.100 - 18.105 MHz - Digital Modes
18.105 - 18.110 MHz - Packet
18.110 - 18.168 MHz - SSB and other wide band modes

15 Meter Band - maximum bandwidth 6 kHz

21.000 - 21.070 MHz - CW
21.070 - 21.090 MHz - Digital Modes
21.090 - 21.125 MHz - Packet
21.100 - 21.150 MHz - CW and SSB
21.150 - 21.335 MHz - SSB and other wide band modes
21.335 - 21.345 MHz - SSTV
21.345 - 21.450 MHz - SSB and other wide band modes

12 Meter Band - Maximum bandwidth 6 kHz

24.890 - 24.930 MHz - CW
24.920 - 24.925 MHz - Digital Modes
24.925 - 24.930 MHz - Packet
24.930 - 24.990 MHz - SSB and other wide band modes

10 Meter Band - Maximum band width 20 kHz

28.000 - 28.200 MHz - CW
28.070 - 28.120 MHz - Digital Modes
28.120 - 28.190 MHz - Packet
28.190 - 28.200 MHz - Beacons
28.200 - 29.300 MHz - SSB and other wide band modes
29.300 - 29.510 MHz - Satellite
29.510 - 29.700 MHz - SSB, FM and repeaters

160 Meters (1.8-2.0 MHz)

1.800 - 2.000 CW
1.800 - 1.810 Digital Modes
1.810 CW QRP
1.843-2.000 SSB, SSTV and other wideband modes
1.910 SSB QRP
1.995 - 2.000 Experimental
1.999 - 2.000 Beacons

80 Meters (3.5-4.0 MHz)

3.590 RTTY/Data DX
3.570-3.600 RTTY/Data
3.790-3.800 DX window
3.845 SSTV
3.885 AM calling frequency

40 Meters (7.0-7.3 MHz)

7.040 RTTY/Data DX
7.080-7.125 RTTY/Data
7.171 SSTV
7.290 AM calling frequency

30 Meters (10.1-10.15 MHz)

10.130-10.140 RTTY
10.140-10.150 Packet

20 Meters (14.0-14.35 MHz)

14.070-14.095 RTTY
14.095-14.0995 Packet
14.100 NCDXF Beacons
14.1005-14.112 Packet
14.230 SSTV
14.286 AM calling frequency

17 Meters (18.068-18.168 MHz)

18.100-18.105 RTTY
18.105-18.110 Packet

15 Meters (21.0-21.45 MHz)

21.070-21.110 RTTY/Data
21.340 SSTV

12 Meters (24.89-24.99 MHz)

24.920-24.925 RTTY
24.925-24.930 Packet

10 Meters (28-29.7 MHz)

28.000-28.070 CW
28.070-28.150 RTTY
28.150-28.190 CW
28.200-28.300 Beacons
28.300-29.300 Phone
28.680 SSTV
29.000-29.200 AM
29.300-29.510 Satellite Downlinks
29.520-29.590 Repeater Inputs
29.600 FM Simplex
29.610-29.700 Repeater Outputs

6 Meters (50-54 MHz)

50.0-50.1 CW, beacons
50.060-50.080 beacon subband
50.1-50.3 SSB, CW
50.10-50.125 DX window
50.125 SSB calling
50.3-50.6 All modes
50.6-50.8 Nonvoice communications
50.62 Digital (packet) calling
50.8-51.0 Radio remote control (20-kHz channels)
51.0-51.1 Pacific DX window
51.12-51.48 Repeater inputs (19 channels)
51.12-51.18 Digital repeater inputs
51.5-51.6 Simplex (six channels)
51.62-51.98 Repeater outputs (19 channels)
51.62-51.68 Digital repeater outputs
52.0-52.48 Repeater inputs (except as noted; 23 channels)
52.02, 52.04 FM simplex
52.2 TEST PAIR (input)
52.5-52.98 Repeater output (except as noted; 23 channels)
52.525 Primary FM simplex
52.54 Secondary FM simplex
52.7 TEST PAIR (output)
53.0-53.48 Repeater inputs (except as noted; 19 channels)
53.0 Remote base FM simplex
53.02 Simplex
53.1, 53.2, 53.3, 53.4 Radio remote control
53.5-53.98 Repeater outputs (except as noted; 19 channels)
53.5, 53.6, 53.7, 53.8 Radio remote control
53.52, 53.9 Simplex

2 Meters (144-148 MHz)

144.00-144.05 EME (CW)
144.05-144.10 General CW and weak signals
144.10-144.20 EME and weak-signal SSB
144.200 National calling frequency
144.200-144.275 General SSB operation
144.275-144.300 Propagation beacons
144.30-144.50 New OSCAR subband
144.50-144.60 Linear translator inputs
144.60-144.90 FM repeater inputs
144.90-145.10 Weak signal and FM simplex (145.01,03,05,07,09 are widely used for packet)
145.10-145.20 Linear translator outputs
145.20-145.50 FM repeater outputs
145.50-145.80 Miscellaneous and experimental modes
145.80-146.00 OSCAR subband
146.01-146.37 Repeater inputs
146.40-146.58 Simplex
146.52 National Simplex Calling Frequency
146.61-146.97 Repeater outputs
147.00-147.39 Repeater outputs
147.42-147.57 Simplex
147.60-147.99 Repeater inputs

1.25 Meters (222-225 MHz)

222.0-222.150 Weak-signal modes
222.0-222.025 EME
222.05-222.06 Propagation beacons
222.1 SSB & CW calling frequency
222.10-222.15 Weak-signal CW & SSB
222.15-222.25 Local coordinator's option; weak signal, ACSB, repeater inputs, control
222.25-223.38 FM repeater inputs only
223.40-223.52 FM simplex
223.52-223.64 Digital, packet
223.64-223.70 Links, control
223.71-223.85 Local coordinator's option; FM simplex, packet, repeater outputs
223.85-224.98 Repeater outputs only

70 Centimeters (420-450 MHz)

420.00-426.00 ATV repeater or simplex with 421.25 MHz video carrier control links and experimental
426.00-432.00 ATV simplex with 427.250-MHz video carrier frequency
432.00-432.07 EME (Earth-Moon-Earth)
432.07-432.10 Weak-signal CW
432.10 70-cm calling frequency

432.10-432.30 Mixed-mode and weak-signal work
432.30-432.40 Propagation beacons
432.40-433.00 Mixed-mode and weak-signal work
433.00-435.00 Auxiliary/repeater links
435.00-438.00 Satellite only (internationally)
438.00-444.00 ATV repeater input with 439.250-MHz video carrier frequency and repeater links
442.00-445.00 Repeater inputs and outputs (local option)
445.00-447.00 Shared by auxiliary and control links, repeaters and simplex (local option)
446.00 National simplex frequency
447.00-450.00 Repeater inputs and outputs (local option)

33 Centimeters (902-928 MHz)

902.0-903.0 Narrow-bandwidth, weak-signal communications
902.0-902.8 SSTV, FAX, ACSSB, experimental
902.1 Weak-signal calling frequency
902.8-903.0 Reserved for EME, CW expansion
903.1 Alternate calling frequency
903.0-906.0 Digital communications
906-909 FM repeater inputs
909-915 ATV
915-918 Digital communications
918-921 FM repeater outputs
921-927 ATV
927-928 FM simplex and links

23 Centimeters (1240-1300 MHz)

1240-1246 ATV #1
1246-1248 Narrow-bandwidth FM point-to-point links and digital, duplex with 1258-1260.
1248-1258 Digital Communications
1252-1258 ATV #2
1258-1260 Narrow-bandwidth FM point-to-point links digital, duplexed with 1246-1252
1260-1270 Satellite uplinks, reference WARC '79
1260-1270 Wide-bandwidth experimental, simplex ATV
1270-1276 Repeater inputs, FM and linear, paired with 1282-1288, 239 pairs every 25 kHz, e.g. 1270.025, .050, etc.
1271-1283 Non-coordinated test pair
1276-1282 ATV #3
1282-1288 Repeater outputs, paired with 1270-1276
1288-1294 Wide-bandwidth experimental, simplex ATV
1294-1295 Narrow-bandwidth FM simplex services, 25-kHz channels
1294.5 National FM simplex calling frequency
1295-1297 Narrow bandwidth weak-signal communications (no FM)
1295.0-1295.8 SSTV, FAX, ACSSB, experimental
1295.8-1296.0 Reserved for EME, CW expansion

1296.00-1296.05 EME-exclusive
1296.07-1296.08 CW beacons
1296.1 CW, SSB calling frequency
1296.4-1296.6 Crossband linear translator input
1296.6-1296.8 Crossband linear translator output
1296.8-1297.0 Experimental beacons (exclusive)
1297-1300 Digital Communications

2300-2310 and 2390-2450 MHz

2300.0-2303.0 High-rate data
2303.0-2303.5 Packet
2303.5-2303.8 TTY packet
2303.9-2303.9 Packet, TTY, CW, EME
2303.9-2304.1 CW, EME
2304.1 Calling frequency
2304.1-2304.2 CW, EME, SSB
2304.2-2304.3 SSB, SSTV, FAX, Packet AM, Amtor
2304.30-2304.32 Propagation beacon network
2304.32-2304.40 General propagation beacons
2304.4-2304.5 SSB, SSTV, ACSSB, FAX, Packet AM, Amtor experimental
2304.5-2304.7 Crossband linear translator input
2304.7-2304.9 Crossband linear translator output
2304.9-2305.0 Experimental beacons
2305.0-2305.2 FM simplex (25 kHz spacing)
2305.20 FM simplex calling frequency
2305.2-2306.0 FM simplex (25 kHz spacing)
2306.0-2309.0 FM Repeaters (25 kHz) input
2309.0-2310.0 Control and auxiliary links
2390.0-2396.0 Fast-scan TV
2396.0-2399.0 High-rate data
2399.0-2399.5 Packet
2399.5-2400.0 Control and auxiliary links
2400.0-2403.0 Satellite
2403.0-2408.0 Satellite high-rate data
2408.0-2410.0 Satellite
2410.0-2413.0 FM repeaters (25 kHz) output
2413.0-2418.0 High-rate data
2418.0-2430.0 Fast-scan TV
2430.0-2433.0 Satellite
2433.0-2438.0 Satellite high-rate data
2438.0-2450.0 WB FM, FSTV, FMTV, SS experimental

3300-3500 MHz

3456.3-3456.4 Propagation beacons

5650-5925 MHz
5760.3-5760.4 Propagation beacons

10.00-10.50 GHz
10.368 Narrow band calling frequency 10.3683-10.3684 Propagation beacons
10.3640 Calling frequency

Now that you have your license (you do, don't you?), and your equipment, you are ready to go live. Below is a suggested start.

1) Assuming you have the HT set up to the appropriate frequency, and offset, press the mic button on the HT and say, "KK4HWX listening." Replace the KK4HWX with your own call sign, the one assigned to you by the FCC (it's the law). If no one responds to your call, you may wish to try again. Hopefully someone will respond to your call.

2) Once you get a response, it will be in the form of something like, "KK4HWX this is ??1??? in Eastport returning. My name is Florence. Back to you. ??1???" then a tone. Let us examine the response more closely. She first acknowledged your call sign (KK4HWX), then identified hers (??1???). From the 1 in her call sign, you know that she first got her license in Region 1, meaning she got it while a resident of CT, ME, MA, NH, RI, or VT. She then told you where she's transmitting from (Eastport). The term "returning" means that she is returning your call. Her name is Florence. The phrase, "Back to you" indicates that she is turning over the conversation to you. She then repeats her call sign. The tone indicates to you that it is okay to proceed with your response. BTW if she had used the term "Over" instead of "Back to you," it would mean the same thing, just fewer words.

3) At this point, press the mic button and continue with the conversation. You should restate your call sign often during the conversation (perhaps every 10 minutes or less and whenever you begin transmitting). Don't forget to say, "Over" or "Back to you" whenever you are giving Florence control of the conversation again.

4) When you are ready to stop the conversation, you should say goodbye or use the phrase "73", meaning "best wishes." Your conversation would end something like, "??1??? 73, this is KK4HWX clear and monitoring." The "clear and monitoring" indicates that you are going to continue to monitor the frequency. If you are not going to continue monitoring, you may wish to end the conversation with Florence with, "clear and QRT" instead. The QRT means that you are stopping transmissions.

Call Sign Phonics

Because of different accents of various people, sometimes it is difficult to understand call sign letters when spoken. For this reason, most ham operators verbalize their call sign using phonics. Below is a table listing the accepted phonics for letters and numbers.

A = ALFA
B = BRAVO
C = CHARLIE
D = DELTA
E = ECHO
F = FOXTROT
G = GOLF
H = HOTEL
I = INDIA
J = JULIETT
K = KILO
L = LIMA
M = MIKE
N = NOVEMBER
O = OSCAR
P = PAPA (PA-PA')
Q = QUEBEC (KAY-BEK')
R = ROMEO

S = SIERRA
T = TANGO
U = UNIFORM
V = VICTOR
W = WHISKEY
X = X-RAY
Y = YANKEE
Z = ZULU (ZED)
1 = ONE
2 = TWO
3 = THREE (TREE)
4 = FOUR
5 = FIVE (FIFE)
6 = SIX
7 = SEVEN
8 = EIGHT
9 = NINE (NINER)
0 = ZERO

The words in parentheses are the pronunciation or the alternate pronunciations for the words or numbers, but you will hear both used. With the letter Z, (ZED) is by far the most commonly used. With the number 9, NINER is the most common and easiest to understand ON THE AIR.

If you wish to use Morse code (CW) instead of voice communication, the "conversation" would follow the same steps, with a few modifications. To type out each word would require a lot of typing and translating. If you are like this author, more means more, i.e., more typing means more typos are likely. To help with this situation, CW enthusiasts have developed a language all their own – they use abbreviations for common phrases. Below is a chart showing some of these abbreviations.

Abbreviation	Use
AR	Over
de	From or "this is"
ES	And
GM	Good Morning
K	Go
KN	Go only
NM	Name
QTH	Location
RPT	Report
R	Roger
SK	Clear
tnx	Thanks
UR	Your, you are
73	Best Wishes

Morse Code and Amateur Radio

If you wish to use CW, but are concerned about accuracy, you might consider purchasing a Morse code translator. This is an electronic device that you place in front of your speakers. It takes the CW sounds and translates them into English and displays the transmission on an LCD display. For the reverse, you can pick up a CW keyboard. With the keyboard, you type in your message and it converts the text to Morse code. The translator does not need to be attached to your ham equipment, whereas the keyboard would.

For your convenience, below is a table showing the Morse code signals and their meaning.

Character	Code
A	· —
B	— · · ·
C	— · — ·
D	— · ·
E	·
F	· · — ·
G	— — ·
H	· · · ·
I	· ·
J	· — — —
K	— · —
L	· — · ·
M	— —
N	— ·
O	— — —
P	· — — ·
Q	— — · —
R	· — ·
S	· · ·
T	—
U	· · —
V	· · · —
W	· — —
X	— · · —
Y	— · — —
Z	— — · ·
0	— — — — —
1	· — — — —
2	· · — — —
3	· · · — —
4	· · · · —
5	· · · · ·

6	— · · · ·
7	— — · · ·
8	— — — · ·
9	— — — — ·
Ampersand [&], Wait	· — · · ·
Apostrophe [']	· — — — — ·
At sign [@]	· — — · — ·
Colon [:]	— — — · · ·
Comma [,]	— — · · — —
Dollar sign [$]	· · · — · · —
Double dash [=]	— · · · —
Exclamation mark [!]	— · — · — —
Hyphen, Minus [-]	— · · · · —
Parenthesis closed [)]	— · — — · —
Parenthesis open [(]	— · — — ·
Period [.]	· — · — · —
Plus [+]	· — · — ·
Question mark [?]	· · — — · ·
Quotation mark ["]	· — · · — ·
Semicolon [;]	— · — · — ·
Slash [/], Fraction bar	— · · — ·
Underscore [_]	· · — — · —

An advantage of using Morse Code is that when broadcasting CW, you are using reduced power, thereby saving your battery. Your battery is used only while actually transmitting or receiving.

International Call Sign Prefixes

As was stated earlier, all ham radio call signs begin with letters (or numbers) taken from blocks assigned to each country of the world by the *ITU - International Telecommunications Union,* a body controlled by the United Nations. The following chart indicates which call sign series are allocated to which countries.

Call Sign Series	Allocated to
AAA-ALZ	**United States of America**
AMA-AOZ	Spain
APA-ASZ	Pakistan (Islamic Republic of)
ATA-AWZ	India (Republic of)
AXA-AXZ	Australia
AYA-AZZ	Argentine Republic
A2A-A2Z	Botswana (Republic of)
A3A-A3Z	Tonga (Kingdom of)
A4A-A4Z	Oman (Sultanate of)
A5A-A5Z	Bhutan (Kingdom of)

A6A-A6Z	United Arab Emirates
A7A-A7Z	Qatar (State of)
A8A-A8Z	Liberia (Republic of)
A9A-A9Z	Bahrain (State of)
BAA-BZZ	China (People's Republic of)
CAA-CEZ	Chile
CFA-CKZ	Canada
CLA-CMZ	Cuba
CNA-CNZ	Morocco (Kingdom of)
COA-COZ	Cuba
CPA-CPZ	Bolivia (Republic of)
CQA-CUZ	Portugal
CVA-CXZ	Uruguay (Eastern Republic of)
CYA-CZZ	Canada
C2A-C2Z	Nauru (Republic of)
C3A-C3Z	Andorra (Principality of)
C4A-C4Z	Cyprus (Republic of)
C5A-C5Z	Gambia (Republic of the)
C6A-C6Z	Bahamas (Commonwealth of the)
C7A-C7Z	World Meteorological Organization
C8A-C9Z	Mozambique (Republic of)
DAA-DRZ	Germany (Federal Republic of)
DSA-DTZ	Korea (Republic of)
DUA-DZZ	Philippines (Republic of the)
D2A-D3Z	Angola (Republic of)
D4A-D4Z	Cape Verde (Republic of)
D5A-D5Z	Liberia (Republic of)
D6A-D6Z	Comoros (Islamic Federal Republic of the)
D7A-D9Z	Korea (Republic of)
EAA-EHZ	Spain
EIA-EJZ	Ireland
EKA-EKZ	Armenia (Republic of)
ELA-ELZ	Liberia (Republic of)
EMA-EOZ	Ukraine
EPA-EQZ	Iran (Islamic Republic of)
ERA-ERZ	Moldova (Republic of)
ESA-ESZ	Estonia (Republic of)
ETA-ETZ	Ethiopia (Federal Democratic Republic of)
EUA-EWZ	Belarus (Republic of)
EXA-EXZ	Kyrgyz Republic
EYA-EYZ	Tajikistan (Republic of)
EZA-EZZ	Turkmenistan
E2A-E2Z	Thailand
E3A-E3Z	Eritrea
E4A-E4Z	Palestinian Authority

E5A-E5Z	New Zealand - Cook Islands (WRC-07)
E7A-E7Z	Bosnia and Herzegovina (Republic of) (WRC-07)
FAA-FZZ	France
GAA-GZZ	United Kingdom of Great Britain and Northern Ireland
HAA-HAZ	Hungary (Republic of)
HBA-HBZ	Switzerland (Confederation of)
HCA-HDZ	Ecuador
HEA-HEZ	Switzerland (Confederation of)
HFA-HFZ	Poland (Republic of)
HGA-HGZ	Hungary (Republic of)
HHA-HHZ	Haiti (Republic of)
HIA-HIZ	Dominican Republic
HJA-HKZ	Colombia (Republic of)
HLA-HLZ	Korea (Republic of)
HMA-HMZ	Democratic People's Republic of Korea
HNA-HNZ	Iraq (Republic of)
HOA-HPZ	Panama (Republic of)
HQA-HRZ	Honduras (Republic of)
HSA-HSZ	Thailand
HTA-HTZ	Nicaragua
HUA-HUZ	El Salvador (Republic of)
HVA-HVZ	Vatican City State
HWA-HYZ	France
HZA-HZZ	Saudi Arabia (Kingdom of)
H2A-H2Z	Cyprus (Republic of)
H3A-H3Z	Panama (Republic of)
H4A-H4Z	Solomon Islands
H6A-H7Z	Nicaragua
H8A-H9Z	Panama (Republic of)
IAA-IZZ	Italy
JAA-JSZ	Japan
JTA-JVZ	Mongolia
JWA-JXZ	Norway
JYA-JYZ	Jordan (Hashemite Kingdom of)
JZA-JZZ	Indonesia (Republic of)
J2A-J2Z	Djibouti (Republic of)
J3A-J3Z	Grenada
J4A-J4Z	Greece
J5A-J5Z	Guinea-Bissau (Republic of)
J6A-J6Z	Saint Lucia
J7A-J7Z	Dominica (Commonwealth of)
J8A-J8Z	Saint Vincent and the Grenadines
KAA-KZZ	**United States of America**
LAA-LNZ	Norway
LOA-LWZ	Argentine Republic

LXA-LXZ	Luxembourg
LYA-LYZ	Lithuania (Republic of)
LZA-LZZ	Bulgaria (Republic of)
L2A-L9Z	Argentine Republic
MAA-MZZ	United Kingdom of Great Britain and Northern Ireland
NAA-NZZ	**United States of America**
OAA-OCZ	Peru
ODA-ODZ	Lebanon
OEA-OEZ	Austria
OFA-OJZ	Finland
OKA-OLZ	Czech Republic
OMA-OMZ	Slovak Republic
ONA-OTZ	Belgium
OUA-OZZ	Denmark
PAA-PIZ	Netherlands (Kingdom of the)
PJA-PJZ	Netherlands (Kingdom of the) - Netherlands Antilles
PKA-POZ	Indonesia (Republic of)
PPA-PYZ	Brazil (Federative Republic of)
PZA-PZZ	Suriname (Republic of)
P2A-P2Z	Papua New Guinea
P3A-P3Z	Cyprus (Republic of)
P4A-P4Z	Netherlands (Kingdom of the) - Aruba
P5A-P9Z	Democratic People's Republic of Korea
RAA-RZZ	Russian Federation
SAA-SMZ	Sweden
SNA-SRZ	Poland (Republic of)
SSA-SSM	Egypt (Arab Republic of)
SSN-STZ	Sudan (Republic of the)
SUA-SUZ	Egypt (Arab Republic of)
SVA-SZZ	Greece
S2A-S3Z	Bangladesh (People's Republic of)
S5A-S5Z	Slovenia (Republic of)
S6A-S6Z	Singapore (Republic of)
S7A-S7Z	Seychelles (Republic of)
S8A-S8Z	South Africa (Republic of)
S9A-S9Z	Sao Tome and Principe (Democratic Republic of)
TAA-TCZ	Turkey
TDA-TDZ	Guatemala (Republic of)
TEA-TEZ	Costa Rica
TFA-TFZ	Iceland
TGA-TGZ	Guatemala (Republic of)
THA-THZ	France
TIA-TIZ	Costa Rica
TJA-TJZ	Cameroon (Republic of)
TKA-TKZ	France

TLA-TLZ	Central African Republic
TMA-TMZ	France
TNA-TNZ	Congo (Republic of the)
TOA-TQZ	France
TRA-TRZ	Gabonese Republic
TSA-TSZ	Tunisia
TTA-TTZ	Chad (Republic of)
TUA-TUZ	Côte d'Ivoire (Republic of)
TVA-TXZ	France
TYA-TYZ	Benin (Republic of)
TZA-TZZ	Mali (Republic of)
T2A-T2Z	Tuvalu
T3A-T3Z	Kiribati (Republic of)
T4A-T4Z	Cuba
T5A-T5Z	Somali Democratic Republic
T6A-T6Z	Afghanistan (Islamic State of)
T7A-T7Z	San Marino (Republic of)
T8A-T8Z	Palau (Republic of)
UAA-UIZ	Russian Federation
UJA-UMZ	Uzbekistan (Republic of)
UNA-UQZ	Kazakhstan (Republic of)
URA-UZZ	Ukraine
VAA-VGZ	Canada
VHA-VNZ	Australia
VOA-VOZ	Canada
VPA-VQZ	United Kingdom of Great Britain and Northern Ireland
VRA-VRZ	China (People's Republic of) - Hong Kong
VSA-VSZ	United Kingdom of Great Britain and Northern Ireland
VTA-VWZ	India (Republic of)
VXA-VYZ	Canada
VZA-VZZ	Australia
V2A-V2Z	Antigua and Barbuda
V3A-V3Z	Belize
V4A-V4Z	Saint Kitts and Nevis
V5A-V5Z	Namibia (Republic of)
V6A-V6Z	Micronesia (Federated States of)
V7A-V7Z	Marshall Islands (Republic of the)
V8A-V8Z	Brunei Darussalam
WAA-WZZ	**United States of America**
XAA-XIZ	Mexico
XJA-XOZ	Canada
XPA-XPZ	Denmark
XQA-XRZ	Chile
XSA-XSZ	China (People's Republic of)
XTA-XTZ	Burkina Faso

XUA-XUZ	Cambodia (Kingdom of)
XVA-XVZ	Viet Nam (Socialist Republic of)
XWA-XWZ	Lao People's Democratic Republic
XXA-XXZ	China (People's Republic of) - Macao (WRC-07)
XYA-XZZ	Myanmar (Union of)
YAA-YAZ	Afghanistan (Islamic State of)
YBA-YHZ	Indonesia (Republic of)
YIA-YIZ	Iraq (Republic of)
YJA-YJZ	Vanuatu (Republic of)
YKA-YKZ	Syrian Arab Republic
YLA-YLZ	Latvia (Republic of)
YMA-YMZ	Turkey
YNA-YNZ	Nicaragua
YOA-YRZ	Romania
YSA-YSZ	El Salvador (Republic of)
YTA-YUZ	Serbia (Republic of) (WRC-07)
YVA-YYZ	Venezuela (Republic of)
Y2A-Y9Z	Germany (Federal Republic of)
ZAA-ZAZ	Albania (Republic of)
ZBA-ZJZ	United Kingdom of Great Britain and Northern Ireland
ZKA-ZMZ	New Zealand
ZNA-ZOZ	United Kingdom of Great Britain and Northern Ireland
ZPA-ZPZ	Paraguay (Republic of)
ZQA-ZQZ	United Kingdom of Great Britain and Northern Ireland
ZRA-ZUZ	South Africa (Republic of)
ZVA-ZZZ	Brazil (Federative Republic of)
Z2A-Z2Z	Zimbabwe (Republic of)
Z3A-Z3Z	The Former Yugoslav Republic of Macedonia
2AA-2ZZ	United Kingdom of Great Britain and Northern Ireland
3AA-3AZ	Monaco (Principality of)
3BA-3BZ	Mauritius (Republic of)
3CA-3CZ	Equatorial Guinea (Republic of)
3DA-3DM	Swaziland (Kingdom of)
3DN-3DZ	Fiji (Republic of)
3EA-3FZ	Panama (Republic of)
3GA-3GZ	Chile
3HA-3UZ	China (People's Republic of)
3VA-3VZ	Tunisia
3WA-3WZ	Viet Nam (Socialist Republic of)
3XA-3XZ	Guinea (Republic of)
3YA-3YZ	Norway
3ZA-3ZZ	Poland (Republic of)
4AA-4CZ	Mexico
4DA-4IZ	Philippines (Republic of the)
4JA-4KZ	Azerbaijani Republic

4LA-4LZ	Georgia (Republic of)
4MA-4MZ	Venezuela (Republic of)
4OA-4OZ	Montenegro (Republic of) (WRC-07)
4PA-4SZ	Sri Lanka (Democratic Socialist Republic of)
4TA-4TZ	Peru
4UA-4UZ	United Nations
4VA-4VZ	Haiti (Republic of)
4WA-4WZ	Democratic Republic of Timor-Leste (WRC-03)
4XA-4XZ	Israel (State of)
4YA-4YZ	International Civil Aviation Organization
4ZA-4ZZ	Israel (State of)
5AA-5AZ	Libya (Socialist People's Libyan Arab Jamahiriya)
5BA-5BZ	Cyprus (Republic of)
5CA-5GZ	Morocco (Kingdom of)
5HA-5IZ	Tanzania (United Republic of)
5JA-5KZ	Colombia (Republic of)
5LA-5MZ	Liberia (Republic of)
5NA-5OZ	Nigeria (Federal Republic of)
5PA-5QZ	Denmark
5RA-5SZ	Madagascar (Republic of)
5TA-5TZ	Mauritania (Islamic Republic of)
5UA-5UZ	Niger (Republic of the)
5VA-5VZ	Togolese Republic
5WA-5WZ	Samoa (Independent State of)
5XA-5XZ	Uganda (Republic of)
5YA-5ZZ	Kenya (Republic of)
6AA-6BZ	Egypt (Arab Republic of)
6CA-6CZ	Syrian Arab Republic
6DA-6JZ	Mexico
6KA-6NZ	Korea (Republic of)
6OA-6OZ	Somali Democratic Republic
6PA-6SZ	Pakistan (Islamic Republic of)
6TA-6UZ	Sudan (Republic of the)
6VA-6WZ	Senegal (Republic of)
6XA-6XZ	Madagascar (Republic of)
6YA-6YZ	Jamaica
6ZA-6ZZ	Liberia (Republic of)
7AA-7IZ	Indonesia (Republic of)
7JA-7NZ	Japan
7OA-7OZ	Yemen (Republic of)
7PA-7PZ	Lesotho (Kingdom of)
7QA-7QZ	Malawi
7RA-7RZ	Algeria (People's Democratic Republic of)
7SA-7SZ	Sweden
7TA-7YZ	Algeria (People's Democratic Republic of)

7ZA-7ZZ	Saudi Arabia (Kingdom of)
8AA-8IZ	Indonesia (Republic of)
8JA-8NZ	Japan
8OA-8OZ	Botswana (Republic of)
8PA-8PZ	Barbados
8QA-8QZ	Maldives (Republic of)
8RA-8RZ	Guyana
8SA-8SZ	Sweden
8TA-8YZ	India (Republic of)
8ZA-8ZZ	Saudi Arabia (Kingdom of)
9AA-9AZ	Croatia (Republic of)
9BA-9DZ	Iran (Islamic Republic of)
9EA-9FZ	Ethiopia (Federal Democratic Republic of)
9GA-9GZ	Ghana
9HA-9HZ	Malta
9IA-9JZ	Zambia (Republic of)
9KA-9KZ	Kuwait (State of)
9LA-9LZ	Sierra Leone
9MA-9MZ	Malaysia
9NA-9NZ	Nepal
9OA-9TZ	Democratic Republic of the Congo
9UA-9UZ	Burundi (Republic of)
9VA-9VZ	Singapore (Republic of)
9WA-9WZ	Malaysia
9XA-9XZ	Rwandese Republic
9YA-9ZZ	Trinidad and Tobago

Third-Party Communications and Amateur Radio

If all of this information about ham radios is somewhat intimidating, do not despair. "You" can still use ham radios for communications without being a licensed operator. Yes, you do have to have a ham license in order to legally transmit by ham equipment (or be under the direct supervision of someone else who is licensed), but there is an alternative – third-party communication.

Third-party communications occur when a licensed operator sends either written or verbal messages on behalf of unlicensed persons or organizations. There are two "controls" on third-party communication.

First, the communication must be noncommercial and of a personal nature. Asking a ham operator to contact another ham operator located in an area just hit by tornados and, because of being without power, phones do not work in Grandma Sally's city so you can check up on her, is okay. Asking a ham to send a message out that you have an old Chevy for sale would not be okay.

Second, the message must be going to a permitted area. Transmitting from a US location to another US location is okay, but transmitting from the US to another country may not. Because third-party communications bypass a country's normal telephone and postal systems, many foreign governments forbid such communications. In order to transmit from one country to another, the other country must have signed a third-party agreement with the US. What follows is a list of those countries that do have third-party a communications agreement with the US.

V2	Antigua / Barbuda
LU	Argentina
VK	Australia
V3	Belize
CP	Bolivia
T9	Bosnia-Herzegovina
PY	Brazil
VE	Canada
CE	Chile
HK	Colombia
D6	Comoros (Federal Islamic Republic of)
TI	Costa Rica
CO	Cuba
HI	Dominican Republic
J7	Dominica
HC	Ecuador
YS	El Salvador
C5	Gambia, The
9G	Ghana
J3	Grenada
TG	Guatemala
8R	Guyana
HH	Haiti
HR	Honduras
4X	Israel
6Y	Jamaica
JY	Jordan
EL	Liberia
V7	Marshall Islands
XE	Mexico
V6	Micronesia, Federated States of
YN	Nicaragua
HP	Panama
ZP	Paraguay
OA	Peru
DU	Philippines
VR6	Pitcairn Island

V4	St. Christopher / Nevis
J6	St. Lucia
J8	St. Vincent and the Grenadines
9L	Sierra Leone
ZS	South Africa
3DA	Swaziland
9Y	Trinidad / Tobago
TA	Turkey
GB	United Kingdom
CX	Uruguay
YV	Venezuela
4U1ITUITU	Geneva
4U1VICVIC	Vienna

Remember, before TSHTF, keep your pantry well stocked, your powder dry, and your batteries fully charged. 73

APPENDIX A

American Radio Relay League

Affiliated Amateur Radio Clubs in

California

ARRL Affiliated Club	Lodi Amateur Radio Club
City:	Acampo, CA
Call Sign:	N6SJV
Section:	SJV
Links:	lodiamateurradioclub.org/, www.qsl.net/ac4us/LodiARC/index.htm

ARRL Affiliated Club	Amateur Radio Club Of Alameda
City:	Alameda, CA
Call Sign:	K6QLF
Section:	EB
Links:	www.arcaham.org

ARRL Affiliated Club	Society of Amateur Radio Operators
City:	Albany, CA
Call Sign:	W6AEX
Section:	EB

ARRL Affiliated Club	Pasadena Radio Club
City:	Altadena, CA
Call Sign:	W6KA
Section:	LAX
Links:	www.qsl.net/w6ka/

ARRL Affiliated Club	Anaheim Amateur Radio Assn.
City:	Anaheim, CA
Call Sign:	K6SYU
Section:	ORG
Links:	www.aara.org

ARRL Affiliated Club	Calaveras Amateur Radio Society, Inc.
City:	Angels Camp, CA
Call Sign:	N6FRG
Section:	SJV
Links:	www.calaverasars.org

ARRL Affiliated Club	Anza Valley Radio Club
City:	Anza, CA
Call Sign:	WB6UBG
Links:	www.anzavalleyradioclub.com, www.avrc.us

ARRL Affiliated Club	Fremont Peak Repeater Association
City:	Aromas, CA
Section:	SCV

ARRL Affiliated Club	Paso Robles Arc
City:	Atascadero, CA
Call Sign:	W6LKF
Section:	SB
Links:	www.pasoroblesarc.org

ARRL Special Service Club	Sierra Foothills Amateur Radio Club
City:	Auburn, CA
Call Sign:	W6EK
Section:	SV
Links:	www.w6ek.org, www.sf-arc.org

ARRL Affiliated Club	Kern County Central Valley Amateur Radio Club
City:	Bakersfield, CA
Call Sign:	W6LIE
Section:	SJV
Links:	www.w6lie.org

ARRL Affiliated Club	Bakersfield Amateur Radio Association
City:	Bakersfield, CA
Call Sign:	W6BAR
Section:	SJV

ARRL Affiliated Club	San Gorgonio Pass Amateur Radio Club
City:	Banning, CA
Call Sign:	W6PRC
Section:	ORG
Links:	www.W6PRC.org

ARRL Affiliated Club	Barstow Amateur Radio Club
City:	Barstow, CA
Call Sign:	WA6TST
Section:	ORG
Links:	www.wa6tst.org

ARRL Affiliated Club	Benicia Amateur Radio Club
City:	Benicia, CA
Call Sign:	KB6EOC
Section:	EB
Links:	www.beniciaccc.org/races

ARRL Affiliated Club	Northern Alameda County ARES
City:	Berkeley, CA
Section:	EB
Links:	www.pdarrl.org/ebsec/nalco/

ARRL Affiliated Club	Big Bear Amateur Radio Club
City:	Big Bear Lake, CA
Call Sign:	K6BB
Section:	ORG
Links:	www.bbarc.org

ARRL Affiliated Club	Bishop Amateur Radio Club
City:	Bishop, CA
Call Sign:	N6OV
Section:	ORG
Links:	n6ov.com

ARRL Affiliated Club	Desert Waves Amateur Radio Club
City:	Blythe, CA
Call Sign:	KR7AZ
Section:	ORG

ARRL Affiliated Club	Intermountain Amateur Radio Club
City:	Burney, CA
Call Sign:	KI6YJR
Section:	SV

ARRL Affiliated Club	Calexico Amateur Radio Society
City:	Calexico, CA
Call Sign:	K6CLX
Section:	SDG

ARRL Affiliated Club	U.H.F. Associates
City:	Calimesa, CA
Call Sign:	WB6ZOD
Section:	ORG
Links:	www.qrz.com/db/wb6zod, www.qrz.com/wb6zod

ARRL Affiliated Club	Valley Emergency Radio Assn.
City:	Camarillo, CA
Call Sign:	K6VER
Section:	SB
Links:	vera.k6iyk.net

ARRL Affiliated Club	SMRA Emergency Repeater Network
City:	Camarillo, CA
Call Sign:	K6ERN
Section:	SB
Links:	www.smravc.org

ARRL Affiliated Club	Foothills Amateur Radio Society (FARS)
City:	Campbell, CA
Call Sign:	K6YA
Section:	SCV
Links:	www.fars.k6ya.org

ARRL Affiliated Club	Sun City Amateur Radio Club
City:	Canyon Lake, CA
Section:	ORG

ARRL Affiliated Club	Friends & Amateur Radio Communications Enthusiasts
City:	Carmichael, CA
Call Sign:	KF6NNM
Section:	SV
Links:	www.kf6nnm.net

ARRL Affiliated Club	United Radio Amateur Club
City:	Carson, CA
Call Sign:	K6AA
Section:	LAX
Links:	www.k6aa.org

ARRL Affiliated Club	220 MHZ Spectrum Management Assn.
City:	Chatsworth, CA
Section:	LAX
Links:	www.220sma.org

ARRL Affiliated Club	Golden Empire Amateur Radio Society
City:	Chico, CA
Call Sign:	W6RHC
Section:	SV
Links:	www.gearsw6rhc.org

ARRL Affiliated Club	South Bay Amateur Radio Society
City:	Chula Vista, CA
Call Sign:	K6QM
Section:	SDG
Links:	www.sobars.org
ARRL Affiliated Club	Tri-County Amateur Radio Association
City:	Claremont, CA
Call Sign:	K6AGF
Section:	LAX
Links:	www.tcara.org
ARRL Affiliated Club	Clovis Amateur Radio Pioneers
City:	Clovis, CA
Call Sign:	K6ARP
Section:	SJV
Links:	www.k6arp.org
ARRL Affiliated Club	Crest Communications, Inc. Amateur Radio Club
City:	Corona, CA
Call Sign:	KE6TZJ
Section:	ORG
Links:	www.CrestCom.org
ARRL Affiliated Club	Corona Police CSV Team
City:	Corona, CA
Call Sign:	W6CPD
Section:	ORG
Links:	discovercorona.com/City-Departments/Police-Department/Communication-Specialist-Volunteers.asp
ARRL Affiliated Club	Calnet Repeater Group
City:	Corona, CA
Section:	ORG
Links:	www.cal-net.org
ARRL Affiliated Club	Coronado Emergency Radio Operators
City:	Coronado, CA
Call Sign:	W6MLI
Section:	SDG
Links:	www.ceroinc.org
ARRL Affiliated Club	West Coast Amateur Radio Club
City:	Costa Mesa, CA
Call Sign:	WC6ARC
Section:	ORG
Links:	www.qsl.net/wcarc/
ARRL Affiliated Club	HP Silicon Valley Radio Club
City:	Cupertino, CA
Call Sign:	WW6HP
Section:	SCV
Links:	www.pdarrl.org/clubs/hpsvrc/

ARRL Affiliated Club
City:
Call Sign:
Section:
Links:

Northern California 900 Repeater System
Diamond Springs, CA
NC9RS
SV
www.nc9rs.com

ARRL Affiliated Club
City:
Call Sign:
Section:
Links:

Downey Amateur Radio Club, Inc.
Downey, CA
W6TOI
LAX
www.downeyarc.org

ARRL Affiliated Club
City:
Call Sign:
Section:
Links:

Amateur Radio Club of El Cajon
El Cajon, CA
WA6BGS
SDG
www.WA6BGS.US

ARRL Affiliated Club
City:
Call Sign:
Section:
Links:

East Bay Amateur Radio Club Inc.
El Cerrito, CA
W6CUS
EB
www.eastbayarc.org

ARRL Affiliated Club
City:
Call Sign:
Section:
Links:

Hughes Amateur Radio Club
El Segundo, CA
W6HA
LAX
Pending

ARRL Affiliated Club
City:
Call Sign:
Section:
Links:

Contra Costa Communications Club
El Sobrante, CA
WA6KQB
EB
www.wd6ezc.org/

ARRL Affiliated Club
City:
Call Sign:
Section:
Links:

Vaca Valley Radio Club
Elmira, CA
W6VVR
EB
w6vvr.net

ARRL Affiliated Club
City:
Call Sign:
Section:
Links:

San Diego DX Club
Escondido, CA
W6PT
SDG
www.sddxc.org

ARRL Affiliated Club
City:
Call Sign:
Section:
Links:

San Diego DX Club
Escondido, CA
W6PT
SDG
www.sddxc.org

ARRL Affiliated Club	Humboldt Amateur Radio Club
City:	Eureka, CA
Call Sign:	W6ZZK
Section:	SF
Links:	www.humboldt-arc.org

ARRL Affiliated Club	Fallbrook Amateur Radio Club
City:	Fallbrook, CA
Call Sign:	N6FQ
Section:	SDG
Links:	www.fallbrookarc.org

ARRL Affiliated Club	San Lorenzo Valley Amateur Radio Club
City:	Felton, CA
Call Sign:	WR6AOK
Section:	SCV
Links:	www.slvarc.org

ARRL Affiliated Club	Redwood Amateur Radio Club
City:	Fortuna, CA
Call Sign:	KF6SYK
Section:	SF

ARRL Affiliated Club	Foster City Amateur Radio Emergency Service
City:	Foster City, CA
Call Sign:	K6FOS
Section:	SCV
Links:	www.fcares.org

ARRL Affiliated Club	Sam's Radio Hams
City:	Fountain Valley, CA
Call Sign:	K6SRH
Section:	ORG
Links:	www.srhams.org

ARRL Affiliated Club	Fountain Valley Amateur Comm. Team
City:	Fountain Valley, CA
Call Sign:	WA6FV
Section:	ORG
Links:	www.qsl.net/fvraces/

ARRL Affiliated Club	Sam's Radio Hams
City:	Fountain Valley, CA
Call Sign:	K6SRH
Section:	ORG
Links:	www.srhams.org

ARRL Affiliated Club	South Bay Amateur Radio Association
City:	Fremont, CA
Call Sign:	KU6S
Section:	EB
Links:	www.sbara.org

ARRL Affiliated Club	West Mesa DX and Contest Club
City:	Fresno, CA
Call Sign:	WM6DX
Section:	SJV

ARRL Affiliated Club	Fresno Amateur Radio Club, Inc.
City:	Fresno, CA
Call Sign:	W6TO
Section:	SJV
Links:	www.w6to.com

ARRL Affiliated Club	Central California DX Club
City:	Fresno, CA
Call Sign:	W6MEL
Section:	SJV
Links:	www.ccdxc.org

ARRL Affiliated Club	Amateur Radio Association of Central California
City:	Fresno, CA
Call Sign:	KI6GIL
Section:	SJV
Links:	www.aracc.org

ARRL Affiliated Club	Central CA Amateur Communications
City:	Fresno, CA
Call Sign:	KE6VFU
Section:	SJV

ARRL Affiliated Club	San Joaquin Valley Amateur Radio Society
City:	Fresno, CA
Call Sign:	WA6SJV
Section:	SJV
Links:	www.sjvars.com

ARRL Affiliated Club	Super System
City:	Fullerton, CA
Call Sign:	WA6TWF
Section:	ORG
Links:	wa6twf.com

ARRL Affiliated Club	Western Amateur Radio Association
City:	Fullerton, CA
Call Sign:	N6ME
Section:	ORG
Links:	www.warahams.net, www.n6me.org/

ARRL Affiliated Club	Fullerton Radio Club
City:	Fullerton, CA
Call Sign:	W6ULI
Section:	ORG
Links:	www.fullertonradioclub.org

ARRL Affiliated Club	Catalina Amateur Repeater Association
City:	Garden Grove, CA
Call Sign:	WC6ARA
Section:	ORG
Links:	www.cara.nu

ARRL Affiliated Club	Kennedy High School
City:	Granada Hills, CA
Call Sign:	KF6KIJ
Section:	LAX

ARRL Affiliated Club	Nevada County Amateur Radio Club
City:	Grass Valley, CA
Call Sign:	W6DD
Section:	SV
Links:	www.ncarc.org

ARRL Affiliated Club	Anchor Bay Amateur Radio Club
City:	Gualala, CA
Call Sign:	W6ABR
Section:	SF
Links:	www.abarc.net

ARRL Affiliated Club	Kings Amateur Radio Club, Inc.
City:	Hanford, CA
Call Sign:	KA6Q
Section:	SJV
Links:	www.qsl.net/ka6q

ARRL Affiliated Club	Hayward Radio Club Inc.
City:	Hayward, CA
Call Sign:	K6EAG
Section:	EB
Links:	www.k6eag.org

ARRL Affiliated Club	Hermosa Beach Amateur Radio Association
City:	Hermosa Beach, CA
Call Sign:	K6HBC
Section:	LAX
Links:	www.hbara.org/

ARRL Affiliated Club	Clairemont Repeater Association
City:	Huntington Beach, CA
Call Sign:	N6SLD
Section:	ORG
Links:	www.145220.com

ARRL Affiliated Club	Mile High Radio Club
City:	Idyllwild, CA
Call Sign:	KD6OI
Section:	ORG
Links:	www.milehighradioclub.org/

ARRL Affiliated Club	Lake County Amatuer Radio Society
City:	Kelseyville, CA
Call Sign:	W6ZK
Section:	SF

ARRL Affiliated Club	Crescenta Valley Radio Club
City:	La Canada Flintridge, CA
Call Sign:	WB6ZTY
Section:	LAX
Links:	www.qsl.net/cvrc

ARRL Affiliated Club   Mountain Repeater Assn.
City: La Crescenta, CA
Call Sign: K6VE
Section: LAX
Links: www.mraradio.org

ARRL Affiliated Club   Southern California DX Club
City: La Habra, CA
Call Sign: W6AM
Section: ORG

ARRL Affiliated Club   SC4 Amateur Radio Club
City: La Honda, CA
Call Sign: W6SCF
Section: SCV
Links: www.sc4arc.org, www.sc4arc.org/

ARRL Affiliated Club   Arcadia Amateur Radio Public Service Corp.
City: La Puente, CA
Call Sign: KI6UJB
Section: LAX

ARRL Affiliated Club   California Amateur Radio Linking Assn.
City: Lafayette, CA
Call Sign: K6LNK
Section: EB
Links: www.carlaradio.net

ARRL Affiliated Club   Laguna Woods Amateur Radio Club
City: Laguna Woods, CA
Call Sign: W6LY
Section: ORG
Links: www.qsl.net/w6ly

ARRL Affiliated Club   Sequoia Amateur Radio Group
City: Lake Isabella, CA
Call Sign: N6KRV
Section: SJV
Links: www.n6krv.org, www.sarg-krv.org/

ARRL Affiliated Club   Antelope Valley Amateur Radio Club
City: Lancaster, CA
Call Sign: K6OX
Section: LAX
Links: www.avarc.av.org

ARRL Affiliated Club   Western Placer Amateur Radio Club
City: Lincoln, CA
Call Sign: K6PAC
Section: SV
Links: www.wparc.us/, www.wparc.org/

ARRL Affiliated Club   Livermore Amateur Radio Klub
City: Livermore, CA
Call Sign: WA6ODP
Section: EB
Links: www.livermoreark.org/

ARRL Affiliated Club	Jerry Pettis VA Amateur Radio Club
City:	Loma Linda, CA
Call Sign:	W6VAH
Section:	ORG

ARRL Affiliated Club	Associated Radio Amateurs of Long Beach
City:	Long Beach, CA
Call Sign:	W6RO
Section:	LAX
Links:	www.aralb.org/

ARRL Affiliated Club	Southern Peninsula Emergency Communications System
City:	Los Altos, CA
Call Sign:	W6ASH
Section:	SCV
Links:	www.specsnet.org

ARRL Affiliated Club	Boy Scouts of America Troop 5
City:	Los Angeles, CA
Call Sign:	KT5BSA
Section:	LAX
Links:	www.qrz.com/db/kt5bsa

ARRL Affiliated Club	Hollywood Hills QRP Contest Club
City:	Los Angeles, CA
Section:	LAX

ARRL Affiliated Club	Los Angeles Amateur Radio Club
City:	Los Angeles, CA
Call Sign:	W6QET
Section:	LAX
Links:	www.kd6olh.org/laarcpg.htm

ARRL Affiliated Club	Baldwin Hills Amateur Radio Club
City:	Los Angeles, CA
Call Sign:	N6EW
Section:	LAX

ARRL Affiliated Club	Loma Prieta Amateur Radio Club
City:	Los Gatos, CA
Section:	SCV
Links:	www.lparc.org

ARRL Affiliated Club	Estro Radio Club, Inc.
City:	Los Osos, CA
Call Sign:	W6JU
Section:	SB
Links:	www.sloradio.net

ARRL Affiliated Club	Madera County Amateur Radio Club
City:	Madera, CA
Call Sign:	W6WGZ
Section:	SJV
Links:	www.w6wgz.org

ARRL Affiliated Club	Ladies Amateur Radio Association of Orange County
City:	Manhattan Beach, CA
Section:	LAX

ARRL Affiliated Club	Manteca Amateur Radio Club
City:	Manteca, CA
Call Sign:	K6MAN
Section:	SJV
Links:	sjham.com/

ARRL Affiliated Club	Monterey Bay Amateur Radio Association
City:	Marina, CA
Call Sign:	N6IJ
Section:	SCV
Links:	www.n6ij.org

ARRL Affiliated Club	Martinez Amateur Radio Club
City:	Martinez, CA
Call Sign:	KF6HTE
Section:	EB

ARRL Affiliated Club	Palo Alto Amateur Radio Association
City:	Menlo Park, CA
Call Sign:	W6OTX
Section:	SCV
Links:	www.PAARA.org/

ARRL Affiliated Club	Northern California DX Club
City:	Menlo Park, CA
Call Sign:	W6TI
Section:	SCV
Links:	www.ncdxc.org

ARRL Affiliated Club	Marin Amateur Radio Society
City:	Mill Valley, CA
Call Sign:	W6SG
Section:	SF
Links:	www.w6sg.net

ARRL Affiliated Club	Millbrae Amateur Radio Club
City:	Millbrae, CA
Call Sign:	KB6TR
Section:	SCV

ARRL Affiliated Club	South Orange Amateur Radio Assoc.
City:	Mission Viejo, CA
Call Sign:	K6SOA
Section:	ORG
Links:	www.soara.org

ARRL Affiliated Club	Stanislaus Amateur Radio Association
City:	Modesto, CA
Call Sign:	WD6EJF
Section:	SJV
Links:	www.saraclub.net/index.html

ARRL Affiliated Club	Moorpark High School Amateur Radio Club
City:	Moorpark, CA
Call Sign:	W6MHS
Section:	SB
Links:	www.mhsweather.org

ARRL Affiliated Club	Moreno Valley Amateur Radio Association
City:	Moreno Valley, CA
Call Sign:	AB6MV
Section:	ORG
Links:	www.mvaranet.org

ARRL Affiliated Club	Mount Shasta Amateur Radio Club
City:	Mount Shasta, CA
Call Sign:	W6BML
Section:	SV
Links:	w6bml.com

ARRL Affiliated Club	Blackberry React, Incorporated
City:	Mountain View, CA
Call Sign:	WZ6BBR
Section:	SCV
Links:	www.blackberryreact.org

ARRL Affiliated Club	Silverado Amateur Radio Society
City:	Napa, CA
Call Sign:	W6CO
Section:	EB
Links:	www.napasars.org

ARRL Affiliated Club	Corona Norco Amateur Radio Club
City:	Norco, CA
Call Sign:	W6PWT
Section:	ORG
Links:	www.w6pwt.org

ARRL Affiliated Club	Valley Good Guys
City:	North Hollywood, CA
Call Sign:	K6VGG
Section:	LAX
Links:	www.geocities.com/vggarc/

ARRL Affiliated Club	San Fernando Valley Amateur Radio Club
City:	Northridge, CA
Call Sign:	W6SD
Section:	LAX
Links:	www.w6sd.net

ARRL Affiliated Club	Mountain Amateur Radio Club
City:	Oakhurst, CA
Call Sign:	W6BW
Section:	SJV
Links:	www.w6bw.org

ARRL Affiliated Club	Oakland Radio Communication Association
City:	Oakland, CA
Call Sign:	WW6OR
Section:	EB
Links:	www.ww6or.com
ARRL Special Service Club	Inland Empire Amateur Radio Club
City:	Ontario, CA
Call Sign:	W6IER
Section:	ORG
Links:	www.w6ier.org
ARRL Affiliated Club	Two-Meter Area Spectrum Management Assn.
City:	Orange, CA
Section:	ORG
Links:	www.tasma.org
ARRL Affiliated Club	Autonetics Radio Club
City:	Orange, CA
Call Sign:	K6NX
Section:	ORG
Links:	www.qsl.net/k6nx
ARRL Affiliated Club	Orange County Council Of Aro
City:	Orange, CA
Section:	ORG
Links:	www.occaro.org/
ARRL Affiliated Club	Oroville Amateur Radio Society
City:	Oroville, CA
Call Sign:	W6AF
Section:	SV
Links:	www.w6af.org
ARRL Affiliated Club	Ventura County Amateur Radio Club
City:	Oxnard, CA
Call Sign:	K6MEP
Section:	SB
Links:	www.qsl.net/k6mep
ARRL Affiliated Club	Coastside Amateur Radio Club
City:	Pacifica, CA
Call Sign:	WA6TOW
Section:	SCV
Links:	www.coastsidearc.org
ARRL Affiliated Club	Coachella Valley Amateur Radio Club
City:	Palm Desert, CA
Call Sign:	NR6P
Section:	ORG
Links:	www.qsl.net/k6bsc
ARRL Affiliated Club	Desert Rats of Palm Springs, CA
City:	Palm Springs, CA
Call Sign:	WD6RAT
Section:	ORG
Links:	desertrats.x.am

ARRL Affiliated Club Palos Verdes Amateur Radio Club
City: Palos Verdes Penin, CA
Call Sign: K6PV
Section: LAX
Links: www.palosverdes.com/pvarc/

ARRL Affiliated Club Redwood Empire DX Assn.
City: Penngrove, CA
Call Sign: W6KB
Section: SF
Links: www.redxa.com/

ARRL Affiliated Club Wizard DX and Amateur Radio Club
City: Phelan, CA
Call Sign: WI6ZRD
Section: ORG

ARRL Affiliated Club Amador County Amateur Radio Club
City: Pine Grove, CA
Call Sign: K6ARC
Section: SV
Links: www.k6arc.org

ARRL Affiliated Club Mother Lode DX/Contest Club
City: Pine Grove, CA
Call Sign: K6AO
Section: SV
Links: www.mldxcc.org/

ARRL Affiliated Club El Dorado County Amateur Radio Club
City: Placerville, CA
Call Sign: AG6AU
Section: SV
Links: www.edcarc.net

ARRL Affiliated Club Mount Diablo Amateur Radio Club
City: Pleasant Hill, CA
Call Sign: W6CX
Section: EB
Links: www.mdarc.org

ARRL Affiliated Club Alameda City Sherriff's Comm. Team
City: Pleasanton, CA
Call Sign: W6VOM
Section: EB

ARRL Affiliated Club Porterville Amateur Repeater Assn.
City: Porterville, CA
Call Sign: KE6WDX
Section: SJV
Links: www.qsl.net/ke6wdx

ARRL Affiliated Club Poway Amateur Radio Society
City: Poway, CA
Call Sign: N6PWY
Section: SDG

ARRL Affiliated Club	Plumas Amateur Radio Club
City:	Quincy, CA
Call Sign:	K6PLU
Section:	SV

ARRL Affiliated Club	Inland Empire Homeschoolers Amateur Radio Club
City:	Rancho Cucamonga, CA
Section:	ORG

ARRL Affiliated Club	Southern Humboldt Arc
City:	Redway, CA
Section:	SF
Links:	sharc-ca.org

ARRL Affiliated Club	Troop 27 & Crew 27 Amateur Radio Club
City:	Redwood City, CA
Call Sign:	KG6WFO
Section:	SCV
Links:	www.v27.org/HamRadio.asp

ARRL Affiliated Club	Rialto Amateur Radio Club
City:	Rialto, CA
Call Sign:	K6RIA
Section:	ORG
Links:	www.k6ria.net

ARRL Affiliated Club	Red Oak Victory Amateur Radio Club
City:	Richmond, CA
Call Sign:	K6YVM
Section:	EB
Links:	www.qsl.net/redoakarc/

ARRL Affiliated Club	Sierra Amateur Radio Club of The High Mojave
City:	Ridgecrest, CA
Call Sign:	WA6YBN
Section:	SJV
Links:	www.qsl.net/wa6ybn/

ARRL Affiliated Club	San Bernardino Microwave Society
City:	Ridgecrest, CA
Call Sign:	W6IFE
Section:	SJV
Links:	www.ham-radio.com/sbms/, www.ham-radio.com/sbms/

ARRL Affiliated Club	Trilogy Radio Club
City:	Rio Vista, CA
Call Sign:	K6TRL
Section:	EB
Links:	Trilogy Radio Club

ARRL Affiliated Club	Riverside County Amateur Radio Association
City:	Riverside, CA
Call Sign:	W6TJ
Section:	ORG
Links:	www.w6tj.org

ARRL Affiliated Club	Sacramento Amateur Radio Club, Inc.
City:	Sacramento, CA
Call Sign:	W6AK
Section:	SV
Links:	www.w6ak.org

ARRL Affiliated Club	Mount Vaca Radio Club
City:	Sacramento, CA
Call Sign:	K6MVR
Section:	SV
Links:	www.mvrc.org

ARRL Affiliated Club	Military Mazagine Amateur Radio Club
City:	Sacramento, CA
Call Sign:	W6MIL
Section:	SV

ARRL Affiliated Club	North Hills Radio Club
City:	Sacramento, CA
Call Sign:	K6IS
Section:	SV
Links:	www.k6is.org

ARRL Special Service Club	River City Amateur Radio Communications Society
City:	Sacramento, CA
Call Sign:	N6NA
Section:	SV
Links:	www.n6na.org

ARRL Affiliated Club	Citrus Belt Amateur Radio Club
City:	San Bernardino, CA
Call Sign:	W6JBT
Section:	ORG
Links:	www.w6jbt.org, www.qsl.net/w6jbt

ARRL Affiliated Club	San Diego A R Council
City:	San Diego, CA
Call Sign:	W6SLF
Section:	SDG
Links:	www.sandarc.org

ARRL Affiliated Club	San Diego Repeater Association (SANDRA)
City:	San Diego, CA
Call Sign:	WB6WLV
Section:	SDG
Links:	www.wb6wlv.com

ARRL Affiliated Club	Spider Amateur Radio Club
City:	San Diego, CA
Call Sign:	AF6DX
Section:	SDG
Links:	www.qsl.net/af6dx

ARRL Affiliated Club	Convair/220 Amateur Radio Club
City:	San Diego, CA
Call Sign:	W6UUS
Section:	SDG

ARRL Affiliated Club	North Shores Amateur Radio Club
City:	San Diego, CA
Call Sign:	K6HAI
Section:	SDG

ARRL Affiliated Club	San Francisco Amateur Radio Club Inc.
City:	San Francisco, CA
Call Sign:	W6PW
Section:	SF
Links:	www.sfarc.org

ARRL Affiliated Club	San Francisco Ham Radio Club
City:	San Francisco, CA
Call Sign:	NO6PW
Section:	SF
Links:	www.qsl.net/no6pw/

ARRL Affiliated Club	San Francisco Ham Radio Club
City:	San Francisco, CA
Call Sign:	NO6PW
Section:	SF
Links:	www.qsl.net/no6pw/

ARRL Affiliated Club	Lee De Forest Amateur Radio Club
City:	San Jacinto, CA
Call Sign:	N7OD
Section:	ORG
Links:	www.ld-arc.org

ARRL Affiliated Club	Santa Clara County Amateur Radio Association
City:	San Jose, CA
Call Sign:	W6UW
Section:	SCV
Links:	www.qsl.net/sccara

ARRL Affiliated Club	West Valley
City:	San Jose, CA
Call Sign:	W6PIY
Section:	SCV
Links:	www.wvara.org

ARRL Affiliated Club	San Leandro Radio Club
City:	San Lorenzo, CA
Call Sign:	W6ZB
Section:	EB

ARRL Special Service Club	Cal Poly Amateur Radio Club
City:	San Luis Obispo, CA
Call Sign:	W6BHZ
Section:	SB
Links:	www.w6bhz.org

ARRL Affiliated Club	San Mateo Radio Club Inc.
City:	San Mateo, CA
Call Sign:	W6UQ
Section:	SCV
Links:	clubs.triyada.com/w6uq/, www.w6uq.org

ARRL Affiliated Club	Bay Area Educational Amateur Radio Society
City:	San Mateo, CA
Section:	SCV
Links:	baears.com

ARRL Affiliated Club	South County ARES Inc.
City:	San Mateo, CA
Call Sign:	K6MPN
Section:	SCV
Links:	k6mpn.org

ARRL Affiliated Club	SS Lane Victory Amateur Radio Club
City:	San Pedro, CA
Call Sign:	W6LV
Section:	LAX
Links:	www.lanevictory.org/

ARRL Affiliated Club	Hamilton Wireless Assn.
City:	San Rafael, CA
Call Sign:	K6BW
Section:	SF
Links:	www.k6bw.org

ARRL Affiliated Club	Amateur Radio Club at University of CA Santa Barbara
City:	Santa Barbara, CA
Call Sign:	W6RFU
Section:	SB
Links:	www.ece.ucsb.edu/~long/W6RFU/index.htm

ARRL Affiliated Club	Santa Barbara Amateur Radio Club
City:	Santa Barbara, CA
Call Sign:	K6TZ
Section:	SB
Links:	www.sbarc.org

ARRL Affiliated Club	Santa Clarita Amateur Radio Club
City:	Santa Clarita, CA
Call Sign:	W6JW
Section:	LAX
Links:	www.w6jw.org

ARRL Affiliated Club	Santa Cruz County Amateur Radio Club, Inc.
City:	SANTA CRUZ, CA
Call Sign:	K6BJ
Section:	SCV
Links:	www.k6bj.org

ARRL Affiliated Club	Sonoma County Radio Amateurs
City:	Santa Rosa, CA
Call Sign:	K6SON
Section:	SF
Links:	www.sonomacountyradioamateurs.com/

ARRL Affiliated Club	Saratoga Amateur Radio Association
City:	Saratoga, CA
Call Sign:	K6SA
Section:	SCV
Links:	www.k6sa.net
ARRL Affiliated Club	Naval Postgraduate School Amateur Radio Club
City:	Seaside, CA
Call Sign:	K6LY
Section:	SCV
Links:	www.k6ly.org
ARRL Affiliated Club	Simi Settlers Amateur Radio Club
City:	Simi Valley, CA
Call Sign:	W6SVS
Section:	SB
Links:	www.simisettlers.org
ARRL Affiliated Club	Valley of The Moon Amateur Radio Club
City:	Sonoma, CA
Call Sign:	W6AJF
Section:	SF
Links:	www.vomarc.org
ARRL Affiliated Club	T.C.A.R.E.S
City:	Sonora, CA
Call Sign:	K6TUO
Section:	SJV
Links:	www.lodelink.com/tcares
ARRL Affiliated Club	Tahoe Amateur Radio Assn.
City:	South Lake Tahoe, CA
Section:	SV
Links:	TahoeAmateurRadio.com
ARRL Affiliated Club	Stanford Radio Club
City:	Stanford, CA
Call Sign:	W6YX
Section:	SCV
Links:	www-w6yx.stanford.edu
ARRL Affiliated Club	Stockton-Delta Amateur Radio Club
City:	Stockton, CA
Call Sign:	W6SF
Section:	SJV
Links:	www.w6sf.org
ARRL Affiliated Club	Southern California Contest Club
City:	Studio City, CA
Section:	LAX
Links:	sccc.contesting.com/
ARRL Affiliated Club	Northern California Contest Club
City:	Sunnyvale, CA
Call Sign:	K6ZM
Section:	SCV
Links:	www.nccc.cc

ARRL Affiliated Club	Association of Silicon Valley Amateur Radio Organization
City:	Sunnyvale, CA
Section:	SCV
Links:	www.asvaro.org

ARRL Affiliated Club	SARES-RG
City:	Sunnyvale, CA
Call Sign:	K6SNY
Section:	SCV

ARRL Affiliated Club	50 Mhz & Up Group of N CA
City:	Sunnyvale, CA
Call Sign:	KF6JJL
Section:	SCV
Links:	www.50mhzandup.org

ARRL Affiliated Club	Lassen Amateur Radio Club
City:	Susanville, CA
Call Sign:	K6LRC
Section:	SV
Links:	www.qsl.net/k6lrc/

ARRL Affiliated Club	Southern Sierra Amateur Radio Society
City:	Tehachapi, CA
Section:	SJV

ARRL Affiliated Club	Rabbit Radio Network
City:	Thousand Oaks, CA
Call Sign:	W6RRN
Section:	SB
Links:	rabbitradio.org

ARRL Affiliated Club	Conejo Valley Amateur Radio Club Inc.
City:	Thousand Oaks, CA
Call Sign:	AA6CV
Section:	SB
Links:	www.cvarc.org

ARRL Affiliated Club	Ventura County Amateur Radio Society
City:	Thousand Oaks, CA
Call Sign:	K6VCS
Section:	SB
Links:	www.vcars.org

ARRL Special Service Club	South Bay Amateur Radio Club
City:	Torrance, CA
Call Sign:	W6SBA
Section:	LAX
Links:	www.w6sba.org

ARRL Affiliated Club	Radiobakervegas Club
City:	Torrance, CA
Call Sign:	W7RBV
Section:	LAX
Links:	www.b2v.org

ARRL Affiliated Club	LA Area Council of Amateur Radio Club
City:	Torrance, CA
Section:	LAX
Links:	www.qsl.net/laacarc

ARRL Affiliated Club	Turlock Amateur Radio Club
City:	Turlock, CA
Call Sign:	W6BXN
Section:	SJV
Links:	www.w6bxn.org

ARRL Affiliated Club	Orange County Amateur Radio Club
City:	Tustin, CA
Call Sign:	W6ZE
Section:	ORG
Links:	www.w6ze.org

ARRL Affiliated Club	North Bay Amateur Radio Assn.
City:	Vallejo, CA
Call Sign:	K6LI
Section:	EB
Links:	www.nbara.org, www.geocities.com/k6livallejo/

ARRL Affiliated Club	Satellite Amateur Radio Club
City:	Vandenberg A F B, CA
Call Sign:	W6AB
Section:	SB
Links:	www.SatelliteARC.com

ARRL Affiliated Club	Ventura Radio Club, Inc.
City:	Ventura, CA
Call Sign:	W6VRC
Section:	SB
Links:	www.w6vrc.org/, www.w6vrc.org

ARRL Affiliated Club	Santa Barbara Section Council of Clubs
City:	Ventura, CA
Section:	SB
Links:	www.qsl.net/arrlsbclubs/

ARRL Affiliated Club	VICTOR VALLEY Amateur Radio Club
City:	Victorville, CA
Call Sign:	K6QWR
Section:	ORG
Links:	www.vvarc.org

ARRL Affiliated Club	Tulare County Amateur Radio Club
City:	Visalia, CA
Call Sign:	WA6BAI
Section:	SJV
Links:	www.tcarc.net

ARRL Affiliated Club	Palomar Amateur Radio Club Inc.
City:	Vista, CA
Call Sign:	W6NWG
Section:	SDG
Links:	www.palomararc.org/

ARRL Affiliated Club	So Cal Amateur Transmitter Society
City:	West Covina, CA
Call Sign:	WB6LRU
Section:	LAX
Links:	www.SCATS.org

ARRL Affiliated Club	Rio Hondo Amateur Radio Club
City:	Whittier, CA
Call Sign:	W6GNS
Section:	LAX
Links:	www.rharc.org/

ARRL Affiliated Club	Golden Triangle Amateur Radio Club
City:	Wildomar, CA
Call Sign:	W6GTR
Section:	ORG
Links:	www.gtarc.org

ARRL Affiliated Club	Willits Amateur Radio Society
City:	Willits, CA
Call Sign:	W6MMM
Section:	SF
Links:	www.k6mhe.com/wars

ARRL Affiliated Club	Glenn Amateur Radio Society
City:	Willows, CA
Call Sign:	KJ6HCG
Section:	SV
Links:	garshamradio2010.org

ARRL Affiliated Club	Berryessa Amateur Radio Klub
City:	Woodland, CA
Call Sign:	KE6YUV
Section:	SV
Links:	www.barkradio.org

ARRL Affiliated Club	Siskiyou County Amateur Radio Assn.
City:	Yreka, CA
Call Sign:	K6SIS
Section:	SV
Links:	k6sis.com

ARRL Affiliated Club	Yuba-Sutter Amateur Radio Club
City:	Yuba City, CA
Section:	SV
Links:	www.ysarc.org

ARRL Affiliated Club	Yucaipa Valley Amateur Radio Club
City:	Yucaipa, CA
Call Sign:	K6YRC
Section:	ORG
Links:	www.yvarc.org

APPENDIX B

Amateur Radio License Holders

in

California: Northern Region
(by City)

FCC Amateur Radio Licenses in Adin

Call Sign: KD6YXA
Allen J Johnson
680525 Butte Creek Rd
Adin CA 96006

Call Sign: W6RXX
Harvey L Overland
67 Hideway Ln
Adin CA 96006

Call Sign: KC6FLU
Lura Yowell
Adin CA 960060113

FCC Amateur Radio Licenses in Albion

Call Sign: N6MAN
Martin D Moilanen
28214 Albion Ridg Rd
Albion CA 95410

Call Sign: KB8MMG
Nancy L Mokry
25700 Albion Ridge Rd
Albion CA 954100081

Call Sign: KI6CGZ
Juliet N Way
26900 Albion Ridge Rd
Albion CA 95410

Call Sign: NX6I
George F Drake
Albion CA 95410

Call Sign: N1EDH
James C Heid
Albion CA 95410

Call Sign: KE6ACW
Joseph M Goforth
Albion CA 95410

Call Sign: KF6CBH
Marlene E Goforth
Albion CA 954100677

Call Sign: KG6ZUX
Frances Kohler
Albion CA 954100884

Call Sign: K6KOH
Frances Kohler
Albion CA 954100884

Call Sign: KD6AEX
Rodric A Lorimer
Albion CA 95410

Call Sign: KF6CBG
Mark R Matthews I
Albion CA 954100492

Call Sign: KJ6IAI
John Passykva
Albion CA 954100563

Call Sign: KI6CHA
Jane D Tate
Albion CA 95410

Call Sign: KI6GGD
Erif Thunen
Albion CA 95410

FCC Amateur Radio Licenses in Alderpoint

Call Sign: KI6PQY
Robin R Craig
Alderpoint CA 95511

FCC Amateur Radio Licenses in Alturas

Call Sign: KE6BGR

John M Hakanson
412 Archer Ave
Alturas CA 96101

Call Sign: K6TBW
Clarence E Wager
Hc 1 Box 11334
Alturas CA 96101

Call Sign: KE6UZO
Dale O Hadley
Hc 4 Box 43028
Alturas CA 96101

Call Sign: KI6CPE
Dale O Hadley
Hc 4 Box 43028
Alturas CA 96101

Call Sign: KJ6JW
Ronny K Greve
Hc 04 Box 44033
Alturas CA 96101

Call Sign: WA6HXB
Doris E Huvar
Hcr 4 Box 44042
Alturas CA 961019510

Call Sign: W6GBF
Cyril F Huvar Jr
Hcr 4 Box 44042
Alturas CA 961019510

Call Sign: N7ERC
Ronald P Sharpless
Hc 3 Box 514
Alturas CA 96101

Call Sign: N6DQN
Christine M Sutter El Berins
Hc 3 Box 543
Alturas CA 96101

Call Sign: N6SVV
Donna J Ferguson
Hcr 3 Box 543
Alturas CA 96101

Call Sign: WA6QNV
Robert C Maupin
112 McDowell
Alturas CA 96101

Call Sign: K6RN
Harold G McRoberts
1304 Spruce St
Alturas CA 96101

Call Sign: K6QQ
John R Moriarity
151 Wayside Dr
Alturas CA 96101

Call Sign: NT6K
Dave E Bullard
Alturas CA 96101

Call Sign: WB6ZFM
Lorene Carnevale
Alturas CA 96101

Call Sign: WB6IUU
Richard D Shepherd
Alturas CA 96101

Call Sign: KB6MD
Dennis R Rothe
Alturas CA 96101

Call Sign: KC6MEI
Judith Bullard
Alturas CA 96101

Call Sign: K6YXE
Daniel R Frey
Alturas CA 96101

Call Sign: KG6OJB

Tyler J Froeming
Alturas CA 96101

Call Sign: NU6C
Tyler J Froeming
Alturas CA 96101

Call Sign: N6KMR
James R Hertel
Alturas CA 96101

Call Sign: WA6IMD
Charles F Keeney
Alturas CA 96101

Call Sign: K6YKY
Charles F Keeney
Alturas CA 96101

Call Sign: WB6HMD
Alwin E Mazet
Alturas CA 96101

Call Sign: KI6YPS
Win J Mccracken Jr
Alturas CA 96101

Call Sign: KC6RST
Bernhard H Schmidt
Alturas CA 96101

Call Sign: NX6G
Bernd H Schmidt
Alturas CA 96101

Call Sign: KG6RUJ
Karin M Schmidt
Alturas CA 96101

Call Sign: KA6RIN
Karin M Schmidt
Alturas CA 96101

Call Sign: KI6YPU
Belinda N Shaver

Alturas CA 96101

Call Sign: KI6YPT
Lindsay N Shaver
Alturas CA 96101

Call Sign: KD6QMW
Lindsay N Shaver
Alturas CA 96101

Call Sign: KB5THH
Cheryl A Stevens
Alturas CA 96101

Call Sign: KJ6JHL
Jacqueline A Tillery
Alturas CA 96101

FCC Amateur Radio Licenses in Anchor Bay

Call Sign: K6UGN
Glenn A Funk
35351 Woodside Ct
Anchor Bay CA 95445

FCC Amateur Radio Licenses in Anderson

Call Sign: KE6POQ
John E Von Brandt
1155 3rd St
Anderson CA 96007

Call Sign: KC6CKT
Richard A Spry
1455 3rd St
Anderson CA 96007

Call Sign: KD6KVE
Ernest E Swartz Jr
1388 Andrew Ave
Anderson CA 96007

Call Sign: KD6VFN

Rolland R Henry
19343 Anna Rd
Anderson CA 96007

Call Sign: KJ6FOD
Yvonne N Keefauver
1381 Aspen Dr
Anderson CA 96007

Call Sign: KI6LMP
Ben C Swim
3015 Aster St
Anderson CA 96007

Call Sign: KE6VFQ
Debra A Waligorski
5295 Balls Ferry
Anderson CA 96007

Call Sign: WA6EVX
Raymond E Ault
4621 Balls Ferry Rd
Anderson CA 96007

Call Sign: N6RZR
Brian K Waligorski
5295 Balls Ferry Rd
Anderson CA 96007

Call Sign: KQ6YX
Gary N Fryer
7034 Bohn Blvd
Anderson CA 96007

Call Sign: KG6THY
Igo Miners Radio Club
7034 Bohn Blvd
Anderson CA 96007

Call Sign: KC6UEG
Charles W Jamison
7329 Bohn Blvd
Anderson CA 96007

Call Sign: KI6SUY

Gaylynn H Robinson
5950 Bourbon Ln
Anderson CA 96007

Call Sign: WD6DCJ
Thomas H Copeland
Rt 1 Box 1898A Pheasant
Dr
Anderson CA 96007

Call Sign: KE6WYB
Dale W White
1577 Bruce Dr Apt A
Anderson CA 96007

Call Sign: W6OHB
Raulino Silveira
4776 C St
Anderson CA 96007

Call Sign: KF6QMV
John F Perez
5081 Chestnut St
Anderson CA 96007

Call Sign: WD6DCJ
John F Perez
5081 Chestnut St
Anderson CA 96007

Call Sign: KI6JGX
Patricia R Day
16351 China Gulch Dr
Anderson CA 96007

Call Sign: KJ6RGK
Owen R Spencer
17072 China Gulch Dr
Anderson CA 96007

Call Sign: N6GRG
Michael J Shreeve Sr
15901 Cloverdale Rd
Anderson CA 96007

Call Sign: K6MR
Kenneth A Beals
14853 Cobblestone Ln
Anderson CA 96007

Call Sign: KI6YVT
Scott A Dunton
17229 Coyote Ln
Anderson CA 96007

Call Sign: KF6VAO
Michael W Brockman
3080 Driftstone Dr
Anderson CA 96007

Call Sign: KD5BJT
David L Minear
281 Fern St
Anderson CA 96007

Call Sign: W6GPM
James R Mcwhorter
16757 Fortune Way
Anderson CA 96007

Call Sign: KD6YFE
Lloyd J St John Jr
17654 Fuzzy Ln
Anderson CA 96007

Call Sign: KF6YIS
Bruce C Legassie
3538 Gardenia St
Anderson CA 96007

Call Sign: KI6PSB
Patrick M Hart
22141 Haller Ln
Anderson CA 96007

Call Sign: KC6YJS
Robin W Paulson
6365 Harrington Ln
Anderson CA 96007

Call Sign: WA7OBG
Glenn H Henderson
16840 Hawthorne Ave
Anderson CA 960070898

Call Sign: KB6VAW
Maxine Tomei
21633 Holt Canyon Rd
Anderson CA 96007

Call Sign: WA6EPG
Selmo Tomei
21633 Hout Canyon Rd
Anderson CA 96007

Call Sign: KE6KMT
Eric M Fletcher
2885 Iris St
Anderson CA 96007

Call Sign: KF6PCN
James M Riddell
7020 Jacobs Way
Anderson CA 960078502

Call Sign: KE6NYI
Brian E Bokkin
19502 Jacqueline St
Anderson CA 96007

Call Sign: KF6LCL
Dennis M McCoy
17039 Jay Dee Ln
Anderson CA 96007

Call Sign: KO6CU
William A Richter
4907 Kristy Ln
Anderson CA 96007

Call Sign: KF6MSJ
William M Richter Jr
4907 Kristy Ln
Anderson CA 96007

Call Sign: KJ6PZR
Jason W Keen
22 La Colina Ter
Anderson CA 96007

Call Sign: W6VLE
Augustine Silva
29 La Colina Ter
Anderson CA 96007

Call Sign: KE6EID
William B Nelson
30 La Colina Ter
Anderson CA 96007

Call Sign: KJ6EYN
Tyler A Dodge
5733A Lalley Ln
Anderson CA 96007

Call Sign: KA6RNI
Joyce L Gooch
16752 Lassen Ave
Anderson CA 96007

Call Sign: KF6AN
Bennett L Gooch
16752 Lassen Ave
Anderson CA 96007

Call Sign: KN6KI
David W Paulson
6455 Ledgestone Ct
Anderson CA 96007

Call Sign: K6NEV
Barbara P Paulson
6455 Ledgestone Ct
Anderson CA 96007

Call Sign: KI6NWK
Jonathan Paulson
6455 Ledgestone Ct
Anderson CA 96007

Call Sign: KD6YXI
John E Elsemore
22235 Lone Tree Rd 9
Anderson CA 96007

Call Sign: W0VO
Oscar E Means Jr
18330 Majestic View Dr
Anderson CA 96007

Call Sign: KC6IME
Charles M Fulghum
5346 Maybelle Wy
Anderson CA 96007

Call Sign: W6SUE
Sue Elsemore
1721 Mill St
Anderson CA 96007

Call Sign: WA6OZZ
John H Elsemore
1721 Mill St
Anderson CA 96007

Call Sign: KF6DDC
John R Schwerin
6580 Mossom Ln
Anderson CA 96007

Call Sign: KC6CLK
David J Bradley
6591 Mossom Ln
Anderson CA 96007

Call Sign: KF6MDC
David P Sprague
2636 Northway St
Anderson CA 96007

Call Sign: W6WAZ
James R Bakeman Sr
2639 Northway St
Anderson CA 96007

Call Sign: K6JIM
Ronald E Nelson
17490 Olinda Rd
Anderson CA 96007

Call Sign: KE6VFR
Ronnie J Nilson
17490 Olinda Rd
Anderson CA 96007

Call Sign: KI6UZS
Connie R Nilson
17490 Olinda Rd
Anderson CA 96007

Call Sign: KG6QT
Scott I Brear
18837 Olinda Rd
Anderson CA 96007

Call Sign: K6KIQ
Robert L Rice
5515 Olive St
Anderson CA 96007

Call Sign: W6PAS
Patsy S Styers
17234 Palm Ave
Anderson CA 960078641

Call Sign: W6CSS
Clarence S Styers Jr
17234 Palm Ave
Anderson CA 960078641

Call Sign: KG6AIC
David A Burruss
5550 Panther Rd
Anderson CA 96007

Call Sign: KG6BBV
Jeanette E Burruss
5550 Panther Rd
Anderson CA 96007

Call Sign: KE6WDH
Aaron J Unger
4773 Pheasant Dr
Anderson CA 96007

Call Sign: KA6BCA
Donald E Ostrander
1263 Pinon Ave
Anderson CA 96007

Call Sign: KA6QMA
Tim W Palmer
1787 Pinon Ave
Anderson CA 96007

Call Sign: KE6RBL
Arthur W Arnold
1920 Pinon Ave 25
Anderson CA 960070129

Call Sign: KC6OVV
Marilyn J Garneau
2501 Red Bud Lne B 23
Anderson CA 96007

Call Sign: KJ6UKM
Dana E Manuel
7090 Rio Rancho Rd
Anderson CA 96007

Call Sign: KC6DKK
Mark R Warnock
7240 River Crest Dr
Anderson CA 96007

Call Sign: KJ6HJM
John V Tasello
3358 Riverside Dr
Anderson CA 96007

Call Sign: KO6OF
Richard T Cole
1723 Shasta St
Anderson CA 96007

Call Sign: KF6QOQ
Jason E White
21122 Shelley Ln
Anderson CA 960078374

Call Sign: KE6ALG
Zane Epps
6526 Shortcake Dr
Anderson CA 96007

Call Sign: KJ6NUX
Mark D Hazeltine
3175 Silver St
Anderson CA 96007

Call Sign: KI6WBJ
Roger L Schreibeer
1942 Spruce Cir
Anderson CA 96007

Call Sign: N6PNK
David L Momsen
1545 Spruce St Apt G
Anderson CA 96007

Call Sign: N6YNV
Joel E Northrup
3616 Stingy Ln
Anderson CA 96007

Call Sign: K6OJN
Joel E Northrup
3616 Stingy Ln
Anderson CA 96007

Call Sign: KE6DOB
Cory T Marks
6885 Sullivan Dr
Anderson CA 96007

Call Sign: KJ6JHK
David Mitchell
7170 Sylvan Ln
Anderson CA 96007

Call Sign: KB6YMF
Delbert O Dalton
3344 Twin Oaks Ln
Anderson CA 96007

Call Sign: KD6KOU
Robin R McDowell
7270 Whitehouse Dr 47
Anderson CA 96007

Call Sign: KO6JT
Bobby L Hutcherson
7330 Whitehouse Dr 8
Anderson CA 96007

Call Sign: KI6NPM
Rob Santry
2165 Willow Glen Dr
Anderson CA 96007

Call Sign: KQ6J
Guy S Cole
Anderson CA 96007

Call Sign: KD6HVV
Charles K Johnson
Anderson CA 96007

Call Sign: KD6SNI
Joe S Parks
Anderson CA 96007

Call Sign: N6BJ
Albert E Simants
Anderson CA 96007

Call Sign: WB6JOB
George W Whipp
Anderson CA 96007

Call Sign: WD6BPZ
Donald G Bowden
Anderson CA 96007

Call Sign: K6TES

William F Mason Jr
Anderson CA 96007

Call Sign: KJ6UAG
Khris R Rulon
Anderson CA 96007

Call Sign: WB6JOZ
Leonard D Tucker
Anderson CA 96007

Call Sign: WA6OZY
Donald J Wiens
Anderson CA 96007

FCC Amateur Radio Licenses in Arcata

Call Sign: W6FYX
Robert M Ensminger
2133 11th St
Arcata CA 95521

Call Sign: N6LQC
Edward A Forsyth
318 12th St
Arcata CA 955215914

Call Sign: KG6LHG
William Chandler-Klein
1070 12th St
Arcata CA 95521

Call Sign: KG6LHH
Daniel Chandler-Klein
1070 12th St
Arcata CA 95521

Call Sign: KD6LME
Gregg J Gold
860 12th St 2
Arcata CA 95521

Call Sign: KF6FKW
Benjamin H Meninga

896 13th St
Arcata CA 95521

Call Sign: KF6OEH
James M Cotton
1971 27th St
Arcata CA 95521

Call Sign: KF6VLO
Deanna L Dizmang
474 4th St
Arcata CA 95521

Call Sign: KG6JUI
Andrius D Ilgunas
664 B 5th St
Arcata CA 95521

Call Sign: KF6OUR
Patrick L Spurling
801 A St
Arcata CA 95521

Call Sign: KE6PAM
Thomas M Thee
2042 Adams Ct
Arcata CA 95521

Call Sign: KE6PAP
Diane C Thee
2042 Adams Ct
Arcata CA 95521

Call Sign: KD6VUB
Donovan W Tolman
3259 Alliance Rd
Arcata CA 95521

Call Sign: KD6AAJ
Norman E Burton II
2575 Alliance Rd Apt 6E
Arcata CA 95521

Call Sign: KF6FLB
David S Jolson

2294 Alliance Rd F
Arcata CA 95521

Call Sign: KI6ZQU
Dawn C Albrecht
2313 Ariel Way
Arcata CA 95521

Call Sign: KF6NUH
Liza M Smith
841 Bayside Rd 24
Arcata CA 95521

Call Sign: W6NQE
Curtis J Siats
4346 Belmont Ct
Arcata CA 955214512

Call Sign: KG6GKF
Michael D Weaver
1637 Benjamin Ct
Arcata CA 95521

Call Sign: KD6LM
Gregg J Gold
1513 Beverly Dr
Arcata CA 95521

Call Sign: KG6JAY
Wyatt A Ledbetter
1468 Buttermilk Ln
Arcata CA 95521

Call Sign: KG6JAZ
Rod C Ledbetter
1468 Buttermilk Ln
Arcata CA 95521

Call Sign: KG6LHI
Gail Ledbetter
1468 Buttermilk Ln
Arcata CA 955216910

Call Sign: KI6DVM
Craig J Redwine

2777 Buttermilk Ln
Arcata CA 95521

Call Sign: W6BBN
Samuel H Jansen
304 California Ave
Arcata CA 95521

Call Sign: KM6WB
Michael A Kapitan
640 California Ave
Arcata CA 95521

Call Sign: KI6ULF
Rusty R Burke
545 Cedar Hill Ln
Arcata CA 95521

Call Sign: KI6EOT
James C Mccurtain
640 Cedar Hill Ln
Arcata CA 95521

Call Sign: KF6FLE
Kevin R Hamblin
3630 Coombs Ct
Arcata CA 95521

Call Sign: KF6RZP
John K Erickson
85 Crescent Way
Arcata CA 95521

Call Sign: KJ6D
George E Epperson
801 Crescent Way Ste 1
Arcata CA 95521

Call Sign: KJ6PEO
Charles D Chamberlain
1990 Daniels St
Arcata CA 95521

Call Sign: K6XG
David A Abell

1021 Diamond Dr
Arcata CA 955218349

Call Sign: KG6LHJ
Alicia W Abell
1021 Diamond Dr
Arcata CA 955218349

Call Sign: KG6LJ
Alicia W Abell
1021 Diamond Dr
Arcata CA 955218349

Call Sign: KG6MDZ
Van C Hare
726 Dorothy Ct
Arcata CA 95521

Call Sign: KJ6NFY
Sherry K Constancio
2885 Dunbar Ct
Arcata CA 95521

Call Sign: KG6GKC
Joseph G Fini
450 Elizabeth Dr
Arcata CA 955219252

Call Sign: N6OTL
Bent Christensen
611 Elizabeth Dr
Arcata CA 95521

Call Sign: KF6LZV
David J Brown
2012 Ernest Way
Arcata CA 95521

Call Sign: KE6UWI
Cathy L Enis
37 F St
Arcata CA 95521

Call Sign: KG6MQK
John D Longshore

1347 F St	928 H St	3172 Janes Rd
Arcata CA 95521	Arcata CA 95521	Arcata CA 95521

Call Sign: KE6LOV
Le Anna M Carson Hansen
1200 Fernwood Dr
Arcata CA 95521

Call Sign: KA6LJL
Michael D Seeber
1350 Hallen Dr 4
Arcata CA 95521

Call Sign: KC6MMA
Cerina K Gastineau
1362 K St 3
Arcata CA 95521

Call Sign: KF6AAL
Dean T Moore
2175 Fickle Hill Rd
Arcata CA 95521

Call Sign: K1HSU
HSU Radio Club
HSU 1 Harpts St
Arcata CA 955218299

Call Sign: KJ6PYR
Jerome K Carman
1233 Lincoln Ave
Arcata CA 95521

Call Sign: WA6HFC
Linda L Myers
2715 Fickle Hill Rd
Arcata CA 95521

Call Sign: KG6VAO
HSU Radio Club
HSU 1 Harpts St
Arcata CA 955218299

Call Sign: KF6MAH
Barry A Johnson
350 Lynn St
Arcata CA 95521

Call Sign: KG6JUJ
Eric J Eichelberger
1033 G St
Arcata CA 95521

Call Sign: KG6JUH
Adam R Gourley
1285 I St
Arcata CA 95521

Call Sign: K6BAJ
Barry A Johnson
350 Lynn St
Arcata CA 95521

Call Sign: KF6RZN
Gene C Smith
2715 Green Briar Ln
Arcata CA 95521

Call Sign: KA6AFO
Colman C Fockens
1390 I St
Arcata CA 95521

Call Sign: KG6GKB
Tyler J Buwalda
2065 Margaret Ln
Arcata CA 95521

Call Sign: KF6RZO
Jerret H Smith
2715 Greenbriar Ln
Arcata CA 95521

Call Sign: KG6OCI
Troy C Fowler
1494 I St
Arcata CA 95221

Call Sign: KF6UTY
Larry A Buwalda
2065 Margaret Ln
Arcata CA 95521

Call Sign: N6ZQE
Nicole A West
652B Grotzman Rd
Arcata CA 95521

Call Sign: KF6CMN
Joe E Rouvier
1156 J St
Arcata CA 95521

Call Sign: KO6EB
Grady Ward
3449 Martha Ct
Arcata CA 95521

Call Sign: KF6AAO
Melvin J Forrester
112 H St
Arcata CA 95521

Call Sign: KQ6RD
Lloyd L Buckley
3501 James Rd
Arcata CA 95521

Call Sign: KF6OEJ
Lan Sing Wu
178 Myrtle Ct
Arcata CA 95521

Call Sign: KF6OEI
David F Hitchcock

Call Sign: KG6LNV
Robert E Ruehl

Call Sign: KF6ZVC
Teresa L Michael

198 Myrtle Ct
Arcata CA 95521

1233 Poplar Dr
Arcata CA 95521

550 Union St A 3
Arcata CA 95521

Call Sign: KF6WMT
Craig H Scott
198 Myrtle Ct
Arcata CA 95521

Call Sign: WA6TBP
Jay M Davis
3456 Ribeiro Ln
Arcata CA 95521

Call Sign: KD6JMV
Robert G Manny Jr
550 Union St Apt B4
Arcata CA 95521

Call Sign: KI6RVH
Jared A Nipper
1062 N St
Arcata CA 95521

Call Sign: W9OKQ
John C Schaefer
1734 Roberts Way
Arcata CA 95521

Call Sign: KF6OEG
Bruce Thuel Chassaigne
4534 Valley W Blvd
Arcata CA 95521

Call Sign: KI6IMB
Jason W Moore
1192 Oasis St
Arcata CA 95521

Call Sign: KI6EGO
Ervyl E Pigg
1834 Roberts Way
Arcata CA 95521

Call Sign: W6HPM
Darrell M Wright
4517 Valley W Blvd C
Arcata CA 95521

Call Sign: KA6OQJ
James A Ruegg
1524 Old Arcata Rd
Arcata CA 95521

Call Sign: KE6IDR
Teresa A Matsumoto
2087 Scott Ct
Arcata CA 955215460

Call Sign: WA6DYJ
George Ritscher
1721 Victor Blvd
Arcata CA 95521

Call Sign: KB6RPX
Brenda S Ruegg
1524 Old Arcata Rd
Arcata CA 95521

Call Sign: KA6KJN
Mosby L Simmons IV
222 Simmons Ln
Arcata CA 95521

Call Sign: WB6QPG
Robert A Rocha
1365 Virginia Way
Arcata CA 95521

Call Sign: KF6FY
Irma D Ruegg
1524 Old Arcata Rd
Arcata CA 95521

Call Sign: KG6JUK
Jon D Forsyth
1298 Spring St
Arcata CA 95521

Call Sign: KG6LFS
John H Kafel
153 Wagon Jack Ln
Arcata CA 95521

Call Sign: KI6ULE
Claudia L Johnson
2176 Palomino Ln
Arcata CA 95521

Call Sign: KE6DBL
Barry J Gerdts
5059 Spruce Way
Arcata CA 95521

Call Sign: WA6POF
John H Kafel
153 Wagon Jack Ln
Arcata CA 95521

Call Sign: W6GNC
Kenneth R Heckman
4977 Ponderosa Way
Arcata CA 955214617

Call Sign: KE6FEI
Lance C Colburn
200 Stamps Ln
Arcata CA 95521

Call Sign: N6HGG
Robert E Reed Jr
232 Warren Creek Rd
Arcata CA 95521

Call Sign: WD6HEM
Charles S Somers Jr

Call Sign: K6KJN
Steve Savetz

Call Sign: KJ6IBY
Alicia K Mitchell

850A Warren Creek Rd
Arcata CA 95521

Call Sign: WA9TKO
Alicia K Mitchell
850A Warren Creek Rd
Arcata CA 95521

Call Sign: WB6YTM
Bernice E Sisto
2535 Wyatt Ln
Arcata CA 95521

Call Sign: KA6NYM
Peggy B Hans
2859 Wyatt Ln
Arcata CA 95521

Call Sign: KA6NYN
Torsten O Hans
2859 Wyatt Ln
Arcata CA 95521

Call Sign: KD6QIN
Angela M Clayton
Arcata CA 95521

Call Sign: KD7NU
Edwin L Greenwood
Arcata CA 95521

Call Sign: KE6FEG
Michael C Schultz Sr
Arcata CA 95521

Call Sign: KG6JUG
William P Fox
Arcata CA 95521

Call Sign: KF6EFO
John H Baum
Arcata CA 95518

Call Sign: KB6ISS
Marilyn A Bennett

Arcata CA 95518

Call Sign: KF6LZW
Janet A De Pace
Arcata CA 95518

Call Sign: KD6QKH
James H Doherty
Arcata CA 955184861

Call Sign: KJ6ATZ
Michael-Peter A Esko
Arcata CA 95518

Call Sign: KI6EBL
James T Farley
Arcata CA 95518

Call Sign: K6ZOD
James T Farley
Arcata CA 95518

Call Sign: K6YO
James T Farley
Arcata CA 95518

Call Sign: KF6MAI
Geoffrey Gahm
Arcata CA 95518

Call Sign: KI6EBJ
Ryle L Goehausen
Arcata CA 95518

Call Sign: KG6BDV
C Grant Kimbell
Arcata CA 95518

Call Sign: KC6LVO
Linda S Mahoney
Arcata CA 95518

Call Sign: KF6DAS
Shea Mahoney
Arcata CA 95521

Call Sign: KD6LLV
Robert F Neefus
Arcata CA 95518

Call Sign: KJ6PEM
Nanette R Nickerson
Arcata CA 95521

Call Sign: WB6ADU
Harold G Smith
Arcata CA 95521

Call Sign: KG6HXW
John W Warren
Arcata CA 95518

Call Sign: KF6YQR
David J Weaver
Arcata CA 95518

Call Sign: KG6LHW
Anthony F Wiese
Arcata CA 95518

FCC Amateur Radio Licenses in Bayside

Call Sign: KG6MAR
John D Olson
1575 Alex Ln
Bayside CA 95524

Call Sign: WB6DXX
Fred Leslie III
580 Hidden Valley Rd
Bayside CA 955249320

Call Sign: N6IJB
Mr. Gordon Inkeles
1641 Hyland St
Bayside CA 95524

Call Sign: WA6TOE
Dennis R Almand

2506 Jacoby Creek Rd
Bayside CA 95524

Call Sign: KB6HPL
Thomas D Savage
1154 Lombard Rd
Bayside CA 95524

Call Sign: KI6GRU
Forrest A Schafer
1147 Walker Pt Rd
Bayside CA 95524

Call Sign: KF6AAI
Dean L Thomas
1177 Walker Pt Rd
Bayside CA 95524

Call Sign: KD6TGE
Randall E Ackles
Bayside CA 95524

Call Sign: KK6ZY
David W Cook
Bayside CA 95524

Call Sign: K6TPJ
Terrance P Jones
Bayside CA 95524

Call Sign: N6VYD
Samuel B Trumbull
Bayside CA 95524

Call Sign: KF6YWI
Dwuane T Brummell
Bayside CA 95524

Call Sign: KJ6NNC
Roger P Eckart
Bayside CA 95524

**FCC Amateur Radio
Licenses in Bella Vista**

Call Sign: N6JPW
Joseph P Weggeland
24035 Ajax Ln
Bella Vista CA 96008

Call Sign: KF6DDA
Joseph F Lockwood
11770 Bella Vista Ct
Bella Vista CA 96008

Call Sign: N6CKO
Michael F Zeigler
12700 Brookview Manor
Dr
Bella Vista CA 96008

Call Sign: N6GYN
Ann M Murphy
12194 Old Ranch Rd
Bella Vista CA 96008

Call Sign: W6WY
Peter J Murphy
12194 Old Ranch Rd
Bella Vista CA 96008

Call Sign: KD6NZU
Jeffrey S Klotz
13867 Woodman Ln
Bella Vista CA 96008

Call Sign: KJ6GQ
Don L Galusha
Bella Vista CA 96008

Call Sign: KF6YTD
Leann N Brink
Bella Vista CA 96008

Call Sign: N6TVW
Mark A Carpenter
Bella Vista CA 96008

Call Sign: WA7ZXM
Lawrence H Fleming

Bella Vista CA 96008

Call Sign: N3FQ
Lawrence H Fleming
Bella Vista CA 96008

Call Sign: WA6DON
Don L Galusha
Bella Vista CA 96008

Call Sign: KG6GXV
Jeffrey K Gerlach
Bella Vista CA 96008

Call Sign: K6BRD
Jeffrey K Gerlach
Bella Vista CA 96008

Call Sign: WA6QNI
Clifford H Howard
Bella Vista CA 96008

Call Sign: KJ6EZJ
John E Jones
Bella Vista CA 96008

Call Sign: KF6JNN
Jonathan A Lockwood
Bella Vista CA 96008

Call Sign: KB6M
James G Miller
Bella Vista CA 96008

Call Sign: N6BYM
Stephen L Roberts
Bella Vista CA 96008

Call Sign: N6FIZ
Karen A Roberts
Bella Vista CA 96008

Call Sign: KJ6CSA
Rhett C Roberts
Bella Vista CA 96008

Call Sign: KE6ODI
Harold S Thorpe II
Bella Vista CA 960081064

FCC Amateur Radio Licenses in Benbow

Call Sign: KB6VSE
Steve Horvitz
10 Fern Springs Rd
Benbow CA 95542

FCC Amateur Radio Licenses in Bieber

Call Sign: K6JSC
Richard J Patak
Bieber CA 96009

FCC Amateur Radio Licenses in Big Bar

Call Sign: N6NOU
Robert C Hendricks
39 Lilac Ln
Big Bar CA 96010

Call Sign: KD6GDR
David K Lister
Big Bar CA 96010

Call Sign: KD6JVU
Dennis R Mac Kinney
Big Bar CA 96010

Call Sign: AB6KC
William J Ochoa
Big Bar CA 96010

Call Sign: KB6SNW
Anthony M Ochoa
Big Bar CA 96010

Call Sign: KB6SNY

Robert A Pearce
Big Bar CA 96010

Call Sign: KD6GDV
V Ray Sparkman
Big Bar CA 96010

Call Sign: N6TKX
Grace E Harrigan
Big Bar CA 96010

Call Sign: N6TKY
James E Harrigan
Big Bar CA 960100667

Call Sign: N6NOT
Colleen M Hendricks
Big Bar CA 96010

Call Sign: KD6JVR
Elizabeth A Mackinney
Big Bar CA 96010

Call Sign: KB6SNX
Diane D Ochoa
Big Bar CA 96010

Call Sign: KG6DHS
Anthony M Ochoa
Big Bar CA 96010

Call Sign: N6TMC
Carol A Rogan Zust
Big Bar CA 96010

Call Sign: N6TMD
James L Zust
Big Bar CA 96010

Call Sign: W6ZRD
Anthony M Ochoa
Big Bar CA 96010

Call Sign: W6DPO
Diane D Ochoa

Big Bar CA 96010

Call Sign: W6AYW
William J Ochoa
Big Bar CA 96010

FCC Amateur Radio Licenses in Blocksburg

Call Sign: KF6YAC
Margaret F Krefting
Blocksburg CA 955140224

FCC Amateur Radio Licenses in Blue Lake

Call Sign: KF6CMD
Timothy L Carlson
510 Blue Lake Blvd
Blue Lake CA 95525

Call Sign: AB6I
Wayne A Carlson
Blue Lake CA 95525

Call Sign: KB6HNH
Mitchell R Patenaude
Blue Lake CA 95525

Call Sign: KF6CMC
Cynthia L Carlson
Blue Lake CA 95525

Call Sign: KI6DGO
William F Cloud
Blue Lake CA 95535

Call Sign: KF6KAC
Thomas I Graves
Blue Lake CA 95525

Call Sign: KF6KAE
Justin K Graves
Blue Lake CA 95525

Call Sign: KG6WWI
John W Grondalski
Blue Lake CA 955250858

Call Sign: KJ6NZA
Lyle D Huff
Blue Lake CA 95525

Call Sign: KI6ULD
George A Machett
Blue Lake CA 95525

Call Sign: KE6IAZ
Paul W Ray
Blue Lake CA 95525

FCC Amateur Radio Licenses in Boonville

Call Sign: KF6LUY
Robert L Smith
12730 Anderson Valley Way
Boonville CA 95415

Call Sign: KF6LUZ
Jan E Wasson Smith
12730 Anderson Valley Way
Boonville CA 95415

Call Sign: WB6GDV
Lawrence Gaffney
13201 Estate Dr
Boonville CA 95415

Call Sign: WB6QOA
Ruben J Thomasson
13151 Meadow Ln
Boonville CA 95415

Call Sign: WD6EIK
Donald W Smoot
Boonville CA 95415

Call Sign: KJ6IAE
Tanner R Archer
Boonville CA 954150251

Call Sign: KJ6IBN
Angela R Dewitt
Boonville CA 954150443

Call Sign: K2HSV
David Jackness
Boonville CA 95415

Call Sign: KJ6HZY
Justin D Laqua
Boonville CA 954150132

Call Sign: KJ6IAA
Aaron D Martin
Boonville CA 954150251

Call Sign: KI6IST
Suzy Miller
Boonville CA 95415

Call Sign: KG6WMP
John E Newstead
Boonville CA 95415

Call Sign: KF6LUW
James E Nickless
Boonville CA 954150428

Call Sign: KI6IDK
Bob E Nimmons
Boonville CA 95481

FCC Amateur Radio Licenses in Bridgeville

Call Sign: AD6VA
George S Owsley Sr
Bear Creek Rd
Bridgeville CA 95526

Call Sign: KC6EBO

Blake J Stretton
39883 Hwy 36
Bridgeville CA 95526

Call Sign: KJ6SYJ
Sydne A Gladding
33096 Hwy 36
Bridgeville CA 95526

Call Sign: KE6TMG
Dennis L Johnson
46255 State Hwy 36
Bridgeville CA 95526

Call Sign: KF6CMJ
Fred B Hauck
451 Van View Rd
Bridgeville CA 95526

Call Sign: KE6SLZ
Jack A Branham
Bridgeville CA 95526

Call Sign: KE6SLW
James J Shreeve
Bridgeville CA 95526

FCC Amateur Radio Licenses in Burney

Call Sign: N6UNP
Gayla M Juul
20174 Arrowood St
Burney CA 96013

Call Sign: N6RQE
Rick G Voet
20334 Arrowood St
Burney CA 96013

Call Sign: KB6YUA
Addie L Harris
37370 Ash St
Burney CA 96013

Call Sign: KJ6HJR
Charles P Woodrum
20090 Bartel St
Burney CA 96013

Call Sign: KE6DHT
Derek C Hutchinson
20324 Cedar St
Burney CA 96013

Call Sign: N6VDB
David J Perry
37623 Mountain View Rd
Burney CA 96013

Call Sign: N6CPW
Charles P Woodrum
20090 Bartel St
Burney CA 96013

Call Sign: KE6NOT
Gregory D Cross
23413 Chism Tr
Burney CA 96013

Call Sign: K6KVL
Manford L Root
37098 Park Ave
Burney CA 96013

Call Sign: KB6DLU
Lois J Henry
20120 Bartel St
Burney CA 96013

Call Sign: KG6FDX
Kate M Drenon
20259 Fir St
Burney CA 96013

Call Sign: W6KAR
Karen A Root
37098 Park Ave
Burney CA 96013

Call Sign: K6VCO
Stuart E Neblett
20141 Bartel St
Burney CA 960131196

Call Sign: KG6WYL
Justin D Arendt
20260 Fir St
Burney CA 96013

Call Sign: KJ6PD
Kurt O Taylor
20075 Peridot Ln
Burney CA 96013

Call Sign: KG6ETG
Raymond R Skidmore
37336 Birch St
Burney CA 96013

Call Sign: KI6FDQ
Maxie N Bullard
37084 Galena Cir
Burney CA 96013

Call Sign: KD6WLJ
Christine C Toland Taylor
20075 Peridot Ln
Burney CA 96013

Call Sign: KF6JRE
Kenneth J Miller Jr
20442 Butte St
Burney CA 96013

Call Sign: N6SFK
Roland P Winter
Garden Ln
Burney CA 96013

Call Sign: KF6VYJ
Jeremy W Winkelman
20220 Tamarack Ave
Burney CA 96013

Call Sign: KC6HNC
Edward F O Brien
37282 Carson St
Burney CA 96013

Call Sign: KE6PQP
Cordelia M Sardoch
21925 Goose Creek Rd
Burney CA 96013

Call Sign: KI6UNN
Michael E Rogers
20293 Tamarack Ave
Burney CA 96013

Call Sign: KD6MS
Larry L Hutchinson
20324 Cedar St
Burney CA 96013

Call Sign: KI6LNP
John M Westlund
20526 Hudson St
Burney CA 96013

Call Sign: WD6BXN
Charles E Evans
37498 Toronto St
Burney CA 96013

Call Sign: KD6PTB
Sherrie Hutchinson
20324 Cedar St
Burney CA 96013

Call Sign: WA6TSH
Stephen C Vaughn
37305 Main St
Burney CA 96013

Call Sign: WD6FGE
Philip J Beaudet
37268 Vedder Rd
Burney CA 96013

Call Sign: N6PJB
Philip J Beaudet
37268 Vedder Rd
Burney CA 96013

Call Sign: WD6BPX
Burney High ARC
Burney CA 96013

Call Sign: KB6SCX
Curtis A Carpenter
Burney CA 96013

Call Sign: KB6WNI
Barbara A Clark
Burney CA 96013

Call Sign: KC6SUU
Arthur W Davis
Burney CA 96013

Call Sign: KC6NQH
Dale E Hackney
Burney CA 96013

Call Sign: KB6REC
Theresa A Harris
Burney CA 96013

Call Sign: KB6WKH
Cynthia R Ickes
Burney CA 96013

Call Sign: KB6WNH
Bartley D Ickes
Burney CA 96013

Call Sign: KD6EHD
Charles H Oguinn
Burney CA 96013

Call Sign: W6PB
Donald E Perry
Burney CA 96013

Call Sign: KC6SUE
Gerald A Wells
Burney CA 96013

Call Sign: KC6SUV
Virginia L Wells
Burney CA 96013

Call Sign: KD6MJV
Patricia M Winter
Burney CA 96013

Call Sign: WA6HWD
Dan E Nielsen
Burney CA 96013

Call Sign: KC6ECG
Ralph D Boggs
Burney CA 96013

Call Sign: KG6DMU
John J Cannon
Burney CA 96013

Call Sign: W6OLF
John J Cannon
Burney CA 96013

Call Sign: KF6BUY
Trent E Drenon
Burney CA 96013

Call Sign: KF6MQR
Cathy L Drenon
Burney CA 96013

Call Sign: AE6HD
Trent E Drenon
Burney CA 96013

Call Sign: KC6EKX
Robert W Fulk
Burney CA 96013

Call Sign: KF6AHP

Patrick C Gheen
Burney CA 96013

Call Sign: N6FRU
Robert W Sales
Burney CA 96013

FCC Amateur Radio Licenses in Burnt Ranch

Call Sign: N6TAQ
Barbara A Boatman
Burnt Ranch CA 95527

FCC Amateur Radio Licenses in Callahan

Call Sign: KF6IRF
Cliff Russ
9513 S Hwy 3
Callahan CA 96014

Call Sign: KF6KTA
Claudia A Russ
9513 S Hwy 3
Callahan CA 96014

FCC Amateur Radio Licenses in Calpella

Call Sign: KI6JCC
Hiram O Campbell Jr
Calpella CA 954180416

Call Sign: KI6ISS
Doran W Licoln
Calpella CA 95418

Call Sign: KJ6VII
Leonard J Martire Jr
Calpella CA 95418

FCC Amateur Radio Licenses in Canby

Call Sign: N6KEB
Kenneth E Bird
99 Buggy Trace Rd
Canby CA 96015

Call Sign: N7JIL
James I Linden Sr
250 CR 82
Canby CA 96015

Call Sign: KF6LXX
Canby Hot Springs 4H
ARC
Box 125 Hwy 299 E
Canby CA 96015

Call Sign: KD6ITD
Allen H Berg
Hwy 299 E
Canby CA 96015

Call Sign: N8MYU
Christine T Lorimer
Hwy 299 E
Canby CA 96015

Call Sign: KQ6TH
Jo Ann K Welsh
Hwy 299 E
Canby CA 96015

Call Sign: WA7OZP
Harry E Brown
Canby CA 96015

Call Sign: KB6TTI
Roger M Jackson
Canby CA 96015

Call Sign: N6SJY
Deborah J Jackson
Canby CA 96015

Call Sign: KG6JLZ

Chad E Linden
Canby CA 96015

Call Sign: AB6JB
Ruth A Stromquist
Canby CA 960150134

**FCC Amateur Radio
Licenses in Carlotta**

Call Sign: KG6DCN
Melissa Vitello
211 Church Ln
Carlotta CA 95528

Call Sign: KE6JQW
Guy A Vitello
211 Church Ln
Carlotta CA 95528

Call Sign: KF6UGH
Lisa A Vitello
211 Church Ln
Carlotta CA 95528

Call Sign: KG6MDY
Sarah C Vitello
211 Church Ln
Carlotta CA 95528

Call Sign: KG6QVJ
Hannah D Vitello
211 Church Ln
Carlotta CA 95528

Call Sign: KG6QVH
Leslie C Evans
5000 Hwy 36
Carlotta CA 95528

Call Sign: KG6QVG
Leslie K Evans
5000 Hwy 36
Carlotta CA 95528

Call Sign: KB6MLC
Leo N Mares
6761 Hwy 36
Carlotta CA 95528

Call Sign: KG6UQF
Michael C Diebner
6906 Hwy 36
Carlotta CA 95528

Call Sign: WB6UCY
Phillip E Scriver
7131 Hwy 36
Carlotta CA 955289703

Call Sign: AF6LR
Phillip E Scriver
7131 Hwy 36
Carlotta CA 955289703

Call Sign: WB6MOZ
John W Stephens
19691 Hwy 36
Carlotta CA 95528

Call Sign: N6KMT
Henry B Stevens
21260 Hwy 36
Carlotta CA 95528

Call Sign: KE6PAR
Christopher J Westkamper
485 Riverside Park Rd
Carlotta CA 95528

Call Sign: KE6PAS
Anthony E Westkamper
485 Riverside Park Rd
Carlotta CA 95528

Call Sign: KD6UOF
John L Cranfill
Carlotta CA 95528

Call Sign: KG6IRM

Jo A Nelson
Carlotta CA 955280241

FCC Amateur Radio Licenses in Caspar

Call Sign: KI6URI
Mary K Desautels
14975 Caspar Rd Box 44
Caspar CA 95420

Call Sign: KG6UXM
Kent B Pember
Caspar CA 95420

FCC Amateur Radio Licenses in Cassel

Call Sign: KQ6M
Kenneth W Phillips
39936 Pumice Dr
Cassel CA 960160053

Call Sign: KB6LFT
Conrad A Skaggs
39976 Pumice Dr
Cassel CA 96016

Call Sign: WA6PFH
Kenneth W Phillips
39936 Pumice Dr SE
Cassel CA 960160053

Call Sign: WB6YZF
John W Rodman
23416 Sandpit Rd
Cassel CA 96016

Call Sign: KA6ZMU
Jeffrey T Meyers
39575 Thrush Rd
Cassel CA 96016

Call Sign: KC6CUK
Karen E Meyers

39575 Thrush Rd
Cassel CA 96016

Call Sign: KG6ELO
Karen E Meyers
39575 Thrush Rd
Cassel CA 96016

Call Sign: KC6CUK
Karen E Meyers
39575 Thrush Rd
Cassel CA 96016

Call Sign: N6PYX
Catherine J Schmidt
39216 Wild Bird Ln
Cassel CA 96016

Call Sign: KD7ECT
Bessie W Congdon
39224 Wild Bird Ln
Cassel CA 96016

Call Sign: WA6MYI
Rachel A Hamilton
Cassel CA 96016

Call Sign: KB6WNF
Lester J Warner
Cassel CA 96016

Call Sign: W6LKV
Mark E Warnock
Cassel CA 96016

Call Sign: KC6WWS
John R Powell
Castella CA 96017

Call Sign: KC6WYJ
Eleanor E Brumer
Castella CA 96017

Call Sign: KG6WGL
Daniel C Rudie

Castella CA 96017

FCC Amateur Radio Licenses in Cedarville

Call Sign: WA6RBW
Brian E Cain
Cedarville CA 96104

Call Sign: KG6HAU
Steve L Holloman
Cedarville CA 96104

Call Sign: KJ6HGF
David M Schulz
Cedarville CA 96104

Call Sign: KG6VAC
Ruth A Stromquist
Cedarville CA 96104

FCC Amateur Radio Licenses in Central Valley

Call Sign: KA6NPV
Ivan G Petersen
4474 Arrow Rock
Central Valley CA 96019

Call Sign: KB6NWZ
Ace W Clemens
4645 Bonneville St
Central Valley CA 96019

Call Sign: WB6QFX
Edward W Gillis
1137 Hardenbrook
Central Valley CA 96019

Call Sign: KD6CPR
Cathy L Hall
1432 Lassen Ave
Central Valley CA 96019

Call Sign: KB6CDZ
George W Barber
2100 Morning Star Way
Apt 29
Central Valley CA 96019

Call Sign: KA6LEM
Bertie E Blevins
Central Valley CA 96019

Call Sign: KE6ALH
Robert L Pearsall Sr
Central Valley CA 96019

Call Sign: KA6HND
Walter J Wysock
Central Valley CA 96019

FCC Amateur Radio Licenses in Comptche

Call Sign: K6RLW
Ross L Williams
Comptche CA 95427

Call Sign: KK6GE
George L Williams
Comptche CA 95427

Call Sign: W6XYL
Catherine L Williams
Comptche CA 95427

FCC Amateur Radio Licenses in Corning

Call Sign: WD5DZB
Thomas W Freer-Heeter
1240 6th St
Corning CA 96021

Call Sign: KD6AGV
Steven J Schromm
680 Almond St
Corning CA 96021

Call Sign: KI6UQF
Gene R Lazard
4132 Columbia Ave
Corning CA 96021

Call Sign: WD6BUN
Joe O Edwards
4950 Edith Ave
Corning CA 96021

Call Sign: KE6QBR
Utah Z Hardy
5675 Edith Ave
Corning CA 96021

Call Sign: WB7CEE
A Malcholm Staheli
240 Edith Ave 160
Corning CA 96021

Call Sign: KI6NKZ
James C Hilton
728 El Paso Ave
Corning CA 96021

Call Sign: KG6IBH
Robert G Nelson
760 El Paso St
Corning CA 96021

Call Sign: WB6EIK
Chris T Evans
16835 Elder Creek Cir
Corning CA 96021

Call Sign: K6SWL
Robert W Johnson
22658 Finnell Ave
Corning CA 960219760

Call Sign: WA6RLA
Michael J Irwin
3835 Gardiner Ferry Rd Sp
48

Corning CA 96021

Call Sign: KA6WUV
Daniel P Coyle
4549 Hall Rd
Corning CA 96021

Call Sign: KD6ZF
Edward Fistor
4714 Hall Rd
Corning CA 96021

Call Sign: WA3AIJ
John A Dudley
1544 Herbert Ave
Corning CA 96021

Call Sign: KE6VCU
Susan J Eissinger
1544 Herbert Ave
Corning CA 96021

Call Sign: K6VCS
Clotis A Ursuery
1119 2 Hillcrest
Corning CA 96021

Call Sign: KG6MTK
Ronald D Nelson
104 Houghton Ave
Corning CA 96021

Call Sign: KD6HVF
Nathaniel G Hobson
1558 Houghton Ave
Corning CA 96021

Call Sign: KJ6DIF
Joel S Wilson
22388 Kraft Ave
Corning CA 96021

Call Sign: KG6JDY
Mathew R Ryant
383 La Mesa Ct

Corning CA 96021

Call Sign: KI6DXO
Gary L Shook
448 Marguerite Av
Corning CA 96021

Call Sign: KE6QMR
John L Hunt
261 Marty Ct
Corning CA 96021

Call Sign: K6JEX
Cheryl K Jenkins
4455 Mary Ave
Corning CA 960210005

Call Sign: KC7SVU
Donald L Marotz
23649 McLane Ave
Corning CA 960211352

Call Sign: KE6POT
Jeff T McFarlen
24080 McLane Ave
Corning CA 96021

Call Sign: W6AYT
Darrol D Martin
203 Mission Dr
Corning CA 96021

Call Sign: KF6QCE
Leonard F Barbo
433 North St
Corning CA 96021

Call Sign: NZ6N
Kevin M Barbo
433 North St
Corning CA 96021

Call Sign: KF6AFH
Mark E Raby
24090 Orangewood Rd

Corning CA 96021

Call Sign: KF6FOC
Barbara J Witter
24090 Orangewood Rd
Corning CA 96021

Call Sign: KG6AYG
John O Wilson
24190 Orangewood Rd
Corning CA 96021

Call Sign: WD6BAD
Bryant M Lewis
285 Victorian Park Ct
Corning CA 960213706

Call Sign: N6FSN
Richard D Kirby
Corning CA 96021

Call Sign: WA6PPK
Dick K Lourence
Corning CA 96021

Call Sign: KC6NCH
Freda J Crowley
Corning CA 96021

Call Sign: N6WRB
John C Crowley
Corning CA 96021

Call Sign: N6DB
Daniel W Butner
Corning CA 96021

Call Sign: KJ6KCB
Carol Y Butner
Corning CA 96021

Call Sign: KJ6LRC
Michael D Holik
Corning CA 96021

Call Sign: W6JEX
William H Jenkins
Corning CA 960210005

Call Sign: N6YCK
Albert Leyva Sr
Corning CA 96021

Call Sign: KJ6LZT
Marquis W Mason
Corning CA 96021

Call Sign: KF6GTR
Ray G McLaughlin
Corning CA 960215783

Call Sign: W8OLO
Robert B Zimmerman
Corning CA 960211320

FCC Amateur Radio Licenses in Cottonwood

Call Sign: W6TYB
Raymond L Tooker
19105 Adams Rd
Cottonwood CA
960228506

Call Sign: K6YTZ
Harold H Hanesworth
19170 Adams Rd
Cottonwood CA 96022

Call Sign: N6SCC
Shasta County Amateur
Radio Emergency Service
19105 Adams Rd
Cottonwood CA 96022

Call Sign: KC6IPF
Peter G Shegas
18245 Alta Way
Cottonwood CA 96022

Call Sign: K6IPF
Peter G Shegas
18245 Alta Way
Cottonwood CA 96022

Call Sign: KI6ZIO
Teresa M Park
22210 Blacktail Pl
Cottonwood CA 96022

Call Sign: AC0SS
Daniel F Maase
18862 Blythe Way
Cottonwood CA 96022

Call Sign: KF6RPD
Jack R Haller
17095 Bowman Rd
Cottonwood CA 96022

Call Sign: KF6EMP
Ronnie J Vigliotti
18400 Bowman Rd
Cottonwood CA 96022

Call Sign: KC6WBQ
Glenn E Newcome
18431 Bowman Rd
Cottonwood CA 96022

Call Sign: NC6L
Glenn E Newcome
18431 Bowman Rd
Cottonwood CA 96022

Call Sign: WX6K
Charles R Fox II
18277 Bowman Rd
Cottonwood CA 96022

Call Sign: N8SJX
Donald D Duffus
22141 Buckeye Pl
Cottonwood CA 96022

Call Sign: KB6CPJ
Elmer A Butler
19544 Canyon Dam Pl
Cottonwood CA 96022

Call Sign: KD6MPV
Richard D Robuck
3323 Charles St
Cottonwood CA 96022

Call Sign: KF6EMR
Anna M Smith
18810 Cobblestone Dr
Cottonwood CA
960229302

Call Sign: KD6YXN
Ralph W Smith Jr
18810 Cobblestone Dr
Cottonwood CA 96022

Call Sign: KD6WDY
Terry C Navone
3292 Denice Way
Cottonwood CA 96022

Call Sign: KI6WAV
Linda K Mclean
3214 Denice Way
Cottonwood CA 96022

Call Sign: KE6EIA
Bill J Drybread
3825 Drybread Rd
Cottonwood CA 96022

Call Sign: W6NHV
Jack E Drake
17437 Evergreen Rd
Cottonwood CA 96022

Call Sign: KF6IBX
Del Ganeff
17785 Golden Meadow
Cottonwood CA 96022

Call Sign: W6PTO
Del Ganeff
17785 Golden Meadow Trl
Cottonwood CA 96022

Call Sign: KI6KPD
Florence A Ganeff
17785 Golden Meadow Trl
Cottonwood CA 96022

Call Sign: KC6JWO
Joseph C Moeller
16565 Heitman Rd
Cottonwood CA 96022

Call Sign: N6XOU
Patricia A Hickman
16875 Hickman Ln
Cottonwood CA 96022

Call Sign: N7NP
Will C Hickman
16875 Hickman Ln
Cottonwood CA 96022

Call Sign: KG6LNE
Brian P Officer
17905 Hidden Valley Rd
Cottonwood CA 96022

Call Sign: KJ6MUN
Robert D Smith Jr
20003 Indian Tom Dr
Cottonwood CA 96022

Call Sign: WA6PWX
Vernon C Blanke
19250 Kiowa Ln
Cottonwood CA 96022

Call Sign: KC6BWG
Ronald E Herman
19325 Kiowa Ln
Cottonwood CA 96022

Call Sign: N6GPM
Robert M Benesh
19760 Little Ln
Cottonwood CA
960229666

Call Sign: KE6YKU
Norman G Daniels Jr
17360 Little Oak Ln
Cottonwood CA
960229670

Call Sign: KD5HHT
Richard C Rigsby
18050 Little Ridge Ln
Cottonwood CA 96022

Call Sign: KF6IKB
Carson L Pottorff
17085 Lloyd Way
Cottonwood CA 96022

Call Sign: KI6WBC
Donna M Pottorff
17085 Lloyd Way
Cottonwood CA 96022

Call Sign: KT6A
Tom C Pottorff
17085 Lloyd Way
Cottonwood CA 96022

Call Sign: KQ6D
Richard Finneran
3803 Locust Rd
Cottonwood CA 96022

Call Sign: KR6M
Kenna L Finneran
3803 Locust Rd
Cottonwood CA
960220883

Call Sign: KI6UZU

Howard W Watson
18720 Los Palos Dr
Cottonwood CA 96022

Call Sign: KD6HWH
Kenneth L Welch
18845 Luce Griswold Rd
Cottonwood CA 96022

Call Sign: KJ6NTN
Pamela A Kyle
3789 Main St 33
Cottonwood CA 96022

Call Sign: KF6YFZ
Vicki L Dewey
3789 Main St Sp 7
Cottonwood CA 96022

Call Sign: KJ6FOA
Barry White
2846 Majestic Oak Cir
Cottonwood CA 96022

Call Sign: WB6SOO
Robert L Nixon Sr
3536 Park Dr
Cottonwood CA 96022

Call Sign: K6EMB
Jay A Sturges
3191 Ponder Way
Cottonwood CA 96022

Call Sign: KI6SUS
Angela Ford
17915 Quailridge Rd
Cottonwood CA 96022

Call Sign: KG6VN
Timothy Q Andres
3856 Rolland Dr
Cottonwood CA 96022

Call Sign: KG6TAS

Robert N Hubbard
3549 Savage Dr
Cottonwood CA 96022

Call Sign: K6HUB
Robert N Hubbard
3549 Savage Dr
Cottonwood CA 96022

Call Sign: KB7KBT
Garrey F Morford
16555 Shekinah Ct
Cottonwood CA 96022

Call Sign: KI6WAM
Jeff M Henthorn
17522 Starr Rd
Cottonwood CA 96022

Call Sign: KF6VLS
Kenneth A Graves
19641 Stoneyford Pl
Cottonwood CA 96022

Call Sign: KF6YKO
Bridget L Graves
19641 Stoneyford Pl
Cottonwood CA 96022

Call Sign: KI6YNM
John J Delaney
19483 Sweet Brier Pl
Cottonwood CA 96022

Call Sign: KI6YNA
Lance Gingell
19497 Sweet Brier Pl
Cottonwood CA 96022

Call Sign: KA6ADW
Claude R Sparks
19345 Whipple Tree Rd
Cottonwood CA 96022

Call Sign: WB6ENP

Cecil E Critton
19675 Whitehorse Pl
Cottonwood CA 96022

Call Sign: KE6ADB
Roger A Payton
19191 Yar Pl
Cottonwood CA 96022

Call Sign: KE6BPY
Joylyn Payton
19191 Yar Pl
Cottonwood CA 96022

Call Sign: KA6ESI
Albert L Lewis
Cottonwood CA 96022

Call Sign: KE6EIC
Michael L Martin
Cottonwood CA 96022

Call Sign: KG6TYP
Keith A Ryant
Cottonwood CA 96022

Call Sign: KG6TYR
Kevin O Ryant
Cottonwood CA 96022

Call Sign: KG6TYS
Mary A Johnson
Cottonwood CA 96022

Call Sign: KG6URY
Michelle R Hoopes
Cottonwood CA 96022

FCC Amateur Radio Licenses in Covelo

Call Sign: WB6TCS
Denis L Moore
26101 East Ln
Covelo CA 954289622

Call Sign: K6QLT
David L Nixon
71300 Hill Rd
Covelo CA 95428

Call Sign: KJ6VIG
Mary Jane Cummings
72005 Hill Rd
Covelo CA 95428

Call Sign: KJ6VHQ
Ramona J Stewart
77551 Logan Ln
Covelo CA 95428

Call Sign: KJ6VJQ
Robert L Stewart
77551 Logan Ln
Covelo CA 95428

Call Sign: W4SFL
Robert C Arge Sr
76450 Lovell St
Covelo CA 95428

Call Sign: KC6ZUH
Jon J Heimark
Covelo CA 95428

Call Sign: WA6QPG
Jacob E Joyner
Covelo CA 95428

Call Sign: KI6OMB
Cooper R Heppler
Covelo CA 95428

Call Sign: N6JYB
Richard S Saunders
Covelo CA 95428

FCC Amateur Radio Licenses in Crescent

Call Sign: KF6HBW
Theodore L Smith
650 E Washington Blvd 12
Crescent CA 95531

Call Sign: KF6STC
Eugene C Hamilton
655 Pacific Ave Apt 22
Crescent CA 95531

FCC Amateur Radio Licenses in Crescent City

Call Sign: KF6IYY
David R Hopkins
640 4th St 1
Crescent City CA 95531

Call Sign: KF6MZG
Aura M Lower
364 8th St
Crescent City CA 95531

Call Sign: KF6DCL
Charles E Davis
1164 8th St
Crescent City CA 95531

Call Sign: KA6KJT
Morris D Ricks
1568 A St
Crescent City CA 95531

Call Sign: KG6OYA
Henry L Luerra II
1571 A St
Crescent City CA 95531

Call Sign: KG6LTQ
Charles E Hartwick
121 Angel Ln
Crescent City CA 95531

Call Sign: N6CEC
Charles E Hartwick

121 Angel Ln
Crescent City CA 95531

Call Sign: KK6RU
James E Mierkey
105 Annandale Ct
Crescent City CA 95531

Call Sign: KF6PBY
Arlita E Johnson
180 Arnett
Crescent City CA 95531

Call Sign: KJ6ATU
Martin C Kelly
125 Barker St
Crescent City CA 95531

Call Sign: AD6FC
Clyde F Wagner Jr
145 Becky Ct
Crescent City CA 95531

Call Sign: KC6HTA
John H Jackson
800 Bertsch Ave
Crescent City CA 95531

Call Sign: KB6WUF
Michael R Ross
120 Blackberry Ln
Crescent City CA 95531

Call Sign: KD6USE
Nathan M Hubbard
1551 Boulder Ave
Crescent City CA 95531

Call Sign: KD7ON
Robert E Young
161 Breakwater Dr
Crescent City CA 95531

Call Sign: KD6GDZ
Douglas C Mason

210 Breakwater Dr
Crescent City CA 95531

Call Sign: K6DCM
Douglas C Mason
210 Breakwater Dr
Crescent City CA 95531

Call Sign: KG6FAX
Gary A Moore
1385 Breen St
Crescent City CA 95531

Call Sign: KJ6KU
Walter J Mac Phee
255 Brush Creek Rd
Crescent City CA 95531

Call Sign: N6QJR
Sylvia M Mac Phee
255 Brush Creek Rd
Crescent City CA 95531

Call Sign: KJ6ATX
Karen L Ortman
300 Brush Creek Rd
Crescent City CA 95531

Call Sign: KD6ITZ
William C Beard
820 Butte St
Crescent City CA 95531

Call Sign: WA6WFQ
Bill R Beard
820 Butte St
Crescent City CA 95531

Call Sign: KD6VHM
Shirley A Wortell
110 Cannon Dr
Crescent City CA 95531

Call Sign: KB6WUE
Richard P Mello

801 Cessna Dr
Crescent City CA 95531

Call Sign: KI6ZHU
Joel A Bruhns
280 Chevy Chase Way
Crescent City CA 95531

Call Sign: W7VAZ
Albert Deines
125 Colonial Ct
Crescent City CA
955318389

Call Sign: NS6E
Robert J Peterson
1785 Del Mar Rd
Crescent City CA 95531

Call Sign: KB6WUD
Michelle R Duncan
1078 Doran Ct
Crescent City CA 95531

Call Sign: KB6ZRE
Ronald F Gastineau
1078 Doran Ct
Crescent City CA 95531

Call Sign: KJ6UOW
Amy E Cox
200 Dryden Ln
Crescent City CA 95531

Call Sign: KI6PRJ
Trenton A Mitchell
200 Dryden Ln
Crescent City CA 95531

Call Sign: KF6JBS
Donna J Smith
650 E Washington Blvd 32
Crescent City CA 95531

Call Sign: KG6JKL

John R Gray
650 E Washington Blvd Sp
19
Crescent City CA 95531

Call Sign: K6EJM
Homer L Dale
434 East St
Crescent City CA
955313947

Call Sign: NL7GR
Douglas J Allison
260 East St 4
Crescent City CA 95531

Call Sign: W6ACT
Charles A Thunen
Memorial Arc
1301 Eldorado St
Crescent City CA 95531

Call Sign: KB6ZRD
Kenneth D Olson
900 Elk Creek Rd
Crescent City CA 95531

Call Sign: KD6USB
Orion D Mosher
703 Elk Valley Rd
Crescent City CA 95531

Call Sign: KJ6JZQ
Robert A Eslick
740 Elk Valley Rd
Crescent City CA 95531

Call Sign: KD6USD
Janette E Lechuga
1480 Elk Valley Rd
Crescent City CA 95531

Call Sign: WB6HAL
Teryl D Wakeman I
1780 Elk Valley Rd

Crescent City CA 95531

Call Sign: N6ATX
Dorothy M Cory
1900 Elk Valley Rd
Crescent City CA 95531

Call Sign: WA6LUO
Ronald Van Weemen Van
Noord
2835 Elk Valley Rd
Crescent City CA 95531

Call Sign: KJ6UOZ
Paul F Senyszyn
2980 Elk Valley Rd
Crescent City CA 95531

Call Sign: KF6KPG
Sharon K Long
333 Esta Ave
Crescent City CA 95531

Call Sign: KO6QJ
Kenneth C Long
333 Esta Ave
Crescent City CA 95531

Call Sign: KE6QOG
Larry J Folsom
951 Ferndale Ln
Crescent City CA 95531

Call Sign: KE6QOH
Sharline L Folsom
951 Ferndale Ln
Crescent City CA 95531

Call Sign: KB6WUB
Richard L Green
1701 Ferndale Ln
Crescent City CA 95531

Call Sign: KB6WTZ
Robert W Garner

482 G St 6
Crescent City CA 95531

Call Sign: KE6TKN
George O Layton
1168 Gainard St
Crescent City CA 95531

Call Sign: KE6ZIS
Carol C Layton
1168 Gainard St
Crescent City CA 95531

Call Sign: KD6FYV
Clone Runiyon Jr
1244 Gainard St
Crescent City CA 95531

Call Sign: KB6WUA
Michael N McKinnon
1257 Gainard St
Crescent City CA 95531

Call Sign: KB2ZSR
Mary K Saylor
1543 Gainard St
Crescent City CA 95531

Call Sign: KG6DOJ
Gracie C Saylor
1543 Gainard St
Crescent City CA 95531

Call Sign: KB2ZAK
Louis C Saylor Jr
1543 Gainard St
Crescent City CA
955313322

Call Sign: KJ6ATW
Donald A Morrison
1279 Harrold St 3
Crescent City CA 95531

Call Sign: N7FSK

Dwight O Stapleton Sr
105 Hart Ct
Crescent City CA 95531

Call Sign: KF6SFJ
Khristina M Ramirez
155 Hillcrest Ln
Crescent City CA 95531

Call Sign: KE6BVJ
Rachel R Williams
326 Humboldt Rd
Crescent City CA 95531

Call Sign: KA6NBN
Bernard E Rolland
1229 Huntington
Crescent City CA 95531

Call Sign: KB6TAX
Victoria Bates
1401 Huntington
Crescent City CA 95531

Call Sign: KB6WTX
David B Rand
1402 Huntington St
Crescent City CA 95531

Call Sign: KD6SSP
Terry L Towne
1093 Hwy 101 N Sp 8
Crescent City CA 95531

Call Sign: N6GHH
Bill F Bowman
2831 Hwy 199
Crescent City CA 95531

Call Sign: WA6JJH
Howard W McBride
2510 Hwy 199 Sp 42
Crescent City CA 95531

Call Sign: KG6KBD

Paul I Mccreary
577 I St 4
Crescent City CA 95531

Call Sign: WA6YRJ
Clifford C Foote
1403 Inyo St
Crescent City CA
955312150

Call Sign: WA6ZDO
Christie L Rust
1152 Jaccard St
Crescent City CA 95531

Call Sign: N1JG
Jack B German Sr
1177 Jaccard St
Crescent City CA 95531

Call Sign: N6RYB
Ardean E Sveum
1459 Jaccard St
Crescent City CA 95531

Call Sign: KA7PRR
Stephen C Paynter
149 Jackie St
Crescent City CA 95531

Call Sign: KE6IIL
Thomas L Wilson
467 Joaquin St
Crescent City CA 95531

Call Sign: WA6QMP
Rudy W Hammack
110 Karen Way
Crescent City CA 95531

Call Sign: KG6EJO
Theodore H Johnson Jr
510 Keller Ave
Crescent City CA 95531

Call Sign: KE6QOI
Eva M Goodgame
925 Kellogg Rd
Crescent City CA 95531

Call Sign: KC6MLZ
Stephen R Lampl
128 Kerby St
Crescent City CA 95531

Call Sign: KG6VGW
Kevin C Wakeman
3800 Kings Valley Rd
Crescent City CA 95531

Call Sign: KG6WNJ
Susan C D'Errico
6240 Kings Valley Rd
Crescent City CA 95531

Call Sign: KC6YYZ
Derek P Woodbyrne
3420 Kings Valley Rd Sp
32
Crescent City CA 95531

Call Sign: WB6HAJ
Roger L Wakeman
3800 Kingsvalley Rd
Crescent City CA 95531

Call Sign: KJ6VFU
Steven B Spehling
103 Kristian Ln
Crescent City CA 95531

Call Sign: KE7AM
Carl E Young
120 Lafayette Way
Crescent City CA 95531

Call Sign: WB6WNS
Dallas R Andruss
3500 Lake Earl Dr
Crescent City CA 95531

Call Sign: KD6KAN
Griffith H Yamamoto
401 Lakeview Dr
Crescent City CA 95531

Call Sign: KE6UFT
Christopher C Chang
2565 Le Clair
Crescent City CA 95531

Call Sign: WB6TER
Ray J Morisseau
3071 Lesina Rd
Crescent City CA 95531

Call Sign: WA6KLM
Alice M Morisseau
3071 Lesina Rd
Crescent City CA
955318547

Call Sign: KD6USG
Carol A Jefferson
100 Lorenzo
Crescent City CA 95531

Call Sign: KD6USH
John O Jefferson
100 Lorenzo
Crescent City CA 95531

Call Sign: WB6FKZ
William L Stuck
1609 Macken Ave
Crescent City CA 95531

Call Sign: KF6NBL
Timothy J Jackson
135 Madeleine Ln
Crescent City CA 95531

Call Sign: KF6NBK
Christopher N Jackson
135 Madeliene Ln

Crescent City CA 95531

Call Sign: KG6ZVU
Matthew C Tetrick
180 Mason Ct
Crescent City CA 95531

Call Sign: KA6YKH
Theodore H Brown Jr
1232 McNamara Ave
Crescent City CA 95531

Call Sign: KF6SFE
James L Husong
188 Modoc St
Crescent City CA 95531

Call Sign: KF6CVH
Edward L McCartney
2650 Moseley Rd
Crescent City CA 95531

Call Sign: KG6DOX
Janet M Knight
3415 Movie Ln
Crescent City CA 95531

Call Sign: KE6WHH
Earl W Knight
3415 Movie Ln
Crescent City CA 95531

Call Sign: K6EWK
Earl W Knight
3415 Movie Ln
Crescent City CA 95531

Call Sign: WA6FPR
Walter L Klein
130 Mud Hen Rd
Crescent City CA
955319743

Call Sign: KE6UFS
Charlaine A Davis

160 Mud Hen Rd
Crescent City CA 95531

Call Sign: N6IUM
Chad Gagnon
240 Mud Hen Rd
Crescent City CA 95531

Call Sign: KV6RO
Chad Gagnon
240 Mud Hen Rd
Crescent City CA 95531

Call Sign: KF6OFW
Richard M Blair
530 Murphy Ave
Crescent City CA 95531

Call Sign: WA6EJJ
Richard H Strever
4515 N Bank Rd
Crescent City CA 95531

Call Sign: KI6OZR
Kevin D Marsh
6341 N Bank Rd
Crescent City CA 95531

Call Sign: KE6ZWL
David A Aksamit
2051 N Crest Dr 21
Crescent City CA 95531

Call Sign: KJ6UOY
Robin M Payne
2516 Nickel Ave
Crescent City CA 95531

Call Sign: KG6NKZ
Christopher A Corpstein
2625 Nickle Ave
Crescent City CA 95531

Call Sign: KJ6UPA
Robert D Sherman

1950 Northcrest Dr 2
Crescent City CA 95531

Call Sign: AC7BC
Melvin B Cox
1301 B Northcrest Dr 52
Crescent City CA 95531

Call Sign: KG6PAN
Billy J Ward
2331 Old Mill Rd 2
Crescent City CA 95531

Call Sign: KA7CCW
Bernice R Kessler
2331 Old Mill Rd 4
Crescent City CA 95531

Call Sign: KA7CCY
Jack V Lantz
2331 Old Mill Rd 4
Crescent City CA 95531

Call Sign: KG6KUD
Jimmy L Dunn Jr
2331 Old Mill Rd Sp 2
Crescent City CA 95531

Call Sign: KI6DDT
Daren L Shanks
655 Pacific
Crescent City CA 95531

Call Sign: KJ6JZN
Nicholas C Bosteder
752 Pacific Ave
Crescent City CA
955313049

Call Sign: KA6NBB
Roger C Pfahning
1540 Pacific Ave
Crescent City CA 95531

Call Sign: KB6WUC

Bennett L Gooch Jr
1333 Parkway Dr
Crescent City CA 95531

Call Sign: KG6VGX
Patrick G Riley
2971 Parkway Dr
Crescent City CA 95531

Call Sign: KB6ZKP
Eric M Faivre
2620 Peveler Ave
Crescent City CA 95531

Call Sign: KA6SWR
Michael N Mavris
Point St George
Crescent City CA 95531

Call Sign: KA6APF
Willard T Lamade
2341 Railroad Ave
Crescent City CA 95531

Call Sign: KD6KYC
Ronald J Simpson
5661 S Bank
Crescent City CA 95531

Call Sign: KF6KKW
Kelly J Vilven
5630 S Bank Rd
Crescent City CA 95531

Call Sign: KD6SIP
Allis L Simpson
5661 S Bank Rd
Crescent City CA 95531

Call Sign: KD6SIQ
Ronald J Simpson Jr
5661 S Bank Rd
Crescent City CA 95531

Call Sign: W6LQB

John F Phillips
5720 S Bank Rd
Crescent City CA
955319597

Call Sign: KD6VIS
Edwin L Bergren
6565 S Bank Rd
Crescent City CA 95531

Call Sign: WA6ZHP
Michael J Scavuzzo
1127 S Pebble Beach Dr
Crescent City CA
955313556

Call Sign: KI6PV
Sheldon F Crook
1605 S Pebble Beach Dr
Crescent City CA 95531

Call Sign: KD6URY
Donald A Davis
780 Sandhill Rd
Crescent City CA 95531

Call Sign: KJ6JZR
Stephen W Willson
221 Sherwood Ln
Crescent City CA
955316816

Call Sign: KV6G
Richard L Rheinschild
200 Skycrest Dr
Crescent City CA 95531

Call Sign: KG6JBA
Howard Abernathy
205 Stanley Ln
Crescent City CA 95531

Call Sign: KG6VGV
James A Moore Jr
159 Starfish Way

Crescent City CA 95531

Crescent City CA 95531

Crescent City CA 95531

Call Sign: K6BFR
Robert M Henke
400 Sunrise Ave
Crescent City CA 95531

Call Sign: KF6ACQ
Pat S Miller
1385 W Washington Blvd
42
Crescent City CA 95531

Call Sign: KE6GMG
George G Alton
5055 Wonder Stump Rd
Crescent City CA 95531

Call Sign: WD7T
Charles P Jennings
900 Sunset Cir 79
Crescent City CA 95531

Call Sign: KD6URZ
Steen M Day
1385 W Washington Blvd
Apt 6
Crescent City CA 95531

Call Sign: KB6QEN
Dallas M Andruss Jr
4610 Wonderstump Rd
Crescent City CA 95531

Call Sign: KG6IEY
Karin S Guiley
110 Susan Ln
Crescent City CA 95531

Call Sign: KG6NCQ
Renee L Lambert
1385 W Washington Blvd
Apt 98
Crescent City CA 95531

Call Sign: KD6USA
Joe F Hicks
Crescent City CA 95531

Call Sign: K6CC
Clyde M Hutchens
120 Tanbark Ln
Crescent City CA 95531

Call Sign: KD6USC
Jennifer M Hicks
Crescent City CA 95531

Call Sign: KJ6ATT
Cindy G Henderson
105 Willow Glen Ct
Crescent City CA 95531

Call Sign: W1ITX
Albert C Jones
Crescent City CA 95531

Call Sign: KG6QFW
Thomas T Edwards Jr
115 Troyna Ct
Crescent City CA 95531

Call Sign: K6KEN
Kenneth E Cline
4300 Wonder Stamp Rd
Crescent City CA 95531

Call Sign: WB6PHH
Steve P Stone
Crescent City CA 95531

Call Sign: KB6WTY
Brian M Lawless
525 W Cooper Ave
Crescent City CA 95531

Call Sign: K6DIA
Ye Olde Transmitting
Tube Museum
Crescent City CA 95531

Call Sign: KG6NHP
David B Bree
1595 W Jefferson
Crescent City CA 95531

Call Sign: WE6LDS
Del Norte County Local
Disaster Services Arc
4300 Wonder Stump Rd
Crescent City CA 95531

Call Sign: KG6BRB
Robert S Barlow
Crescent City CA 95531

Call Sign: WB6WDH
Kenneth B Knudsen
1535 W Macken Ave
Crescent City CA 95531

Call Sign: KF6UCK
Lynn H Clarke
4700 Wonder Stump Rd
Crescent City CA
955318416

Call Sign: KJ6ATP
Becky L Barlow
Crescent City CA 95531

Call Sign: W6RSZ
Mark P Franusich
144 W Washington Blvd

Call Sign: N6KJT
Alvah J Clark
4721 Wonder Stump Rd

Call Sign: KJ6ATQ
William J Barlow
Crescent City CA 95531

Call Sign: KJ6JZO
David Bosteder
Crescent City CA
955310064

Call Sign: KA6WYW
Kirk L Brown
Crescent City CA 95531

Call Sign: KF6IRM
Michael Y Chang
Crescent City CA 95531

Call Sign: KI6LPV
Christopher C Chang
Crescent City CA 95531

Call Sign: K3LF
Christopher C Chang
Crescent City CA 95531

Call Sign: KF6CML
Mary Chilton
Crescent City CA 95531

Call Sign: KF6BVA
Zane T Curtis
Crescent City CA 95531

Call Sign: W6HY
Del Norte ARC
Crescent City CA 95531

Call Sign: KE6SGA
Joseph P Emond Sr
Crescent City CA 95531

Call Sign: KG6CSA
Dan Fischer
Crescent City CA
955311674

Call Sign: KJ6JZM
Holly Gensaw

Crescent City CA
955311707

Call Sign: KJ6ATS
Misty J Harrison
Crescent City CA 95531

Call Sign: KF6JBT
John G McMillin
Crescent City CA 95531

Call Sign: KF6JRW
Nancy J McMillin
Crescent City CA 95531

Call Sign: KF6JRX
Carissa L McMillin
Crescent City CA 95531

Call Sign: KE6ZYK
Michael F Poole
Crescent City CA 95531

Call Sign: KJ6JZP
Lorie Poole
Crescent City CA
955310264

Call Sign: KE6QOS
Arnold L Stone
Crescent City CA 95531

Call Sign: KF6DUI
Clifford D Threm
Crescent City CA 95531

Call Sign: N6QDS
Nancy A Threm
Crescent City CA 95531

Call Sign: KJ6JZT
Jeffrey L Tinsley
Crescent City CA
955316159

Call Sign: KF6JRV
David A Turner
Crescent City CA 95531

Call Sign: KA6SPQ
William R Wortell
Crescent City CA 95531

FCC Amateur Radio Licenses in Cutten

Call Sign: KB6HDQ
Debbie M Gooch
Cutten CA 95534

Call Sign: W5JXO
Linda W Nellist
Cutten CA 95534

Call Sign: N0KMX
Duane E Isaacson
Cutten CA 95534

Call Sign: KG6VUD
Aaron K Roberts
Cutten CA 95534

Call Sign: N6NZE
Jozef R Van Wyck
Cutten CA 95534

FCC Amateur Radio Licenses in Dorris

Call Sign: KG6VET
Charles H Smith
7026 Sams Neck Rd
Dorris CA 96023

Call Sign: WW6EMS
Charles H Smith
7026 Sams Neck Rd
Dorris CA 96023

Call Sign: KG6VVR

Jeanna L Smith
7026 Sams Neck Rd
Dorris CA 96023

Call Sign: KC6ZVK
Jose M Gamboa
Dorris CA 96023

FCC Amateur Radio Licenses in Dos Rios

Call Sign: KJ6IAB
Gordon K Crawford
11725 Dos Rios Rd
Dos Rios CA 954299113

FCC Amateur Radio Licenses in Douglas City

Call Sign: KF6WLL
Richard M Rapinac
Steiner Flat Rd Box 64
Douglas City CA 96024

Call Sign: KF6LGZ
Neal W Summerhays
Hc 170 Summit Creek Rd
Douglas City CA 96024

Call Sign: W6FOY
Harry L Ivers
395 Union Hill Rd
Douglas City CA 96024

Call Sign: KF6TJ
Dorothy C Cameron
Douglas City CA 96024

Call Sign: W6KOF
William G Rost
Douglas City CA 96024

Call Sign: N6NOM
Ella J Buckley

Douglas City CA
960240207

Call Sign: KF6OAH
Vicki H Riley
Douglas City CA 96024

Call Sign: KF6OAI
Russell B Riley
Douglas City CA 96024

Call Sign: N6NOE
Virginia M Smith
Douglas City CA 96024

Call Sign: WU6R
Robert E Smith
Douglas City CA 96024

Call Sign: W6CE
Norman M Weed
Douglas City CA 96024

Call Sign: KF6MDA
Harvey T Wetterstrom Jr
Douglas City CA 96024

FCC Amateur Radio Licenses in Doyle

Call Sign: N6BBO
John H Marshall
100 Sugar Loaf Rd
Doyle CA 96109

Call Sign: KE6CJB
Charles F Stayton
Doyle CA 96109

FCC Amateur Radio Licenses in Dunsmuir

Call Sign: KF6VYM
Francis J Seitz
4320 Center St

Dunsmuir CA 960251732

Call Sign: N1DHD
Kristyanna Virgona
5941 Dunsmuir Ave
Dunsmuir CA 960252331

Call Sign: NY7M
Richard G Peddicord
5521 Dunsmuir Ave
Dunsmuir CA 96025

Call Sign: KJ6AHU
Mattheu D Fredson
6200 Dunsmuir Ave B
Dunsmuir CA 96025

Call Sign: KK6KF
Kristyanna Virgona
203 Marion St
Dunsmuir CA 96025

Call Sign: WA6BXW
Glenn R Farnsworth
4113 Oak St Apt B
Dunsmuir CA 960252312

Call Sign: KB6VO
James L Connor
110 Rita St
Dunsmuir CA 96025

Call Sign: K6KLG
James L Connor
110 Rita St
Dunsmuir CA 96025

Call Sign: KD6DHX
Alleva L Graham
6282 Scherrer Ave
Dunsmuir CA 96025

Call Sign: KE6JGI
William J Dankson
5918 Shasta Ave

Dunsmuir CA 96025

Call Sign: KR6CA
Austin W Miller
4310 Wells St
Dunsmuir CA 96025

Call Sign: KB6YUI
Richard A Gwinn
Dunsmuir CA 96025

**FCC Amateur Radio
Licenses in Eagleville**

Call Sign: WB6WIS
Robert R Reeves
Eagleville CR 1 Box 19
Eagleville CA 96110

**FCC Amateur Radio
Licenses in Etna**

Call Sign: N6CVU
Harold F Spencer
2600 E Callahan Rd
Etna CA 96027

Call Sign: KB6KLY
David G Webster
4127 French Creek Rd
Etna CA 96027

Call Sign: W6NPS
Carl H Schwarzenberg
7800 French Creek Rd
Etna CA 96027

Call Sign: KB6NFY
Douglas P Blangsted
415 Ida Way
Etna CA 96027

Call Sign: WD6DBI
Ronald L Rhodefer
4936 Island Rd

Etna CA 96027

Call Sign: KI6GVM
Ron Whipple
7827 Island Rd
Etna CA 96027

Call Sign: WA6COD
William A Fowler
400 Naomi Dr
Etna CA 96027

Call Sign: WB6YTZ
David M Nelson
215 Patterson Creek Rd
Etna CA 960279507

Call Sign: N6ZZW
Duane E Stacher
134 Scott St
Etna CA 96027

Call Sign: KI6UXV
Estella O Steele
520 Valley Pines Dr
Etna CA 96027

Call Sign: KJ6CUG
Nora L Barnum
5031 Whitworth Way
Etna CA 96027

Call Sign: KI6HFO
Virginia M Renner
4615 Woods Dr
Etna CA 96027

Call Sign: WA6IHK
Alfred J Kiep Jr
Etna CA 96027

Call Sign: K6ZYR
Mariea L Yoacham
Etna CA 96027

Call Sign: K6PQH
Leon H Yoacham Sr
Etna CA 96027

Call Sign: KF6FRX
Chester R Eastlick
Etna CA 96027

Call Sign: KE6UDB
Wanda R Kiep
Etna CA 96027

Call Sign: KG6ZQY
Alan B Kramer
Etna CA 96027

Call Sign: KJ6ABI
Andrew W Kramer
Etna CA 96027

Call Sign: N6TIY
Edward S Westbrook IV
Etna CA 92007

Call Sign: KE6WVG
Alexis L Williams
Etna CA 96027

Call Sign: KB7BNW
Father Lawrence E
Williams
Etna CA 960270568

**FCC Amateur Radio
Licenses in Eureka**

Call Sign: KB6UZW
Seth C Humbert
1106 10th St
Eureka CA 95501

Call Sign: KE6ONO
Sarah K Humbert
1106 10th St
Eureka CA 95501

Call Sign: N6WHO
Robert B Stretton
1207 10th St 6
Eureka CA 955012075

Call Sign: KE6RKV
Rhonda L Jones Horn
937 8th St
Eureka CA 95501

Call Sign: W6IYN
Joseph P Curless
6166 Beechwood Dr
Eureka CA 95503

Call Sign: KA6NEO
John W Phegley
1905 13th St
Eureka CA 95501

Call Sign: KG6JUF
Larry Brown
3506 Albee St
Eureka CA 95503

Call Sign: KJ6IBW
Eric C Hyer
8011 Berta Rd
Eureka CA 95503

Call Sign: KI6ZQW
Joseph F Lancaster
241 15th St
Eureka CA 95501

Call Sign: AE6JP
Larry Brown
3506 Albee St
Eureka CA 95503

Call Sign: WB6TMY
Warren T Reese
155 Black Snag Rd
Eureka CA 95503

Call Sign: KI6BPN
Sherri S Parish
1109 15th St
Eureka CA 95501

Call Sign: KE6LOW
Edgar L Dickinson
6169 Avalon Dr
Eureka CA 955037504

Call Sign: K6GC
Warren T Reese
155 Black Snag Rd
Eureka CA 95503

Call Sign: KJ6UPC
Christopher A Miller
3538 18th St
Eureka CA 95501

Call Sign: KC6IGY
Billy J Allen
2824 Avery Ln
Eureka CA 95501

Call Sign: WA6NBI
Richard E Fridley
405 Blue Blossom Ln
Eureka CA 95503

Call Sign: KF6GCX
Paul W Peterson
3538 18th St
Eureka CA 95501

Call Sign: KF6CMK
Dora L Allen
2824 Avery Ln
Eureka CA 95501

Call Sign: KI6OEV
Ronald J Den Heyer
180 Blue Spruce Dr
Eureka CA 95503

Call Sign: W6FBK
Richard L Johanson
3543 18th St
Eureka CA 95501

Call Sign: KG6CFE
Elisa M Dallenbach
2924 B St
Eureka CA 95501

Call Sign: KE6FEE
George L Smith
226 Boyle Dr
Eureka CA 95501

Call Sign: W6GGR
Thomas H Monroe Jr
3122 19th St
Eureka CA 95501

Call Sign: WA6YBV
Michael J Furniss
2432 Bainbridge Ln
Eureka CA 95501

Call Sign: AC6YV
James E Shryne Jr
2272 Briarwood Cir
Eureka CA 955037512

Call Sign: KI6PRR
John H Prince
317 3rd St Ste 6
Eureka CA 95501

Call Sign: KG6JAX
Jeffrey R Ross
1321 Bay St
Eureka CA 95501

Call Sign: KE6SDB
Rachael A Shryne
2272 Briarwood Cir
Eureka CA 95503

Call Sign: KY6N
Ronald J Harris
4055 Broadway
Eureka CA 95503

Call Sign: N8MTL
John W Coen Jr
2113 Burns Dr
Eureka CA 95503

Call Sign: KB6GES
Ernest L Millot Jr
3567 California St
Eureka CA 955035170

Call Sign: KB6VWL
William V Hefner
3144 Broadway Ste 3
Eureka CA 95501

Call Sign: KE6LF
Preston L Spruance Jr
2241 Burns Dr
Eureka CA 95503

Call Sign: KE6QKI
Nicholas J Schroeder
2413 B California St
Eureka CA 95501

Call Sign: KI6BPO
Annebeth Lesser
1710 Buhne
Eureka CA 95501

Call Sign: KG6BJI
James L Rossi
749 Burrill
Eureka CA 95503

Call Sign: W6AEY
James E Farr
1701 Campton Rd
Eureka CA 95503

Call Sign: KF6FKZ
Oralia Atteberry
1875 Buhne Dr 41
Eureka CA 95503

Call Sign: N1AWH
Thomas E Mendenhall
215 C St
Eureka CA 95501

Call Sign: W6NLL
Norman D Mudie
3953 Campton Rd
Eureka CA 95503

Call Sign: WB6TSA
Ronald R Atteberry Sr
1875 Buhne Dr 41
Eureka CA 95503

Call Sign: N0REM
Ramona J Butz
2121 C St B
Eureka CA 95501

Call Sign: N6ZOY
P Richard King
1203 Carson St
Eureka CA 95501

Call Sign: KE6TAP
Julie A Reeves
1821 Buhne Dr Sp 41
Eureka CA 95503

Call Sign: KE6QIS
Alan C Bethel
2406 California
Eureka CA 95501

Call Sign: KA1GLA
David A Silverbrand
4163 Cedar St
Eureka CA 95503

Call Sign: KE6TAQ
James E Reeves Sr
1821 Buhne Dr Sp 41
Eureka CA 95503

Call Sign: KJ6IBV
Margaret E Holverson
1330 California Apt C
Eureka CA 95501

Call Sign: KJ6PEQ
Jesse A Boomer
4190 Cedar St
Eureka CA 95503

Call Sign: KD6VUF
Donald C Brown
905 Buhne St
Eureka CA 95501

Call Sign: KJ6AUE
Linda J Kearse
2561 California St
Eureka CA 95501

Call Sign: KQ6AB
Glen G Liscom
1535 Chabot Ct
Eureka CA 95503

Call Sign: KB6YQP
Shailesh P Patel
1308 Buhne St
Eureka CA 95501

Call Sign: WA6TLG
Robert E Baird
2759 California St
Eureka CA 95501

Call Sign: KC6CNI
Marta L Tanner Mason
1569 Chestnut Ct
Eureka CA 95501

Call Sign: KC6OHD
Kimberly A Harris
5600 Christine Dr
Eureka CA 95501

Call Sign: KD6DCP
William A Stein
3436 Dakota St
Eureka CA 95501

Call Sign: KA6JPJ
Kay F Moon
3372 Edgewood Rd
Eureka CA 95501

Call Sign: KI6QYF
Ryan L Larsen
5786 Christine Dr
Eureka CA 95503

Call Sign: KA6VKF
Laura M Brennan
3671 Dolbeer St
Eureka CA 95503

Call Sign: KD6KC
Carl E Moon
3372 Edgewood St
Eureka CA 95501

Call Sign: KE6AFF
Paul R Gustavson
1806 Circle Dr
Eureka CA 95501

Call Sign: KB7VPF
Lowell R Wheeler
213 E Del Norte St
Eureka CA 95501

Call Sign: KA6QQK
Marilyn J Shiflett
3244 Elizabeth St
Eureka CA 95503

Call Sign: KF6KGA
Bruce D Ritz
1558 Coast Guard St
Eureka CA 95501

Call Sign: K6NBC
Pieter J Vanderklis Sr
2550 East St
Eureka CA 95501

Call Sign: KB6WXC
Joao M Figueiredo
6389 Elk River Rd
Eureka CA 95501

Call Sign: K6PKM
Harry E Stevenson
52 Crab St
Eureka CA 95501

Call Sign: K6PKM
Pieter J Vanderklis Sr
2550 East St
Eureka CA 95501

Call Sign: KA6SSY
Joan E McLaughlin
6389 Elk River Rd
Eureka CA 95501

Call Sign: AF6PA
Joseph E Lowe
135 Crab St
Eureka CA 95503

Call Sign: KB6FRI
Paul D Hidy
2703 East St
Eureka CA 95501

Call Sign: KF6QIB
Dale F Bridges
2500 Erie St
Eureka CA 955013332

Call Sign: NU6O
Joseph E Lowe
135 Crab St
Eureka CA 95503

Call Sign: KE6ETM
Charles C Childers
2756 East St
Eureka CA 95501

Call Sign: KI6GRV
Marleen A Bridges
2500 Erie St
Eureka CA 95501

Call Sign: KJ6ICA
Winston E Lowe
135 Crab St
Eureka CA 95503

Call Sign: KI6KJJ
Michael J Black Jr
309 East St 4
Eureka CA 95501

Call Sign: KE6ETI
Charles T Smith
1500 Erin Ct
Eureka CA 95503

Call Sign: KF6MAA
Andrew J Pierce
814 Creighton
Eureka CA 95501

Call Sign: KD6CTJ
John G Hurley
1130 East St Apt 37
Eureka CA 95501

Call Sign: WA6BDS
Gordon E Davis
1530 Erin Ct
Eureka CA 95503

Call Sign: KE6LYD
Adam G Caldwell
2135 F St
Eureka CA 95501

Call Sign: KE6DWZ
George E Isenhart
1175 Freshwater Rd
Eureka CA 95503

Call Sign: KC6IQO
Carol A Hill
214 Grange Rd
Eureka CA 95501

Call Sign: KC6VGX
Roy D Cantu
2705 F St
Eureka CA 95501

Call Sign: KF6AAK
Arthur F Fischer III
2033 G St
Eureka CA 95501

Call Sign: KC6ISQ
Gregory R Hill
214 Grange Rd
Eureka CA 95503

Call Sign: N1FRN
Roy D Cantu
2705 F St
Eureka CA 95501

Call Sign: WN6ACP
D Bert Rigden
2521 G St
Eureka CA 95501

Call Sign: KB6CKG
Wallace I Glavich
1208 Gross St
Eureka CA 95503

Call Sign: KE6GAD
Derek Glavich
1207 F St Apt 4
Eureka CA 95501

Call Sign: KF6HQH
Michael E Biesen
2541 G St
Eureka CA 955014151

Call Sign: KB1JYL
Glen A Lauzon
3353 Gross St
Eureka CA 95503

Call Sign: KF6OEK
Ray A Lewis
2074 Fern St
Eureka CA 95503

Call Sign: W7BHT
Leonard W Harrington
2835 G St
Eureka CA 955014435

Call Sign: KE6CAT
Nathaniel V Kelso
1204 H St
Eureka CA 95501

Call Sign: WA6TVQ
Clemente Cantu
1980 Flora Pl
Eureka CA 955012709

Call Sign: KI6ZQV
Regina W Kerns
3413 G St
Eureka CA 95503

Call Sign: KB6NN
Howard M Lang
3124 H St
Eureka CA 95503

Call Sign: KF6OEL
Brandon E Wallace
2560 Forrest Knoll Ln
Eureka CA 955036233

Call Sign: WB6JVS
Harry A Rouse
3824 G St
Eureka CA 95503

Call Sign: KF6KAD
Maryellen Gibson
3781.5 H St
Eureka CA 95503

Call Sign: AE6UU
Steven L Di Leo
2000 Foxwood Dr
Eureka CA 95503

Call Sign: KA6YOS
Freddie G Smith
1412 Gates
Eureka CA 95501

Call Sign: WB6ZOM
Irving H Rohner
224 Harris
Eureka CA 95501

Call Sign: W6KSY
William F Parker
4718 Frederick Dr
Eureka CA 95503

Call Sign: WB6SJR
William H Rosenthal
1607 Glatt St
Eureka CA 95501

Call Sign: WD6GLQ
Donald E Haffner
1815 Harris
Eureka CA 95501

Call Sign: KC6ITM
Richard Daniels
224 Harris St
Eureka CA 955034343

Call Sign: KE6IBD
William H Richards
805 Herrick Ave
Eureka CA 95502

Call Sign: AA6DX
Mark L Nelson
801 J St
Eureka CA 95501

Call Sign: KA6ULG
Robert L Colburn
1337 Harris St
Eureka CA 95501

Call Sign: KJ6KSO
Brandon J Hilgers
4935 Hidden Meadows Ln
Eureka CA 95503

Call Sign: WL7BZR
Elaine M Nelson
801 J St
Eureka CA 95501

Call Sign: K6MZN
Arthur G Seymour Sr
2020 Harris St
Eureka CA 95503

Call Sign: KE6BVK
Staci D Marshall Mrs
247C Higgins St
Eureka CA 95501

Call Sign: WA6MJB
Elaine M Nelson
801 J St
Eureka CA 95501

Call Sign: N6HNB
William B Montgomery Jr
1400 Harrison 4
Eureka CA 955011355

Call Sign: KA6SYX
James D Crow
931 Hill St No 6
Eureka CA 95501

Call Sign: KG6XU
Ronald P Vetter
2714 J St
Eureka CA 95501

Call Sign: WB6BDF
George W Ingraham
2634 Harrison Ave
Eureka CA 95501

Call Sign: KE6ETH
Rebecca A Simone
449 Howard Hts Rd
Eureka CA 95503

Call Sign: KJ6VHP
Brent S Daugherty
2928 J St
Eureka CA 95501

Call Sign: KJ6EMX
John E Davis
15 Hawthorne
Eureka CA 95501

Call Sign: KF6WMQ
Cary J Christensen
6322 Humboldt Hill Rd
Eureka CA 95503

Call Sign: KG6VSL
Harold G Ricker
3824 Jacobs Ave Sp 26
Eureka CA 95501

Call Sign: KI6MTV
Michael R Hislop
1137 Henderson St
Eureka CA 95501

Call Sign: KE6PAK
Becky L Huston
1005 Huntoon St
Eureka CA 95501

Call Sign: KF6ZUI
Joseph E Thorne
1536 John Hill Rd
Eureka CA 95501

Call Sign: KD6JFF
Milton Marsh
1335 Henderson St
Eureka CA 95501

Call Sign: KC6AIK
Taylor E Robert
326 I St 141
Eureka CA 95501

Call Sign: KI6ULB
Lyle O Kittleson
919 K St
Eureka CA 95501

Call Sign: WB6WBN
Michael J Adams
1525 Henderson St
Eureka CA 95501

Call Sign: KG6GRM
Kevin M Nelson
4238 Ivy Ln
Eureka CA 95503

Call Sign: KE6PAT
David W Pryor
2716 K St
Eureka CA 955014550

Call Sign: KJ6DXX
Reginald W Kennedy
4658 Kincaid Ct
Eureka CA 95503

Call Sign: N1AWL
John A McNiel
1201 King Salmon Ave
Eureka CA 95503

Call Sign: W6FCS
John A McNiel
1201 King Salmon Ave
Eureka CA 95503

Call Sign: KF6KAF
Michael K Barker
1617 L St Apt N
Eureka CA 95501

Call Sign: KF6MAB
Ronald L Marlett
1547 Leeman Ct
Eureka CA 95501

Call Sign: KJ6SHC
James S Armstrong
5246 Leppek Ct
Eureka CA 95503

Call Sign: KW6JIM
James S Armstrong
5246 Leppek Ct
Eureka CA 95503

Call Sign: KE6FTC
Kerry R Glavich
5262 Leppek Ct
Eureka CA 95503

Call Sign: KE6TMF
Marcia L Glavich
5262 Leppek Ct
Eureka CA 95503

Call Sign: KE6MMX
Merijean E Matteoli
Glavich
5262 Leppek Ct
Eureka CA 95503

Call Sign: WD9GFL
Michael J Cent
1240 Leslie Rd
Eureka CA 95503

Call Sign: KD6YUP
James L Gayner
4380 Liberty Bell Ct
Eureka CA 955038913

Call Sign: KF6CME
Eleanor A Gayner
4380 Liberty Bell Ct
Eureka CA 955038913

Call Sign: K6VHP
Lloyd D Shallenberger
6835 Linda Rd
Eureka CA 955037132

Call Sign: KC6UUX
Sanna J Wood
6835 Linda Rd
Eureka CA 95503

Call Sign: K6ZJR
Radio Ranch Amateur
Radio Museum
6835 Linda Rd
Eureka CA 95503

Call Sign: W5YO
Robert D Sullivan
3209 Lowell St
Eureka CA 955035220

Call Sign: KG6RBT
Donald O Nelson

2265 Mabelle Ave
Eureka CA 95503

Call Sign: WA6NBG
Donald O Nelson
2265 Mabelle Ave
Eureka CA 95503

Call Sign: KB2ZSQ
Elisabeth A Saylor
1393 Marsh Rd
Eureka CA 95501

Call Sign: KE6FVH
Mark D Heddleston
1405 McCullens Ave
Eureka CA 95503

Call Sign: KG6WWK
Sally Marx
1356 McFarlan
Eureka CA 95501

Call Sign: W6AQR
Leon E Savage Sr
1415 McFarlan
Eureka CA 95501

Call Sign: KD6VAU
Alice J Hensley Jr
2351 Meadow Brook Dr
Eureka CA 95503

Call Sign: KD7JPL
Stacie M Munro
4715 Meyers Ave
Eureka CA 95513

Call Sign: KI6NTQ
Daniel D Freitas
3542 Middlefield Ln
Eureka CA 955012719

Call Sign: KA6UWT
Daniel D Freitas

3542 Middlefield Ln
Eureka CA 95501

7660 Myrtle Ave Sp 69
Eureka CA 95503

2024 P St
Eureka CA 95501

Call Sign: KE6HEC
Donald S Campbell
1633 Mike Ln
Eureka CA 95501

Call Sign: W6GZ
Henry F Mauro
3560 N St
Eureka CA 95503

Call Sign: KF6ZUJ
Paul J Abernathy
3033 Park St
Eureka CA 95501

Call Sign: KE6IAU
Marcelina S Campbell
1633 Mike Ln
Eureka CA 95501

Call Sign: KF6LGG
Hagen Steinhagen
1648 Nedra St
Eureka CA 95501

Call Sign: KA6QHS
Alvin A Lopez
3402 Park St
Eureka CA 95501

Call Sign: WB6TIS
Taylor E Robert
1646 Mike Ln
Eureka CA 95501

Call Sign: KG6NAN
David B Flemmons
5433 Noe Ave
Eureka CA 95503

Call Sign: KE6SLR
Ronald F Angell
4794 Patricia Dr
Eureka CA 95503

Call Sign: KI6ZQY
Lawrence L Labranche
3389 Mitchell Heights Dr
Eureka CA 95503

Call Sign: KI6GRT
Stephen M Hamon
5468 Noe Ave
Eureka CA 95503

Call Sign: KD6FIP
Anthony E Pelley
3970 Pennsylvania Ave
Eureka CA 95501

Call Sign: KJ6SYH
Ruth A Labranche
3389 Mitchell Hts Dr
Eureka CA 95503

Call Sign: KF6IWW
Kevin P McMillan
238 Northview Ln
Eureka CA 95503

Call Sign: KC6OGA
Alling C Foreman
22 Perch St
Eureka CA 95503

Call Sign: KJ6SYF
Harry A Majors
3389 Mitchell Hts Dr
Eureka CA 95503

Call Sign: WD6DCG
John F Erker Jr
2534 O St
Eureka CA 95501

Call Sign: KE6ETN
Kathryn A Trabue
1603 Pine St 1
Eureka CA 95501

Call Sign: AE6R
Brent N Cordes
4343 Mitchell Rd
Eureka CA 95503

Call Sign: KF6NFJ
William F Seramin
2269 Ohio St
Eureka CA 95501

Call Sign: KJ6LUC
Donna Marie Ayala
910 Pine St 2
Eureka CA 95501

Call Sign: KF6MNC
G Barrett Mace
315 Monroe Ln
Eureka CA 95503

Call Sign: KC6SLG
Rodney I Thomsen
3656 Old Arcata Rd 25
Eureka CA 95501

Call Sign: KF6TWL
Merdina D Tatum
400 Pleasant Ave
Eureka CA 95503

Call Sign: KG6AQR
Amelia E Shannon-Holm

Call Sign: KF6FKX
Edwin Stuart Sundet

Call Sign: KF6TWM
John D Tatum

400 Pleasant Ave
Eureka CA 95503

Call Sign: KE6PAQ
Earl D Rutledge
2766 Pleasant Ave
Eureka CA 955033460

Call Sign: KF6GAW
Nancie S Rutledge
2766 Pleasant Ave A
Eureka CA 955033460

Call Sign: KF6WMO
Benjamin J E Hood
3213 Prospect Apt A
Eureka CA 95503

Call Sign: KF6QIE
James L Hood
3213 Prospect Ave A
Eureka CA 95503

Call Sign: KG6NMU
Hidetomo Katsura
6209 Pryor St
Eureka CA 95503

Call Sign: N6LPM
Clarence J Mills Jr
6225 Pryor St
Eureka CA 95503

Call Sign: N6PSX
Wendi A Grammer
6108 Purdue Dr
Eureka CA 95503

Call Sign: KE6JQU
Robert E Noel
6336 Purdue Dr
Eureka CA 95503

Call Sign: K6OBL
C Lou Gooch

2010 Quaker St
Eureka CA 955012729

Call Sign: W6HHP
Thomas H Gooch
2010 Quaker St
Eureka CA 955012729

Call Sign: KD6NOO
Herbert E Bloomfield
2175 Quaker St
Eureka CA 95501

Call Sign: KG6FWT
James N Falls
2605 R St
Eureka CA 95501

Call Sign: K6FWT
James N Falls
2605 R St
Eureka CA 95501

Call Sign: KD6TGF
Mary G Greenwood
759 Redmond Rd
Eureka CA 95503

Call Sign: AL7EP
Arthur S Neumann
759 Redmond Rd
Eureka CA 95503

Call Sign: KD6JFE
Linda M Neumann
759 Redmond Rd
Eureka CA 95503

Call Sign: KE6SLT
Mark Y Phelps III
1911 Ridgewood Dr
Eureka CA 95503

Call Sign: NH6FX
Carol Lee Pinto

2287 Ridgewood Dr
Eureka CA 95503

Call Sign: KF6FKY
Frederick W Lumbert
4398 Roberts Dr
Eureka CA 95503

Call Sign: KD6YVP
Helen B Hui
3006 S St
Eureka CA 95501

Call Sign: KD6YVR
Jonathan C Hui
3006 S St
Eureka CA 95501

Call Sign: WB6GUU
David A Fleming
1534 Santa Clara St
Eureka CA 95501

Call Sign: WB6IUD
Ira A Smith
1265 Searles
Eureka CA 95501

Call Sign: KG6BDU
Craig Smith
1805 Second St
Eureka CA 95501

Call Sign: KE6PAO
Mel R Carlson
3008 Simmons Rd
Eureka CA 95503

Call Sign: KB7FMM
Janet S Bradshaw
2557 Skyline Dr
Eureka CA 95503

Call Sign: KN6DE
Robert N Finley

2708 Skyline Dr
Eureka CA 95503

2205 Tydd St
Eureka CA 95501

4044 V St Apt 1
Eureka CA 95503

Call Sign: KG6ZGV
Julie A Owens
62 Sole St
Eureka CA 95503

Call Sign: KE6IAY
William E Craig
2141 Tydd St Apt 119
Eureka CA 95501

Call Sign: WA6BRV
Kenneth M Estes
1479 Vernon St
Eureka CA 95501

Call Sign: KF6HQF
Laura J Williston
2888 Spears Rd
Eureka CA 95503

Call Sign: WB6VXR
Floyd Powers
2141 Tydd St Apt 516
Eureka CA 95501

Call Sign: W6FCO
Neil H Morse
1121 Vista
Eureka CA 95501

Call Sign: KG6LNT
Guy P Drebing
300 Startare Dr
Eureka CA 95501

Call Sign: KG6LNW
Laurie R Koch
2215 Tydd St Apt 7B
Eureka CA 95501

Call Sign: KG6TNV
Raymond F Thompson
1154 Vista Dr
Eureka CA 95503

Call Sign: KD6RXR
Susan C Vaughn
3546 Summer Ave
Eureka CA 95503

Call Sign: W6RLY
Paul E Flatt Sr
4896 Union
Eureka CA 95501

Call Sign: KG6SAC
Tina M Orton
204 W Del Norte St Apt D
Eureka CA 95501

Call Sign: W6FKP
Simon L Beattie Jr
3332 Summer St
Eureka CA 95501

Call Sign: KC0WQ
Thomas D Turner
2836 Union St
Eureka CA 95503

Call Sign: KJ6PEN
James S Harvey
728 W Everding St
Eureka CA 95503

Call Sign: N6DXQ
Harvey E Jossem
1432 Sunny Ave
Eureka CA 95501

Call Sign: KC6ISA
Glen N Nash
3314 Union St
Eureka CA 95501

Call Sign: KE6FYM
Daniel H Slone
135 W Grant St
Eureka CA 95501

Call Sign: KE6CDD
Neil G Pettit
44 Sunshine Way
Eureka CA 95503

Call Sign: W6DHE
Frederick L Zerlang
3408 Union St
Eureka CA 95503

Call Sign: KE6ETJ
Georgette C Thomas
322 W Grant St
Eureka CA 95501

Call Sign: KC5GOH
Lisa C Polack
1678 Terrace Way
Eureka CA 95501

Call Sign: KB6FIW
Dustin P Smith
3421 Union St
Eureka CA 955035119

Call Sign: KG6EFA
Jennifer Hood
621 W Harris St
Eureka CA 95503

Call Sign: KF6AAM
Richard S Kelly

Call Sign: KG6UUG
Nancy L Hampton

Call Sign: W6ARK
Albert P Rovelli

123 W Simpson St
Eureka CA 95501

Call Sign: AA6GO
Gary D Fluno
234 W Sonoma St
Eureka CA 95501

Call Sign: KF6QID
Paul A Leslie
3223 W St
Eureka CA 95503

Call Sign: KI6NIE
Samuel F Sanders
28 W Wadash Ave
Eureka CA 95501

Call Sign: KG6QPE
Jonathan D Taggart
4056 Walnut Apt D
Eureka CA 95503

Call Sign: N7CFD
Raymond H Rathjen
5815 Walnut Dr
Eureka CA 95501

Call Sign: KF6WMP
Ivie C Dotson
4184 Williams
Eureka CA 95503

Call Sign: WA6RTP
Kenneth J Johnson
4070 Williams St
Eureka CA 955036062

Call Sign: W6CNG
Clifford R King
2804 Windsor St
Eureka CA 955011441

Call Sign: KG6YVR
Susan M Brown

297 Wisteria Ln
Eureka CA 95503

Call Sign: K6TYK
Gerald D Chappelle
1527 Wood St
Eureka CA 95501

Call Sign: N7ISX
Joyce G Johnson
1615 Wood St
Eureka CA 95501

Call Sign: KF6MNE
Susan K Van Hoose
1737 Wood St
Eureka CA 95501

Call Sign: WB6HII
Richard J Van Hoose
1737 Wood St
Eureka CA 95501

Call Sign: KD6VUI
Carlye J Van Hoose
1737 Wood St
Eureka CA 95501

Call Sign: KF6MAF
John Chillinsky III
1 X St
Eureka CA 95501

Call Sign: KC6ANE
Steven E Casassa
Eureka CA 95502

Call Sign: KB6BEW
Darrel W Tomer
Eureka CA 95502

Call Sign: N6AGP
Lydell K Anderson
Eureka CA 95502

Call Sign: KI6ETH
Tyrel D Carver
Eureka CA 95502

Call Sign: AF6TS
Tyrel D Carver
Eureka CA 95502

Call Sign: KI6BGK
Claymond J Castro
Eureka CA 95502

Call Sign: WB6QWG
John W Cooper III III
Eureka CA 95501

Call Sign: W6IES
Michael-Peter A Esko
Eureka CA 95502

Call Sign: K6FWR
Far West Repeater
Association Inc
Eureka CA 95502

Call Sign: KE6SLS
M J Inabnit
Eureka CA 95502

Call Sign: KE6NLH
James A Johnson
Eureka CA 95502

Call Sign: KG6FWU
Dexter Luther
Eureka CA 955028017

Call Sign: AG6DA
Dexter Luther
Eureka CA 955028017

Call Sign: KG6UUF
Ralph J Marx
Eureka CA 95501

Call Sign: KI6DPZ
Mary Ann Murphy
Eureka CA 95502

Call Sign: KF6DRN
Larry A Netz
Eureka CA 95502

Call Sign: KB6NHD
Karl E Newman
Eureka CA 95502

Call Sign: KB6NHE
Ken J Newman
Eureka CA 95502

Call Sign: KE7LBM
Cynthia J Perez
Eureka CA 95502

Call Sign: KJ6SYE
Cynthia J Perez
Eureka CA 95502

Call Sign: AG6IV
Cynthia J Perez
Eureka CA 95502

Call Sign: KI6NXC
Charles D Simpson
Eureka CA 95502

Call Sign: KI6HFN
Marjorie D Simpson
Eureka CA 95502

Call Sign: KI6QYG
Norman C Thompson
Eureka CA 95502

Call Sign: KF6SJV
Aaron A Tilch
Eureka CA 955021234

Call Sign: KI6ZQS

James L Turner
Eureka CA 95502

Call Sign: K6TXH
Steve L Wingate
Eureka CA 95501

Call Sign: KA6TEC
Jesse A Woods
Eureka CA 95502

FCC Amateur Radio Licenses in Fairhaven

Call Sign: KG6LNX
Troy R Nicolini
2573.5 Broadway St
Fairhaven CA 955649505

FCC Amateur Radio Licenses in Fall River Mills

Call Sign: KD1FF
Stephen D Haynes Sr.
43217 4th St
Fall River Mills CA
960280453

Call Sign: KB6WZI
William R Krapf
Box 760 Hwy 299E
Fall River Mills CA 96028

Call Sign: KJ6VB
Gary L Tjaden
25122 Old Reynolds Rd
Fall River Mills CA 96028

Call Sign: KA6HLO
Gordon F Rathburn
27912 Soldier Mountain
Rd
Fall River Mills CA 96028

Call Sign: KE6GEK
Michael B Larrabee
Fall River Mills CA 96028

Call Sign: KB6USW
William J Mayer
Fall River Mills CA 96028

Call Sign: WA6NVY
Dale D Wonder
Fall River Mills CA
960280274

Call Sign: WA6UHO
Larry D Drouin
Fall River Mills CA
960280054

Call Sign: KI6YJR
Intermountain ARC
Fall River Mills CA 96028

FCC Amateur Radio Licenses in Ferndale

Call Sign: KG6DCO
Christopher R Rennercox
8800 Blue Slide Rd
Ferndale CA 95536

Call Sign: KE6ZPF
Kirby L Bay
1907 Crosby Rd
Ferndale CA 95536

Call Sign: KF6JBQ
Nancy L Bay
1907 Crosby Rd
Ferndale CA 95536

Call Sign: KF6SYK
Redwood ARC
1907 Crosby Rd
Ferndale CA 95536

Call Sign: KF6HBY
Spencer L Koch
401 Emerson Ln
Ferndale CA 95536

Call Sign: K6TMY
David L Andersen
48 Francis St
Ferndale CA 95536

Call Sign: KJ6AUM
Curtis Barry
4800 Grizzly Bluff
Ferndale CA 95536

Call Sign: N6PGR
Leslie B Carr
650 Williams Creek Rd
Ferndale CA 95536

Call Sign: WZ6S
David J Carr
650 Williams Creek Rd
Ferndale CA 95536

Call Sign: K6ERQ
William A Beers
Ferndale CA 95536

Call Sign: KC6SJO
Robert E Griggs Jr
Ferndale CA 95536

Call Sign: WA6LMS
Billy D De Foreest
Ferndale CA 95536

Call Sign: N7HQZ
James M Sandford
Ferndale CA 95536

Call Sign: KE6HSG
Catherine E Sandford
Ferndale CA 955361459

Call Sign: KB5ZDL
Quentin L Youngblood
Ferndale CA 95536

FCC Amateur Radio Licenses in Fieldbrook

Call Sign: N6MQE
Lawrence F Robins
5160 11th St
Fieldbrook CA 95519

Call Sign: KG6LFQ
Michael S Welch
2584 Arthur Rd
Fieldbrook CA 95519

Call Sign: KF6HQI
Elaine Y Crandall
955 Ford St
Fieldbrook CA 95519

Call Sign: W6PQ
Starr Kilian
4090 Old Railroad Grade
Rd
Fieldbrook CA 95521

Call Sign: KC6ODF
Nathaniel D Kilian
4090 Old Railroad Grade
Rd
Fieldbrook CA 955199721

Call Sign: KC6ODG
Christopher M Kilian
4090 Old Railroad Grade
Rd
Fieldbrook CA 955199721

Call Sign: N6MGE
Esther M Kilian
4090 Old Railroad Grade
Rd
Fieldbrook CA 955199721

Call Sign: KF6FLC
Steven M Jacobs
800 Sawdust Trl
Fieldbrook CA 95519

FCC Amateur Radio Licenses in Fields Landing

Call Sign: KJ6IBX
Rebecca L Lowe
Fields Landing CA 95537

Call Sign: KJ6NYY
Chris Rothstein
Fields Landing CA 95537

FCC Amateur Radio Licenses in Forks of Salmon

Call Sign: KB6EJR
Carl O Eichenhofer
Star Rt Box 907
Forks Of Salmon CA
96031

FCC Amateur Radio Licenses in Fort Bidwell

Call Sign: AD6OO
Gregory T Small
Fort Bidwell CA 96112

Call Sign: KF6SPT
Derk Steggewentz
Fort Bidwell CA 96112

Call Sign: N2VE
Derk Steggewentz
Fort Bidwell CA 96112

Call Sign: K6MHE
Danny W Richardson
26450 Blueberry Hill Rd
Fort Bragg CA 95437

Call Sign: AG6KL
Richard J Shoop
26401 Blueberry Hill Rd
Fort Bragg CA 95437

Call Sign: KI6ISN
Nita T Ishcomer
16901 Boice Ln
Fort Bragg CA 95437

Call Sign: KV6K
Brian C Bishop
31255 Brush Creek Rd
Fort Bragg CA 954376213

Call Sign: KG6JSA
Nicholas D Bishop
31255 Brush Creek Rd
Fort Bragg CA 95437

Call Sign: KF6YIU
Lowell V Kline
1040 Cedar St
Fort Bragg CA 95437

Call Sign: KC6PNA
Roy R Scott
379 Cypress St
Fort Bragg CA 95437

Call Sign: KI6TNT
Vicki J Ball
301 Cypress St 217
Fort Bragg CA 95437

Call Sign: KG6NXN
Scott P Alexander

175 Dana St
Fort Bragg CA 954374505

Call Sign: KA3WFE
Stewart C Kinner
546 E Laurel St
Fort Bragg CA 95437

Call Sign: KI6YGQ
Gabriel Q Maroney
25800 Fen View Ln
Fort Bragg CA 95437

Call Sign: KB6LZW
Dennis W Murphy
17750 Freitas Ln
Fort Bragg CA 954378363

Call Sign: KC6WDT
Steven Francis
19901 Hanson Rd
Fort Bragg CA 954379210

Call Sign: N6ZVS
Donald F Armstrong
36865 Hillcrest Ter
Fort Bragg CA 95437

Call Sign: KG6IDR
Lesley D Bennett
27750 Hwy 20
Fort Bragg CA 95437

Call Sign: W6AVK
Phillip F Lauer
31700 Hwy 20
Fort Bragg CA 95437

Call Sign: KA6VFL
Jere L Melo
120 Jewett St
Fort Bragg CA 95437

Call Sign: WA6MYR
Jack M Hawkins

21641 John Hyman Rd
Fort Bragg CA 95437

Call Sign: AC6AB
Carl E Nicholson
33009 Lassen Dr
Fort Bragg CA 95437

Call Sign: KE6ORK
Kathleen D Benson
33400 Little Valley Rd
Fort Bragg CA 95437

Call Sign: KC6OPK
Roger L Latner
32850 Mill Creek 14
Fort Bragg CA 95437

Call Sign: KF6CBA
Jason R Ross
32801 Mill Creek Dr
Fort Bragg CA 954378429

Call Sign: KF6CBB
Philip R Ross
32801 Mill Creek Dr
Fort Bragg CA 954378429

Call Sign: KA6BXL
Lewis D Stamback
32850 Mill Creek Dr
Fort Bragg CA 95437

Call Sign: KF6CBC
Russ C Smith
16300 Mitchell Creek Dr
Fort Bragg CA 954378727

Call Sign: KF6JNZ
John C Hendrickson
16861 Mitchell Creek Rd
Fort Bragg CA 954378727

Call Sign: KI6IDN
Jeremiah D Waller

810 N Harrison St
Fort Bragg CA 95437

Call Sign: KF6EIY
Deborah A Smith
16401 N Hwy 1
Fort Bragg CA 95437

Call Sign: KF6QAV
Joseph L Wagner
18320 N Hwy 1
Fort Bragg CA 954378740

Call Sign: KF6IP
Robert B Rouse
23131 N Hwy 1
Fort Bragg CA 95437

Call Sign: KM6TG
Brian C Bishop
631 N McPherson St
Fort Bragg CA 95437

Call Sign: WB6OOC
Verl R Lyons
31700 N Mitchell Creek
Rd
Fort Bragg CA 95437

Call Sign: KB2EZO
Donna M Schuler
210 N Whipple St
Fort Bragg CA 95437

Call Sign: W6FSE
Harold R Platt
19100 Neptune Ave
Fort Bragg CA 95437

Call Sign: WA6DCH
Patrick W Lawler
32125 O Bayley Dr
Fort Bragg CA 95437

Call Sign: KB6LOO

Elias Wolfman
33301 Pacific Way
Fort Bragg CA 95437

Call Sign: KJ6IZL
Loren M Rex
24881 Park Dr
Fort Bragg CA 95437

Call Sign: KE6MWW
Malia Nelson
190 Park St
Fort Bragg CA 95437

Call Sign: NA6T
Robert O Smith
320 Park St
Fort Bragg CA 95437

Call Sign: KG6VTI
Cummins Family Radio
Club
16298 Pearson Ln
Fort Bragg CA 95437

Call Sign: WA6SFC
Viola J Goodnough
18830 Porterfield Ln
Fort Bragg CA 95437

Call Sign: WB6VFO
Robert A Bainbridge
31775 Pudding Creek Rd
Fort Bragg CA 95437

Call Sign: WD6HDY
Richard V White
183 S Corry St
Fort Bragg CA 954374336

Call Sign: W6VJH
Charles C Proudfit
19051 S Harbor Dr
Fort Bragg CA 95437

Call Sign: KE6PYD
Brent E Rusert
188 S Harold St
Fort Bragg CA 954373716

Call Sign: AF6D
Sterling A Sorenson
430 S McPherson
Fort Bragg CA 95437

Call Sign: KF6CBF
Jason A Bearden
372 S Whipple St
Fort Bragg CA 954374908

Call Sign: KI6GIQ
Kyle V Nelepovitz
30774 Sherwood Rd
Fort Bragg CA 95437

Call Sign: WA6MYR
Kyle V Nelepovitz
30774 Sherwood Rd
Fort Bragg CA 95437

Call Sign: W6RQH
William E Manley
30500 Simpson Ln
Fort Bragg CA 95437

Call Sign: KF6CBD
Samuel R Bearden
32440 Simpson Ln
Fort Bragg CA 954378705

Call Sign: KA6EHH
Ernest R Messex
30601 Turner Rd
Fort Bragg CA 95437

Call Sign: KI6ISJ
Karen S Emerson
33041 Virgin Creek Ln
Fort Bragg CA 95437

Call Sign: KF6PQP
William S Gillespie
25075 Ward Ave
Fort Bragg CA 95437

Call Sign: KN6HC
Michael K Gillming
25301 Ward Ave
Fort Bragg CA 95437

Call Sign: KC6GMF
James A Gross
715 West St
Fort Bragg CA 95437

Call Sign: WA6ZCJ
Forrest E Welch
16100 Woodside Way
Fort Bragg CA 95437

Call Sign: W6QFX
Henry E Simonson
840 Woodward St
Fort Bragg CA 95437

Call Sign: N6GDV
Ralph R Bentley
Fort Bragg CA 95437

Call Sign: KD6CWD
Larin J Henricksen
Fort Bragg CA 95437

Call Sign: W6UCC
George E Goranson
Fort Bragg CA 95437

Call Sign: KF6JNY
David F Byrnes
Fort Bragg CA 954371058

Call Sign: KF6JNW
Wendy D Chapin
Fort Bragg CA 95437

Call Sign: KG6EYM
Dan J Cotton Sr
Fort Bragg CA 954370314

Call Sign: KI6PFI
Jeff A Diehl
Fort Bragg CA 95437

Call Sign: KI6ISK
Ann Marie Gittings
Fort Bragg CA 95437

Call Sign: KI6ISM
Terry L Hendricks
Fort Bragg CA 95437

Call Sign: KE6EBZ
Derek Hoyle
Fort Bragg CA 95437

Call Sign: KE6TJI
Charles R Johnson
Fort Bragg CA 95437

Call Sign: KF6CBE
Peggy A Johnson
Fort Bragg CA 954370223

Call Sign: KF6ZOK
Cecil D Lale
Fort Bragg CA 95437

Call Sign: KI6CHE
Lloyd E Livingstone
Fort Bragg CA 95437

Call Sign: KE6UZS
Ronald J Rick Jr
Fort Bragg CA 954371294

Call Sign: KB6OBM
Kelly D Silveria
Fort Bragg CA 95437

Call Sign: KB9JRQ

John W Smith
Fort Bragg CA 95437

Call Sign: KE6SAM
Michael P Wilson
Fort Bragg CA 95437

**FCC Amateur Radio
Licenses in Fort Dick**

Call Sign: KF6VXO
Johnny L Vanderhoofven
Fort Dick CA 95538

Call Sign: W6JLV
Johnny L Vanderhoofven
Fort Dick CA 95538

Call Sign: KA7WAK
Clifton B Priddle
Fort Dick CA 95538

Call Sign: KJ6JZS
Sonnie M Rubio
Fort Dick CA 95538

Call Sign: KF6YTJ
Franklin C Vanderhoofven
Fort Dick CA 955380165

Call Sign: W6FCV
Franklin C Vanderhoofven
Fort Dick CA 955380165

**FCC Amateur Radio
Licenses in Fort Jones**

Call Sign: K6OOY
Patrick A Patterson
1019 Aisling Cottage
Fort Jones CA 96032

Call Sign: KE6SXT
Dayna Crow
6516 Doe Run

Fort Jones CA 96032

Call Sign: KD6PML
Michael L Pope
12048 Main St
Fort Jones CA 96032

Call Sign: WB6MER
Donald L Kincanon
12080 Main St
Fort Jones CA 960320008

Call Sign: KE6JCP
Kenneth B Maurer
13635 Meamber Cr Rd
Fort Jones CA 96032

Call Sign: N6UKE
Ardith E Hamilton Jr
8915 N Hwy 3
Fort Jones CA 96032

Call Sign: AA6EL
Frederick A Fox
13609 Quartz Valley Rd
Fort Jones CA 96032

Call Sign: N6OGE
Barry A Filippone
7025 Quartz Valley Rd
Fort Jones CA 96032

Call Sign: N6WIH
Rita M Smith
8714 Scarface Rd
Fort Jones CA 96032

Call Sign: W6LXL
Ruth L Hinkle
5725 Scott River Rd
Fort Jones CA 96032

Call Sign: AA6CE
Patrick J Costello
2945 W Moffett Creek Rd

Fort Jones CA 96032

Call Sign: KF6RVG
Susan A Maurer
Fort Jones CA 960321101

Call Sign: KA6VBA
Ronald L Brink
Fort Jones CA 96032

Call Sign: K6IVD
Leland F Gipson
Fort Jones CA 96032

Call Sign: WA6UUR
Raymond M Skinner
Fort Jones CA 96032

Call Sign: KE6MZQ
David R Crow
Fort Jones CA 96032

Call Sign: KD7FHG
George R May
Fort Jones CA 96032

Call Sign: KE6MZP
Jerry O Crow
Fort Jones CA 96032

Call Sign: KG6RKO
Charles H House
Fort Jones CA 96032

Call Sign: N6FC
Charles H House
Fort Jones CA 96032

Call Sign: KI6WTA
Jo Peterson
Fort Jones CA 96032

Call Sign: KE6LUV
Frederick C Rockstroh
Fort Jones CA 96032

Call Sign: KD6PLY
Jean S Skinner
Fort Jones CA 96032

Call Sign: KE6RQT
James H Slaven
Fort Jones CA 96032

FCC Amateur Radio Licenses in Fortuna

Call Sign: N6AI
William R McBride II
960 14th St
Fortuna CA 955402140

Call Sign: WA6FCS
Collis P Mahan
836 15 St
Fortuna CA 95540

Call Sign: KA6ALA
Barbara J Lewis
925 9th St
Fortuna CA 95540

Call Sign: N6MIX
Anita M Anderson
2310 Acacia Dr
Fortuna CA 95540

Call Sign: WJ6P
Merlin I Anderson
2310 Acacia Dr
Fortuna CA 95540

Call Sign: KF6MNF
Jack R Bernstein
468 Annahy Dr
Fortuna CA 95540

Call Sign: KM6KX
Ronald J Harris
600 Annahy Dr

Fortuna CA 95540

Call Sign: KE6TMJ
Renee M Pulley
1991 Becker Ln
Fortuna CA 95540

Call Sign: KE6TMK
David H Pulley
1991 Becker Ln
Fortuna CA 95540

Call Sign: KB6SLY
Ellen H Dolson
1751 Beech St
Fortuna CA 955402419

Call Sign: WB6TFX
John G Dolson
1751 Beech St
Fortuna CA 955402419

Call Sign: KI6KTX
Alan E Rice
2607 Boone St
Fortuna CA 95540

Call Sign: KJ6HGN
Jason E Kadle
1848 Brandi Ln
Fortuna CA 95540

Call Sign: N6HRL
Joyce B Coomes
1680 Campton Ln
Fortuna CA 95540

Call Sign: KI6JAV
Mark A Mowrey
1727 Cecil Ave
Fortuna CA 95540

Call Sign: KJ6AVJ
John L Wilder
2680 Chism Ct

Fortuna CA 95540

Call Sign: KJ6AVI
Selene K Wilder
2680 Chism Ct
Fortuna CA 95540

Call Sign: K6BMZ
Frank C Cope
3581 Clifton Way
Fortuna CA 95540

Call Sign: KE6FEF
Michael M Ransford
3395 Covey Ct
Fortuna CA 95540

Call Sign: KF6FLA
James V Mortensen
2269 Cresr Dr
Fortuna CA 95540

Call Sign: KF6DNP
Beverly A Dobyns
124 Crest Dr
Fortuna CA 95540

Call Sign: WA6NAA
Charles E Langdon
1514 Crest Dr
Fortuna CA 95540

Call Sign: KG6TZY
Steven L Di Leo
1134 Crestview Dr
Fortuna CA 95540

Call Sign: KE6TML
Kenneth A Mahouski
3427 Drake Hill Rd
Fortuna CA 95540

Call Sign: KD7GSC
Michael S Lee

1242 Elizabeth Barcus
Way
Fortuna CA 95540

Call Sign: AE6BD
Robert L Winkelhaus
180 Empire Dr
Fortuna CA 95540

Call Sign: KJ6AUD
Susan R Dager
196 Empire Dr
Fortuna CA 95540

Call Sign: KC8OU
Richard J Dager
196 Empire Dr
Fortuna CA 95540

Call Sign: KD6IBS
Henry A Schafer
201 Empire Dr
Fortuna CA 95540

Call Sign: N6CMW
Calvin M Weil
487 Francesco Pl
Fortuna CA 955404810

Call Sign: KE6TMI
Eddie P Kemper
213 Franklin Ave
Fortuna CA 95540

Call Sign: WD6CPH
William H Harrison
1004 Garden Ln
Fortuna CA 95540

Call Sign: KJ6AUH
Chester W King
524 Guido Ave
Fortuna CA 95540

Call Sign: W6ZEM

Sydney H Moate
2344 Hannah Ct
Fortuna CA 95540

Call Sign: W9ZVE
Daniel A Armstrong
107 Harlan Way
Fortuna CA 95540

Call Sign: KE6FWN
Lorene G Loudon
2395 Hillside Dr
Fortuna CA 95540

Call Sign: KN6YT
Robert C Loudon II
2395 Hillside Dr
Fortuna CA 95540

Call Sign: KI6ULC
Dawn A Smith
1030 Hilltop Dr
Fortuna CA 95540

Call Sign: KC6BRF
Robert N Brockmann
850 Holman Way
Fortuna CA 95540

Call Sign: KE6ZPE
Gregory J Musson
1369 Home Ave
Fortuna CA 95540

Call Sign: W6NKW
Dudley M Stone
1579 Kings Row
Fortuna CA 95540

Call Sign: KC6MZQ
Robert T Pearson
2720 Kirby St
Fortuna CA 95540

Call Sign: KE6SLY

Lowell C Dobyns
1755 Laurelwood Pl
Fortuna CA 95540

Call Sign: KC6TGS
Robert C Crane
1001 Main St
Fortuna CA 95540

Call Sign: KE6YGW
Marisol Moreno
867 Maxwell St
Fortuna CA 95540

Call Sign: K6BMV
Francis C Callan
229 Meadowbrook
Fortuna CA 95540

Call Sign: KF6QIC
Michael C Johnson
236 Meadowbrook
Fortuna CA 955402602

Call Sign: WB6MQC
Ronald B Jones
5400 Mill St
Fortuna CA 95540

Call Sign: W6RBJ
Ronald B Jones
5400 Mill St
Fortuna CA 95540

Call Sign: KI6SIC
Robert S Freeman
820 N St
Fortuna CA 95540

Call Sign: KB6ZJS
John D Tyler
220 Newell Dr
Fortuna CA 95540

Call Sign: KB6HYS

Vernon A Lindstrom
229 Newell Dr
Fortuna CA 95540

Call Sign: KE6ETL
Donald L Moon
4065 Olsen Ct
Fortuna CA 95540

Call Sign: KG6ZVJ
Lewis M Mccrigler
60 Page Way
Fortuna CA 95540

Call Sign: KF6BVB
Leroy McCrigler
106 Page Way
Fortuna CA 95540

Call Sign: KJ6HGO
Carol L Nichols
188 Palmer Blvd
Fortuna CA 95540

Call Sign: KE6OSN
Richard A Bennett
505 Palmer Blvd
Fortuna CA 95540

Call Sign: AE6XW
Richard A Bennett
505 Palmer Blvd
Fortuna CA 95540

Call Sign: WA6YUD
Donald W Mueller Jr
109 Pampas Ln
Fortuna CA 95540

Call Sign: KE6TMH
Omer L Hooper Jr
145 Paradise Dr
Fortuna CA 955409209

Call Sign: KI6GGK

Robert W Shaw
3700 Renner Dr
Fortuna CA 95540

Call Sign: K6RWS
Robert W Shaw
3700 Renner Dr
Fortuna CA 95540

Call Sign: W6RNA
Jeffrey T Pierce
2189 Riverwalk Dr
Fortuna CA 95540

Call Sign: KE6LPD
Laura E Andrews
3786 Rohner St
Fortuna CA 95540

Call Sign: N6AFT
Laura E Andrews
3786 Rohner St
Fortuna CA 95540

Call Sign: N6AFT
Vernon L Reinke
3786 Rohner St
Fortuna CA 955403182

Call Sign: WD6DQB
Marion L Rowell
4140 Rohnerville Rd
Fortuna CA 95540

Call Sign: K6PXC
John H Rowell Jr
4140 Rohnerville Rd
Fortuna CA 95540

Call Sign: KB5ZUE
Daniel R Andrews
1320 Ronald Ave
Fortuna CA 95540

Call Sign: KF6JBR

Gale L Klinetobe
1735 Ronald Ave
Fortuna CA 95540

Call Sign: KE6VMU
Enoch Ibarra
1741 Ronald Ave
Fortuna CA 95540

Call Sign: KF6EYM
Brandon C Burt
1302 S Main St
Fortuna CA 95540

Call Sign: KF6CMH
George S Owsley Sr
1302 S Main St
Fortuna CA 95540

Call Sign: KF6CMI
George S Owsley Jr
1302 S Main St
Fortuna CA 95540

Call Sign: KJ6AUJ
Margaret J Murray
1943 Scenic Dr
Fortuna CA 95540

Call Sign: KJ6AUI
Michael P Murray
1943 Scenic Dr
Fortuna CA 95540

Call Sign: W6VEJ
Melvin H Murphy
3471 School St
Fortuna CA 95540

Call Sign: KG6HAC
Richard A Childers
2011 Shamrock Dr
Fortuna CA 95540

Call Sign: KB6WBU

Amy E Smith
2130 Smith Ln Apt 30
Fortuna CA 95540

Call Sign: N6ADS
Richard E Poe
2000 Smith Ln E
Fortuna CA 955402748

Call Sign: WB6ZLE
James R Vaughan
1166 Stewart St
Fortuna CA 95540

Call Sign: AE6ZL
James R Vaughan
1166 Stewart St
Fortuna CA 95540

Call Sign: KJ6AUF
Stephanie A Blood
433 Strawberry Ln
Fortuna CA 95540

Call Sign: KJ6AUG
Jared L Blood
433 Strawberry Ln
Fortuna CA 95540

Call Sign: KD7CHF
R Thomas Graham
193 Sunrise Ct
Fortuna CA 95540

Call Sign: WB6ZNZ
Boyett R Helton
1684 Thelma St
Fortuna CA 95540

Call Sign: KG6AQQ
Steven R Hibbard
2865 Thomas St
Fortuna CA 95540

Call Sign: AD6TT

Steven R Hibbard
2865 Thomas St
Fortuna CA 95540

Call Sign: KC6CFF
James E Bilderback
1432 Tompkins Hill Rd
Fortuna CA 95540

Call Sign: KE6VMT
Laurel A Baker
2960 Van Duzen St
Fortuna CA 95540

Call Sign: KQ6HR
Brian E Baker
2960 Van Duzen St
Fortuna CA 95540

Call Sign: K6KGA
Paul C Perrine
1460 Vancil St
Fortuna CA 955401521

Call Sign: KE6KQC
John R Ek
2746 Virginia Ct
Fortuna CA 95540

Call Sign: KE6TMM
Susan C Crane
147 Watson Ln
Fortuna CA 95540

Call Sign: KE6TMN
Stacy C Crane
147 Watson Ln
Fortuna CA 95540

Call Sign: K6PXI
Robert T Miner
1732 Wood Ave
Fortuna CA 95540

Call Sign: K6PIJ

Steven J Rogers
1667 Wood St
Fortuna CA 95540

Call Sign: KC6LVN
Hans Bogusch
1790 Wood St
Fortuna CA 95540

Call Sign: KD6JJD
Curtis A Tidmore Jr
Fortuna CA 95540

Call Sign: KG6IRN
Sherie A Henderson
Fortuna CA 95540

Call Sign: KF6HBZ
Lori G McCrigler
Fortuna CA 95540

Call Sign: WB6PAA
Lillian A Natt
Fortuna CA 95540

Call Sign: KJ6AUK
Jessyca D Rosson
Fortuna CA 95540

Call Sign: KJ6SYG
Donald K Smith
Fortuna CA 95540

**FCC Amateur Radio
Licenses in French Gulch**

Call Sign: KI6SUR
Martha A Daily
14900 Trinity Mt Rd
French Gulch CA 96033

Call Sign: KI6OMT
Steve M Daily
14900 Trinity Mt Rd
French Gulch CA 96033

Call Sign: W6SMD
Steve M Daily
14900 Trinity Mt Rd
French Gulch CA 96033

Call Sign: KD6IYZ
John H Lee
French Gulch CA 96033

**FCC Amateur Radio
Licenses in Garberville**

Call Sign: KC6GAF
Steven K Gill
4030 A Rd
Garberville CA 95542

Call Sign: KF6KMC
Michael C Thompson
2906 Alderpoint Rd
Garberville CA 95542

Call Sign: KJ6OTF
Margaret L Lewis
23 Alice Ave
Garberville CA 95542

Call Sign: N6TBT
Dan L Durham
93 Alice Ave
Garberville CA 95440

Call Sign: KI6IUK
Kitty Lynch
3425 Bell Springs Rd
Garberville CA 95542

Call Sign: KF6IBP
James R Wilson
6525 Briceland Thorn Rd
Garberville CA 95542

Call Sign: KG6BIL
Nancy R Wilson

6525 Briceland Thorn Rd	1025 Kimtu Rd	755 Redwood St
Garberville CA 95542	Garberville CA 95542	Garberville CA 95542
Call Sign: KE6FBQ	Call Sign: KF6KBX	Call Sign: KF6KBW
Malcolm Stebbins	Todd R Barton	Celeste H Boyd
1210 Dutyville Rd	853 Locust St	936 Riverview Ln
Garberville CA 95542	Garberville CA 95542	Garberville CA 95542
Call Sign: N6NKL	Call Sign: KE6PEJ	Call Sign: KG6RHM
William C Roddy	Charles F Morse	Patti S Rose
1581 E Branch Rd	810 M Rd	2190 Spronel Creek Rd
Garberville CA 95542	Garberville CA 95442	Garberville CA 95542
Call Sign: KJ6KZK	Call Sign: KF6IZH	Call Sign: KE6KQA
Bernice C Fladen	Tawny M Morse	Thomas J Snead
2651 Etterburg Rd	810 M Rd	2232 Sprowel Ck Rd
Garberville CA 95542	Garberville CA 95542	Garberville CA 95542
Call Sign: KB6LAB	Call Sign: KF6CYM	Call Sign: KF6KBT
Patricia A Vanek	Ben G Richard	Brian M Ormond
Ettersburg SR	454 Melville Rd	353 Sprower Crk Rd
Garberville CA 95440	Garberville CA 95542	Garberville CA 95542
Call Sign: W0YAU	Call Sign: KF6EKV	Call Sign: KE6KKF
James A Wise	Electra A Richard	Marsha R Arbo Snead
1055 Goodman Ranch Rd	454 Melville Rd	2232 Sprowl Cr Rd
Garberville CA 95542	Garberville CA 95542	Garberville CA 95542
Call Sign: KB7QZO	Call Sign: KE6KKE	Call Sign: KB6WZN
Michael L Wood	Kristin M Vogel	Desmond M Swithenbank
220 Harmony Ln	2500 Old Briceland Rd	2220 Sprowl Creek Rd
Garberville CA 95542	Garberville CA 95542	Garberville CA 95542
Call Sign: KF6WLH	Call Sign: KG6BFQ	Call Sign: KG6PIJ
Stephen W Greel Sr	Jay F Senter	Steven J Rogers
521 Jewett Rd	11700 Old Briueland Dr	750 US Hwy 101
Garberville CA 95542	Garberville CA 95542	Garberville CA 95542
Call Sign: KG6PSA	Call Sign: KD6FES	Call Sign: KE6LHX
Garold L Wellborn	Wilma J Bell	Frank E Haskins
1025 Kimtu Rd	755 Redwood St	257 Wallan Rd
Garberville CA 95542	Garberville CA 95440	Garberville CA 955429405
Call Sign: K6JXM	Call Sign: K7GDW	Call Sign: KB6WZQ
Garold L Wellborn	Warren L Bell	Thomas J Brown

Garberville CA 95440

Call Sign: KB6IFS
Kirk T Carrico
Garberville CA 95542

Call Sign: KD6LWN
Norville W Scott Jr
Garberville CA 95440

Call Sign: WD6FWA
Samuel K Sloane
Garberville CA 95542

Call Sign: KM6TE
John R Foster
Garberville CA 95440

Call Sign: KE6FBP
Margaret L Brown
Garberville CA 95542

Call Sign: KF6IBO
Ronald L Aronson
Garberville CA 955420747

Call Sign: KF6EKW
Fred N Baron
Garberville CA 95542

Call Sign: KG6UCG
James P Courtois
Garberville CA 95542

Call Sign: KF6BLS
David I Dickinson
Garberville CA 95542

Call Sign: KG6BIK
Thomas A Hoffman
Garberville CA 95542

Call Sign: KE6KQB
Craig K Johns
Garberville CA 95542

Call Sign: KJ6KZL
Joshua D Lux
Garberville CA 95542

Call Sign: KF6HUE
Mary Ann L Machi
Garberville CA 95542

Call Sign: KJ6KZM
Jacob C Whitney
Garberville CA 95542

Call Sign: KF6EKX
Brian D Winterberg
Garberville CA 95542

Call Sign: KI6YDI
Elizabeth A Ziganti
Garberville CA 95542

FCC Amateur Radio Licenses in Gasquet

Call Sign: KG6VGY
Ross M Morgan
1401 N Fork Rd
Gasquet CA 95543

Call Sign: KC6QOP
Barry J Henderson
Gasquet CA 95543

Call Sign: KI6FAZ
Theodore H Johnson
Gasquet CA 95543

Call Sign: AA6UN
Gene J Petrik
Gasquet CA 95543

FCC Amateur Radio Licenses in Gazelle

Call Sign: N6YOZ

Justina J Williams
9217 Gazelle Callahan Rd
Gazelle CA 96034

FCC Amateur Radio Licenses in Gerber

Call Sign: KC6BRI
Charles R Irwin
9416 99 W Rd
Gerber CA 96035

Call Sign: KC6BWH
Enan B Irwin
9416 99 W Rd
Gerber CA 96035

Call Sign: KD6MTT
Tony A Nanfito
22381 Dove
Gerber CA 96035

Call Sign: KD6JEO
Michael D Muscio
22620 Dove Ave
Gerber CA 960359762

Call Sign: KC6IPG
Lisa S Hart
7325 Perfect Cir
Gerber CA 96036

Call Sign: KC6GJT
Marion L Hiatt
23025 Reno Ave
Gerber CA 96035

Call Sign: KC6IRL
Imler E Hiatt
23025 Reno Ave
Gerber CA 96035

Call Sign: KC6FRV
Kraig M Morgan
9343 State Hwy 99W

Gerber CA 96035

Call Sign: KD0OQM
Robert E Bruce
Gerber CA 96035

FCC Amateur Radio Licenses in Greenview

Call Sign: KF6QDX
Gary Prince
2608 N Kidder Creek
Greenview CA 96037

Call Sign: KF6RVH
Mark C George
3622 N Kodder Cr Rd
Greenview CA 960370155

Call Sign: K6ED
Edward S Westbrook III
Greenview CA 960370220

Call Sign: KF6ZSY
Blessed Seraphim Rose
Amateur Rad Aux
Greenview CA 96037

Call Sign: KG6ZEI
Leanne J Brown
Greenview CA 96037

Call Sign: KJ6GTT
Austin C Hasemeyer
Greenview CA 96037

Call Sign: K6GYL
Dianne C Hasemeyer
Greenview CA 96037

Call Sign: K6NOD
Donald R Hasemeyer
Greenview CA 96037

Call Sign: KI6LOL

Jefferson Amateur Radio
Society
Greenview CA 96037

Call Sign: KF6MWH
Michael D La Londe
Greenview CA 96037

Call Sign: WA6MJX
Joseph L La Londe
Greenview CA 96037

Call Sign: KF6TMB
Gary D Pollard
Greenview CA 96037

Call Sign: K6JAR
State Of Jefferson Amateur
Radio
Greenview CA 96037

Call Sign: N6STE
Camelia M Westbrook
Greenview CA 960370220

FCC Amateur Radio Licenses in Grenada

Call Sign: KA6JGX
James W Elkins
15109 Hwy 99
Grenada CA 96038

Call Sign: KD6DHW
Larry L Duff
12817 Old Hwy 99
Grenada CA 96038

Call Sign: KE6MZO
Nancy E Duff
12817 Old Hwy 99
Grenada CA 96038

Call Sign: K6BOD
Edward M Davis

12819 Old Hwy 99
Grenada CA 960389610

Call Sign: WA6JCE
Michael S Hennig
724 Shasta Blvd
Grenada CA 96038

Call Sign: KC5OHA
Richard A Ray
6321 Siskiyou Blvd
Grenada CA 96038

Call Sign: KD6LIR
Patrick A O Toole
Grenada CA 96038

Call Sign: WB6WTH
Garry W Korpi
Grenada CA 96038

Call Sign: KG6FBI
Richard F Metcalfe
Grenada CA 96038

Call Sign: KG6ZEB
Kenneth V Metcalfe
Grenada CA 96038

Call Sign: KG6ZEA
Ruby J Metcalfe
Grenada CA 96038

FCC Amateur Radio Licenses in Gualala

Call Sign: N6GGI
Michael H Henderson
Anchor Bay Campground
Gualala CA 95445

Call Sign: K6OFW
Carlton White
45351 Fish Rock Rd
Gualala CA 95445

Call Sign: N6KIP
Jo Ann Harris
34575 Hwy 1
Gualala CA 95445

Call Sign: KE6HVM
Wayne T Buttress
43411 Iversen Rd
Gualala CA 95445

Call Sign: KI6GGC
Robert A Nelson
30150 S Hwy 1
Gualala CA 95445

Call Sign: K7LIM
Loren D Flanagan
34591 S Hwy 1
Gualala CA 95445

Call Sign: K3DH
Donald A Heimburger
36851 S Hwy 1
Gualala CA 954451507

Call Sign: KG6PTW
Richard J Ryder
35501 S Hwy 1 Unit 151
Gualala CA 95445

Call Sign: KE6GHB
Roy K Menning
35501 S Hwy 1 Unit 40
Gualala CA 95445

Call Sign: K6YLW
William T Hartman
35501 S Hwy 1 Unit 51
Gualala CA 95445

Call Sign: KG6YLW
Cathleen J Crosby
46541 Tickled Pink
Gualala CA 954451274

Call Sign: W8CAT
Cathleen J Crosby
46541 Tickled Pink
Gualala CA 954451274

Call Sign: N9UBS
Scott P Baselt
46541 Tickled Pink Dr
Gualala CA 95445

Call Sign: KI6DJI
Linda J Katahara
30316 Woodside Ct
Gualala CA 95445

Call Sign: KC6PKQ
Doris L Bertram
Gualala CA 95445

Call Sign: KD6PPA
James R Bold
Gualala CA 95445

Call Sign: KD6MFC
Donna L De Baets
Gualala CA 95445

Call Sign: KE6GHC
James F De Wilder
Gualala CA 95445

Call Sign: KD6MFB
Ramona L Essoe
Gualala CA 95445

Call Sign: KD6MEV
Ira G Essoe Jr
Gualala CA 95445

Call Sign: KD6MFA
Donald C Geis
Gualala CA 95445

Call Sign: WB6MWZ

James S McLaughlin
Gualala CA 95445

Call Sign: N6MIV
Wiley L Reading Jr
Gualala CA 95445

Call Sign: N6LPN
James N Teale
Gualala CA 95445

Call Sign: AE6U
Scott T Williams
Gualala CA 95445

Call Sign: KI6BEB
Donald R Furr Jr
Gualala CA 95445

Call Sign: KF6AIE
Tyrone A Amersfoort
Gualala CA 954451002

Call Sign: KF6ZSZ
Anchor Bay ARC
Gualala CA 954450465

Call Sign: W6ABR
Anchor Bay ARC
Gualala CA 954450465

Call Sign: KF6AIF
Richard E Balch
Gualala CA 954451409

Call Sign: KI6GGA
Mary E Benton
Gualala CA 95445

Call Sign: KG6HMP
Kathryn L Berleyoung
Gualala CA 954450397

Call Sign: KD6WJT
Christopher D Brown

Gualala CA 95445

Call Sign: KI6IVP
Darla J Buechner
Gualala CA 95445

Call Sign: KE6PXP
George E Bush
Gualala CA 954451528

Call Sign: KG6OHP
Charles J Cappotto
Gualala CA 954451308

Call Sign: KI6DJL
Dennis L Carter
Gualala CA 95445

Call Sign: KI6DJG
Janice L Carter
Gualala CA 95445

Call Sign: KG6TOG
Doris M Causey
Gualala CA 954451349

Call Sign: KG6YLU
Joel B Chaban
Gualala CA 95445

Call Sign: KI6GGI
Pat A Chaban
Gualala CA 95445

Call Sign: KG6KLO
Lewis R Chapman
Gualala CA 95445

Call Sign: KB6YKV
Laura P Cortright
Gualala CA 954451495

Call Sign: KG6NHV
William C Davy
Gualala CA 954451275

Call Sign: KI6HGY
Flavia De Oliveira
Gualala CA 954450212

Call Sign: KJ6DKY
Louise M Dewilder
Gualala CA 95445

Call Sign: WD4NEK
Robert C Diefenbach
Gualala CA 95445

Call Sign: KG6KLR
Robert L Dillon
Gualala CA 95445

Call Sign: W6YJL
Harold G Elzig
Gualala CA 95445

Call Sign: N6UFC
Richard H Emmons
Gualala CA 95445

Call Sign: KG6ULO
Marta N Emmons
Gualala CA 95445

Call Sign: KI2Q
Frank A Field
Gualala CA 954451476

Call Sign: K6CQE
Lawrence D Gaudet
Gualala CA 95445

Call Sign: KG6VHC
Joyce M Gaudet
Gualala CA 95445

Call Sign: KI6CGY
Coralyn Hadden
Gualala CA 95445

Call Sign: KI6DJJ
Suzanne J Hansen
Gualala CA 95445

Call Sign: KG6KLP
Donald A Heimburger
Gualala CA 954451507

Call Sign: KG6NHX
Marcia A Heimburger
Gualala CA 95445

Call Sign: KG6KLN
Johnny N Hiatt
Gualala CA 954451695

Call Sign: KD6MUE
Thomas S Ingersoll
Gualala CA 95445

Call Sign: KG6IPV
Marjory C Ingersoll
Gualala CA 954450483

Call Sign: KG6YLS
Christopher T Jewell
Gualala CA 95445

Call Sign: AE6VW
Christopher T Jewell
Gualala CA 95445

Call Sign: KW6H
Christopher T Jewell
Gualala CA 954451396

Call Sign: KG6YLT
Jan Jewell
Gualala CA 95445

Call Sign: KI6ORO
Jan Jewell
Gualala CA 95445

Call Sign: KG6PTX

James L Johnson
Gualala CA 954451690

Call Sign: KI6RBL
Robert T Juengling
Gualala CA 95445

Call Sign: KI6VEV
Arthur E Juhl
Gualala CA 95445

Call Sign: KG6OHO
Linda Keir
Gualala CA 95445

Call Sign: KG6PTV
Brannon B Klopfer
Gualala CA 95445

Call Sign: KG6PTU
Brent B Klopfer
Gualala CA 95445

Call Sign: W6TXY
James C Lawson
Gualala CA 95445

Call Sign: KG6PTY
Irene E Leidner
Gualala CA 954451275

Call Sign: WA6MUB
James I Long
Gualala CA 95445

Call Sign: KE6YKV
Brent M Mason
Gualala CA 95445

Call Sign: KG6FPJ
Susanna L Matthay
Gualala CA 954451686

Call Sign: KI6IVQ
Alfred J Mcelroy

Gualala CA 95445

Call Sign: KG6FPN
Bridget S Mclaughlin
Gualala CA 95445

Call Sign: KG6FPP
Leighton R Nelsen
Gualala CA 95445

Call Sign: KF6AIH
Alice J Nelsen
Gualala CA 954451386

Call Sign: WA6EXM
Alice J Nelsen
Gualala CA 954451386

Call Sign: KG6YLX
Margaret L Nelson
Gualala CA 95445

Call Sign: KF6APS
Nola A Noriega
Gualala CA 95445

Call Sign: KG6TOF
Joan L O Connell
Gualala CA 95445

Call Sign: KI6GFZ
Lawrence A Pike
Gualala CA 954451671

Call Sign: KI6CHC
Bonnie L Plakos
Gualala CA 95445

Call Sign: KG6FPM
Lin Plescia
Gualala CA 95445

Call Sign: KI6ZOK
Deborah A Plumer
Gualala CA 95445

Call Sign: KI6CHB
Robert L Pounds
Gualala CA 954451455

Call Sign: KG6YLV
Jerry D Rench
Gualala CA 954450962

Call Sign: KE6WC
Kenneth N Reynoldson
Gualala CA 954450465

Call Sign: KI6ZOJ
Barbara S Rice
Gualala CA 95445

Call Sign: KI6VEU
David W Rice
Gualala CA 95445

Call Sign: K6DWR
David W Rice
Gualala CA 95445

Call Sign: KI6GGE
Barbara A Roberts
Gualala CA 95445

Call Sign: KI6IVO
Joost Romeu
Gualala CA 95445

Call Sign: AD6EN
Millard F Schewe
Gualala CA 954450563

Call Sign: KG6NHW
Ralph I Schwartz
Gualala CA 95445

Call Sign: KI6ZOL
Roberta H Smith
Gualala CA 95445

Call Sign: KI6VEW
Frederick R Stange
Gualala CA 95445

Call Sign: KI6DJF
Deann K Steele
Gualala CA 95445

Call Sign: KG6KLQ
Richard C Stover
Gualala CA 95445

Call Sign: N6QNY
David S Torres
Gualala CA 95445

Call Sign: K6URG
Paul A Truelsen
Gualala CA 954451551

Call Sign: KI6KRH
Ravindra C Vasavada
Gualala CA 95445

Call Sign: KI6GGJ
Gerald D Waxman
Gualala CA 95445

Call Sign: N6YBQ
Clayton W Yale
Gualala CA 954451495

Call Sign: KG6TOI
Donna M Yates-Johnson
Gualala CA 954451690

FCC Amateur Radio Licenses in Happy Camp

Call Sign: KF6OFX
Jody E Lohn
63715 Applegate Dr
Happy Camp CA 96039

Call Sign: KF6DPL

Charles A Mayton
63715 Applegate Dr
Happy Camp CA 96039

Call Sign: N6SOJ
William B Worcester
60731 Gordons Ferry Rd
Happy Camp CA 96039

Call Sign: WB6OTV
William B Worcester
60731 Gordons Ferry Rd
Happy Camp CA
960390129

Call Sign: KD7ODL
Jerry D Poeschel
62929 Hwy 96
Happy Camp CA 96039

Call Sign: KG6SAW
Diana S Poeschel
62929 Hwy 96
Happy Camp CA 96039

Call Sign: N6CAS
George W Thorward
4919 Indian Creek Rd
Happy Camp CA 96039

Call Sign: WA6SHD
Charles T McWethy
121 Park Way
Happy Camp CA 96039

Call Sign: KG6SFV
Jerry D Poeschel
4018 Pine Pl
Happy Camp CA 96039

Call Sign: WA6EAR
Michael S Trombetta
Happy Camp CA 96039

Call Sign: WB6QFS

Janice K Trombetta
Happy Camp CA 96039

Call Sign: N6EML
William B Worcester
Happy Camp CA 96039

Call Sign: KI6KFB
Kenneth Baldwin
Happy Camp CA 96039

Call Sign: KJ6ICK
Steve L Burns
Happy Camp CA 96039

Call Sign: K6IEA
Steve L Burns
Happy Camp CA 96039

Call Sign: K6GIG
Steve L Burns
Happy Camp CA 96039

Call Sign: KF6RED
George M Chambers
Happy Camp CA
960390789

Call Sign: KD6WZA
Stanley L Poeschel
Happy Camp CA 96039

Call Sign: W6EAR
Michael S Trombetta
Happy Camp CA 96039

Call Sign: K6RED
Janice K Trombetta
Happy Camp CA 96039

FCC Amateur Radio Licenses in Hat Creek

Call Sign: KG6JY
Page T Perrin

41480 Bidwell Rd
Hat Creek CA 96040

Call Sign: KF6EUT
E James Norman
16957 Hwy 89
Hat Creek CA 96040

Call Sign: KJ6MQT
Robert J Pearce Jr
42463 Leaping Trout Way
Hat Creek CA 96040

Call Sign: KJ6PCU
Robert J Pearce Jr
42463 Leaping Trout Way
Hat Creek CA 96040

FCC Amateur Radio Licenses in Hayfork

Call Sign: KG6ZIM
Robert E Brothers
861 Hwy3
Hayfork CA 96041

Call Sign: KB6WTB
Clinton Guy
Hayfork CA 96041

Call Sign: KB6WMK
Sheila A Judkins
Hayfork CA 96041

Call Sign: KB6WML
Curtis L Judkins Jr
Hayfork CA 96041

Call Sign: KG6BGC
David G Menefee Jr
Hayfork CA 96041

Call Sign: KB6WTA
Stanley C Arnold
Hayfork CA 96041

Call Sign: KF6WLP
Patricia A Arnold
Hayfork CA 96041

Call Sign: KJ6OCL
Leston Karl Fisher
Hayfork CA 960410045

Call Sign: KI6BVP
Clifford N Groman
Hayfork CA 96041

Call Sign: KE6CDQ
Joan C Hamilton
Hayfork CA 96041

Call Sign: KI6WAK
Jonathan A Hanover
Hayfork CA 96041

Call Sign: N0RTA
Robert E Kearbey Jr
Hayfork CA 96041

Call Sign: KE6SLV
Philip J Kearney
Hayfork CA 96041

Call Sign: KI6TRN
Alan R Kernohan
Hayfork CA 96041

Call Sign: WB6GVM
John W Kizziar
Hayfork CA 96041

Call Sign: N6LUA
Frederick C May Jr
Hayfork CA 96041

Call Sign: KF6TWN
Nicholas A Morgan
Hayfork CA 96041

Call Sign: WD6HCO
Steven M Snyder
Hayfork CA 96041

Call Sign: N6TEM
Steven M Snyder
Hayfork CA 96041

Call Sign: KF6WSZ
Robert B Winter
Hayfork CA 960410688

Call Sign: KG6PRJ
Robert E Young
Hayfork CA 96041

FCC Amateur Radio Licenses in Herlong

Call Sign: K7JEU
James B Swaim
112 Tamarack
Herlong CA 96113

Call Sign: KD6STL
Hugh S Jamison
Herlong CA 96113

Call Sign: N7UVK
Thomas H Stoner
Herlong CA 96113

Call Sign: AC6JY
David R Faggard
Herlong CA 96113

Call Sign: KF6ELU
Blake L Hutchinson
Herlong CA 96113

Call Sign: KE6KCE
Bruce B Pfeiffer
Herlong CA 96113

FCC Amateur Radio Licenses in Honeydew

Call Sign: WD8ROV
Allen T Heady
3475 Wilder Ridge Rd
Honeydew CA 95545

Call Sign: KF6PRK
Robert L Fuel
Honeydew CA 955450121

Call Sign: KJ6BVP
Tim C Trower
Honeydew CA 95545

FCC Amateur Radio Licenses in Hopland

Call Sign: KI6URQ
Roy Morelli
360 Ralph Betcher Rd
Hopland CA 95449

Call Sign: KJ6IAC
Nicole M Young
486 St Marys Ave
Hopland CA 954599798

Call Sign: KI6URP
Brock Archer
Hopland CA 95449

Call Sign: KJ6LFK
Marc Brandt
Hopland CA 95449

Call Sign: N6MAB
Marc Brandt
Hopland CA 95449

Call Sign: KI6URL
Danny Contreras
Hopland CA 95449

Call Sign: AG6GG
Gregory W Etchell
Hopland CA 95449

Call Sign: KI6RIW
Doug J Taylor
Hopland CA 95449

FCC Amateur Radio Licenses in Hornbrook

Call Sign: KB6MPI
Kathleen A Jarschke-Schultze
19101 Camp Creek Rd
Hornbrook CA 96044

Call Sign: KG6MM
Robert A Schultze
19101 Camp Creek Rd
Hornbrook CA 96044

Call Sign: KD6EPD
Madeleine Cornwell
2139 Hilt Rd
Hornbrook CA 96044

Call Sign: KD6NAO
Beverly A Cornwell
2139 Hilt Rd
Hornbrook CA 96044

Call Sign: KD6NAP
Jacquelin M Cornwell
2139 Hilt Rd
Hornbrook CA 96044

Call Sign: WA7KSW
George D Essig
4312 Pheasant Pl
Hornbrook CA 96044

Call Sign: W6WR
William S Skeen
12634 Ponderosa St

Hornbrook CA 96044

Call Sign: KF6ERJ
Zeneta Mary Crawford
Hornbrook CA 96044

Call Sign: N6PSJ
Carl C Holst
Hornbrook CA 960440542

Call Sign: KE6MZN
Frank H Norman
Hornbrook CA 96044

FCC Amateur Radio Licenses in Hyampom

Call Sign: K7OOH
Gerald L Miles
Hyampom CA 96046

Call Sign: KJ6MEN
Francis G Moore
Hyampom CA 96046

Call Sign: W6FGM
Francis G Moore
Hyampom CA 96046

FCC Amateur Radio Licenses in Hydesville

Call Sign: W6GLO
Clifford O Evans
3498 A St Sp1
Hydesville CA 95547

Call Sign: KI6HDC
Daniel R Martin
3125 Graybrook Ln
Hydesville CA 95547

Call Sign: AG6JW
Daniel R Martin
3125 Graybrook Ln

Hydesville CA 95547

Call Sign: KD6AXL
Iris J Mattes
3222 Graybrook Ln
Hydesville CA 95547

Call Sign: WB6ZUT
Erwin J Mattes
3222 Graybrook Ln
Hydesville CA 955479406

Call Sign: AD6NX
Erwin J Mattes
3222 Graybrook Ln
Hydesville CA 955479406

Call Sign: KF6GAX
Patricia A Inabnit
Hydesville CA 955470607

FCC Amateur Radio Licenses in Igo

Call Sign: KF6OLE
David J Mayer
1 Gunnysack Rd
Igo CA 96047

Call Sign: KG6TJI
Prudence L Lockhart
14437 Marsha Way
Igo CA 96047

Call Sign: KJ6DMW
Danie A Rowe
8017 Plating Rd
Igo CA 96047

Call Sign: K6YBZ
Jack W Schlotter
7161 Rector Creek Rd
Igo CA 96047

Call Sign: KA6OQI

Virginia M Schlotter
7161 Rector Creek Rd
Igo CA 96047

Call Sign: AA6SZ
Donald A Kujath
Igo CA 96047

Call Sign: KD6GQR
Randy B Mosher
Igo CA 96047

Call Sign: KN6LK
Ron D Mosher
Igo CA 96047

Call Sign: KC6VRS
Robert W Anderson
Igo CA 960470405

Call Sign: KG6CXZ
Michelle D Hannaford
Igo CA 96047

Call Sign: KJ6RFH
Stephen R Morrill
Igo CA 96047

Call Sign: KG6RXV
James E Willson
Igo CA 96047

FCC Amateur Radio Licenses in Janesville

Call Sign: N1KER
Klaus H W Strassmann
461 545 Bovee Ln
Janesville CA 96114

Call Sign: N1QDB
Ulrich E Maitre Jr
461 545 Bovee Ln
Janesville CA 96114

Call Sign: KJ6DUA
Peter R Wilcox
713 727 Cat Cut Hill Rd
Janesville CA 96114

Call Sign: KC6OLJ
William W Black
463 840 Christie St
Janesville CA 96114

Call Sign: KI6NWM
Roger W Krueger
465 855 Cook Rd
Janesville CA 96114

Call Sign: WB6RTV
Sierra L Manatt
466 055 Cook Rd
Janesville CA 96114

Call Sign: W6IWD
Sierra L Manatt
466 055 Cook Rd
Janesville CA 96114

Call Sign: WA6GSG
James E Manatt
466 055 Cook Rd
Janesville CA 96114

Call Sign: KE6WWT
William J Martens Jr
704325 Indians Rd
Janesville CA 96114

Call Sign: KF6QOS
Autumn E Martens
704 325 Indians Rd
Janesville CA 96114

Call Sign: KF6QOT
Freda J Russell
704 325 Indians Rd
Janesville CA 96114

Call Sign: KJ6BQI
Joanna M Zimmermann
459 680 Lakeview Dr
Janesville CA 96114

Call Sign: K6ZLM
Harold B Miner
463 625 Main St
Janesville CA 96114

Call Sign: WB6WIO
Barbara A Albers
709 935 Pine St
Janesville CA 961149672

Call Sign: WA6RPE
Franklin R Albers
709 935 Pine St
Janesville CA 96114

Call Sign: KB7ZCI
William T Adams
459 610 Ponderosa Blvd
Janesville CA 96114

Call Sign: KF6LBK
Rod A Baillie
459 765 Ponderosa Blvd
Janesville CA 96114

Call Sign: KE6VUB
John E Goude
460 235 Ponderosa Blvd
Janesville CA 96114

Call Sign: KJ6BQD
Michael S Riley
711 450 Property Ln
Janesville CA 96114

Call Sign: KI6NWN
John J Ward
712 265 Sunyside Rd
Janesville CA 96114

Call Sign: KI6IFM
Rodney M Jones
714760 Vista Ln
Janesville CA 96114

Call Sign: K7NUU
Stanley R La Pointe
708 720 Warring St
Janesville CA 961149603

Call Sign: W6WMF
George G Bunnell
Janesville CA 96114

Call Sign: K6ME
Terry L Cobb
Janesville CA 96114

Call Sign: AA6QW
Patrick K Collins
Janesville CA 96114

Call Sign: K6LRC
Lassen ARC
Janesville CA 96114

Call Sign: WB6YWU
Robert D Baertschiger
Janesville CA 96114

Call Sign: KF6JBH
Robert E Cobb
Janesville CA 96114

Call Sign: KF6JBI
Gloria M Cobb
Janesville CA 96114

Call Sign: K6GMC
Gloria M Cobb
Janesville CA 96114

Call Sign: K6JBH
Robert E Cobb
Janesville CA 96114

Call Sign: KI6HBS
Christine I Duerksen
Janesville CA 96130

Call Sign: KG6VCS
Devin D Duerksen
Janesville CA 96114

Call Sign: KI6HBR
Laura L Duerksen
Janesville CA 96114

Call Sign: KJ6BQG
Lexie L Feige
Janesville CA 96114

Call Sign: KF6FNG
Mardella B Hardesty
Janesville CA 96114

Call Sign: KJ6MQP
Mary C Johnson
Janesville CA 96114

Call Sign: KJ6HSF
Carol A Montgomery
Janesville CA 96114

Call Sign: KJ6JFS
Don F Montgomery
Janesville CA 96114

Call Sign: KJ6HSG
Jolee D Montgomery
Janesville CA 96114

Call Sign: KJ6BQE
Sarah J North
Janesville CA 96114

Call Sign: KI6JQC
Mark Paytas
Janesville CA 96114

Call Sign: KQ6HA
John G Pryor
Janesville CA 96114

Call Sign: KJ6MQR
Gayle A Triplett
Janesville CA 96114

Call Sign: KI6NWL
Kam Vento
Janesville CA 96114

FCC Amateur Radio Licenses in Junction City

Call Sign: KE6WYP
Rebia N Westbrook
1271 Lake Rd
Junction City CA 96048

Call Sign: KD6PAX
Taylor K Downs
20 Red Hill Rd
Junction City CA
960480279

Call Sign: WD6EDA
Lee F Mayer
Junction City CA 96048

Call Sign: KE6ZIQ
James A Beeler
Junction City CA 96048

Call Sign: WD6FYC
Joel L Horn
Junction City CA 96048

Call Sign: WD6DAA
Gaines K Horn
Junction City CA
960480329

Call Sign: N6MIQ
Kelly S Horn

Junction City CA
960489329

Call Sign: KI6DVO
Christine L Taylor
Junction City CA 96048

Call Sign: KI6DVP
Gregory V Taylor
Junction City CA 96048

FCC Amateur Radio Licenses in Klamath

Call Sign: KI6KEB
Labecca R Nessier
99 Redwood Dr
Klamath CA 95548

Call Sign: W7PXY
Gerald O Connor
472 Ter Wer Riffle Rd
Klamath CA 95548

Call Sign: KI6KEA
Peggy L O'Neill
Klamath CA 95548

Call Sign: KI6PDY
Joanne Benson
16700 Hwy 96
Klamath River CA 96050

FCC Amateur Radio Licenses in Kneeland

Call Sign: KG6WQU
Benedikt Dreier
175 Green Rd
Kneeland CA 95549

Call Sign: KE6OSO
Ruth A Epperson
175 Green Rd
Kneeland CA 95549

Call Sign: KF6CMF
Maureen G Lilleland
3461 Greenwood Hghts
Kneeland CA 95549

Call Sign: KF6CMG
Eric T Lilleland
3461 Greenwood Hghts
Kneeland CA 95549

Call Sign: KJ6IBZ
Ryan T Jameson
4748A Greenwood Hghts
Kneeland CA 95549

Call Sign: KE6PTT
Howard R Burk
2364 Greenwood Hgts D6
Kneeland CA 95549

Call Sign: KE6IAV
Philip M Perez
186 Shale Ln
Kneeland CA 95549

Call Sign: KE6IAW
Caroline K Perez
186 Shale Ln
Kneeland CA 95549

Call Sign: W6DVO
Mark J D Adams
Kneeland CA 95549

FCC Amateur Radio Licenses in Korbel

Call Sign: N5ZEF
James P Clayton
24748 Maple Creek Rd
Korbel CA 95550

Call Sign: KF6NKM
Michael K Cooper

Korbel CA 95550

Call Sign: KI6CPU
Michael E Waterman
19753 Bonnie Vista Ln
Lakehead CA 960519665

Call Sign: WB0CQF
Anthony Grombone
19253 Golden Eagle Rd
Lakehead CA 96051

Call Sign: AE6FA
Anthony Grombone
19253 Golden Eagle Rd
Lakehead CA 96051

Call Sign: W6CQG
Anthony Grombone
19253 Golden Eagle Rd
Lakehead CA 96051

Call Sign: WB7QGI
Erik R Mickelsen
17529 Grey Fawn Trl
Lakehead CA 96051

Call Sign: WA6VLQ
Dale H Rukes
19836 Lakeshore Dr
Lakehead CA 96051

Call Sign: KA6VLR
Lori E King
20714 Lakeshore Dr
Lakehead CA 96051

Call Sign: N6CZV
Rusty D King
20714 Lakeshore Dr
Lakehead CA 96051

Call Sign: KC6IWK
Jonathan K Williams
341 Mammoth Dr
Lakehead CA 96051

Call Sign: KD6DVQ
Jeremy A Williams
20767 Mammoth Dr
Lakehead CA 96051

Call Sign: KA6FXD
Harriette A Zornes
20662 Oak St
Lakehead CA 96051

Call Sign: WA6MSZ
Don E Zornes
20662 Oak St
Lakehead CA 96051

Call Sign: N6QYX
Theodore V Hoyle
20721 Oak St
Lakehead CA 96051

Call Sign: KD6TCV
Isaac Bentley
Lakehead CA 96031

Call Sign: KE6POX
Jack R Thatcher
Lakehead CA 96051

Call Sign: W6FBI
Herman E Voss
Lakehead CA 960510010

Call Sign: KI6FRX
David A White
58500 Bell Springs Rd
Laytonville CA 954549022

Call Sign: N6MNF
Reed W Fowles
7151 Woodman Rd
Laytonville CA 95454

Call Sign: KA6YUH
Ira Pilgrim
Laytonville CA 95454

Call Sign: KD6MFQ
Mary J Radke
Laytonville CA 95454

Call Sign: KD6SBF
Richard M Robinson
Laytonville CA 95454

Call Sign: KD6SEV
Richard L Richter
Laytonville CA 95454

Call Sign: KC6TFL
Clyde G Davis
Laytonville CA 95454

Call Sign: KJ6HZZ
Ray A Blumenthal
Laytonville CA 954540702

Call Sign: KE6WYS
Susan J Davis
Laytonville CA 95454

Call Sign: KJ6VIA
Jane A Evans
Laytonville CA 95454

Call Sign: KF6QAN
Larry C Finch
Laytonville CA 954541357

Call Sign: KG6CTI
Sharon A Finch
Laytonville CA 954541357

Call Sign: KE6RTJ
James E Hagami
Laytonville CA 954541205

Call Sign: KD6LFO
Kevin R Headlee
Laytonville CA 95454

Call Sign: KJ6VIE
Life Jensen
Laytonville CA 95454

Call Sign: N6KYX
Douglas P Jones
Laytonville CA 95454

Call Sign: KE6MUT
James M Kornegay
Laytonville CA 954540102

Call Sign: N6CZY
Michael R Lewis
Laytonville CA 95454

Call Sign: N6IRH
Darlene H Lewis
Laytonville CA 95454

Call Sign: KE6VGA
John Morehouse
Laytonville CA 95454

Call Sign: AC6DL
Joseph R Park II
Laytonville CA 95454

Call Sign: WY1A
Donald A Setzco
Laytonville CA 954541831

Call Sign: KJ6OMM
Ronald L Spence
Laytonville CA 95454

Call Sign: KJ6HKE

Dennis R Wier
Laytonville CA 95454

FCC Amateur Radio Licenses in Leggett

Call Sign: KE6KRL
Barbara Burke
Leggett CA 955850098

Call Sign: KF6LTT
Mark Drake
Leggett CA 95585

Call Sign: KI6PVC
Edward C Permenter
Leggett CA 95585

FCC Amateur Radio Licenses in Lewiston

Call Sign: KA6YGR
Dennis G Zane
125 2nd Ave
Lewiston CA 96052

Call Sign: KG6QGJ
Gene S Maxwell
Hcr 1 Box 85
Lewiston CA 96052

Call Sign: KG6BD
Carroll O Johnson
2995 Goose Ranch Rd
Lewiston CA 96052

Call Sign: W6KWZ
Morton J Kardos
5 Rush Creek Dr
Lewiston CA 960529606

Call Sign: KB6HVY
Robert J Wilson
67400 State Hwy 299W 72
Lewiston CA 96052

Call Sign: KF6JNO
Ronald A Perez
96 Viola Ln
Lewiston CA 96052

Call Sign: KE6EIF
Jack A Scribner
Lewiston CA 96052

Call Sign: KG6BQY
Matthew B Aguilar
Lewiston CA 96052

Call Sign: KI6OQV
John M Hurley
Lewiston CA 960520790

Call Sign: KF6LGX
Katty F Perez
Lewiston CA 96052

Call Sign: KG6OJT
Michael E Walker
Lewiston CA 96052

Call Sign: KG6TJH
Chad A Wyckoff
Lewiston CA 96052

FCC Amateur Radio Licenses in Likely

Call Sign: KA6UTU
Robert A Houghtby
Likely CA 96116

FCC Amateur Radio Licenses in Litchfield

Call Sign: KA6ELH
John A Schaap
Litchfield CA 96117

Call Sign: KD6ZN

John J Sigwing
Litchfield CA 96117

Call Sign: KG6OQX
Paul S Thomas
Litchfield CA 96117

FCC Amateur Radio
Licenses in Little River

Call Sign: W6MJP
Donald R Copeland
43300 Airport Rd 53
Little River CA 95456

Call Sign: KB6LBG
Thomas A Taylor
33001 Frog Pond Rd
Little River CA
954560352

Call Sign: KJ6ZE
Ora G Hollaway
6675 Little River Airport
Rd
Little River CA 95456

Call Sign: N6VGM
Sheila Hollaway
6675 Little River Airport
Rd
Little River CA 95456

Call Sign: KI6KRO
James D Hoover
43300 Little River Airport
Rd 106 Rivendell Rd
Little River CA 95456

Call Sign: W6PEG
Paul E Greene
Little River CA
954560312

Call Sign: KD6MEY

Martha N Taylor
Little River CA 95456

Call Sign: NC6E
Charles P Weikel
Little River CA 95456

Call Sign: KK6W
Gary D Burleson
Little River CA 95456

Call Sign: N6EM
Henry D Eddy
Little River CA 95456

Call Sign: KI6DJH
Carole A Judd-Lamb
Little River CA 95456

Call Sign: KI6IVM
Samuel E Levine
Little River CA 95456

FCC Amateur Radio
Licenses in Loleta

Call Sign: KF6AAT
Harold E Schulman
64 Echo Ln
Loleta CA 95551

Call Sign: KE6PIA
Suzanne E Schmidt
65 Hillcrest
Loleta CA 95551

Call Sign: KF6PRM
Robert L Winkelhaus
560 Peugh Rd
Loleta CA 95551

Call Sign: KE6OSP
Kenneth G Williams
609 Singley Rd
Loleta CA 95551

Call Sign: WB6KGW
Kenneth G Williams
609 Singley Rd
Loleta CA 95551

Call Sign: WA6HZG
Bernard J Christen
Loleta CA 95551

Call Sign: WA6FRN
John S Bond
Loleta CA 955510476

Call Sign: KF6FLF
Claire L Christen
Loleta CA 955510145

Call Sign: KF6NKO
Carrie E Cook
Loleta CA 95551

Call Sign: KG6QVI
Clifford O Evans
Loleta CA 95551

Call Sign: KJ6LHK
Nicholas F Flenghi
Loleta CA 95551

Call Sign: K6LTR
John M Meng
Loleta CA 95551

Call Sign: KI6QYI
Jeff S Robison
Loleta CA 95551

FCC Amateur Radio
Licenses in Lookout

Call Sign: KB6ZZH
Bruce Webb
CR 93
Lookout CA 96054

Call Sign: AD6RV
Bruce Webb
CR 93
Lookout CA 96054

Call Sign: KF6VPX
Andrea J Gifford
Lookout CA 960540079

Call Sign: KI6DVF
John C Joiner
Lookout CA 96054

Call Sign: W7GFN
Charles E Reed
Lookout CA 96054

Call Sign: KB6ZZI
Lorraine H Webb
Lookout CA 96054

FCC Amateur Radio Licenses in Los Molinos

Call Sign: WD6BMU
David F Shields
24850 5th Ave Sp 32
Los Molinos CA 96055

Call Sign: N6IUG
Kittie L Hinek
24515 Clement Ave
Los Molinos CA 96055

Call Sign: N6IUJ
William L Hinek
24515 Clement Ave
Los Molinos CA 96055

Call Sign: WD6DCH
Michael H Chrasta
7461 Hwy 99 E
Los Molinos CA 96055

Call Sign: KG6ETF
Henry H Reno
25510 Lee St
Los Molinos CA 96055

Call Sign: KG6KKI
Ruthe R Reno
25510 Lee St
Los Molinos CA 96055

Call Sign: KD6WXO
Chris R Stuehler
24955 Logans Ln
Los Molinos CA 96055

Call Sign: WA6EDV
Harold G Chandler Jr
25032 Reeves Rd
Los Molinos CA 96055

Call Sign: KI6NPL
Karen R Chandler
25032 Reeves Rd
Los Molinos CA 96055

Call Sign: WB6RXF
Jerry T Short
25253 S Center St
Los Molinos CA 96055

Call Sign: N6FF
Richard J Wolf
25295 Seventh Ave
Los Molinos CA 96055

Call Sign: KO6TW
Raymond A Watkins
8485 Sherwood Blvd
Los Molinos CA 96055

Call Sign: N6HRW
Frederick G Crowe
11043 Singer Ave
Los Molinos CA 96055

Call Sign: KD6VLE
Eric C Weber
24848 Taft St
Los Molinos CA 96055

Call Sign: KJ6TLD
Eric C Weber
24848 Taft St
Los Molinos CA 96055

Call Sign: KC6OZC
Christopher P Heaney
24839 Tehama Vina Rd
Los Molinos CA 96055

Call Sign: N6DVW
Raymond D Brooks
24880 Wanda Ct
Los Molinos CA 96055

Call Sign: KD6CUL
Kenneth E Lane
Los Molinos CA 96055

Call Sign: KA7CBK
Janet S Stetson
Los Molinos CA 96055

Call Sign: KD7NK
Clinton M Stetson
Los Molinos CA 96055

Call Sign: WB6LXQ
Janet S Elmore
Los Molinos CA 96055

FCC Amateur Radio Licenses in MacDoel

Call Sign: W6SOJ
State Of Jefferson
Operators United Relay
Network And Emergency
Radio Soc
3616 Lazy Ranch Rd

MacDoel CA 96058

Call Sign: KG6AMS
State Of Jefferson
Operators United Relay
Network And Emergency
Radio Society
3616 Lazy Ranch Rd
MacDoel CA 96058

Call Sign: KF6USG
Eric L Cross
701 Meiss Lake Rd
MacDoel CA 96058

Call Sign: N6MRX
Frank L Cross
701 Meiss Lake Rd
MacDoel CA 96058

Call Sign: KG6ZEG
Particia F Cross
701 Meiss Lake Rd
MacDoel CA 96058

Call Sign: WB6VSZ
Cloy V Williamson
13520 Tennant Rd
MacDoel CA 96058

Call Sign: K6VX
Raymond D Balch
MacDoel CA 96058

Call Sign: KD6OWT
Roman Grasiano Perez
MacDoel CA 96058

Call Sign: KD6OWU
Rogasiano Perez
MacDoel CA 96058

Call Sign: KD6OWX
Jose S Perez
MacDoel CA 96058

Call Sign: KD6OWZ
Silvia Perez
MacDoel CA 96058

Call Sign: KD6OWY
Antonio Perez Sr
MacDoel CA 96058

Call Sign: KC6HOY
David W Thorne
MacDoel CA 96058

Call Sign: W7OTF
Linden D Bahnsen
MacDoel CA 96058

Call Sign: KF6WZX
Martha R Cherry
MacDoel CA 96058

Call Sign: WA6FEF
Marcia I Malmin
MacDoel CA 96058

Call Sign: KE6MZT
Nannette S Thorne
MacDoel CA 96058

Call Sign: K6SOJ
David W Thorne
MacDoel CA 96058

Call Sign: KI6ASO
World Radio Relay League
Inc
MacDoel CA 96058

Call Sign: W7RRL
World Radio Relay League
Inc
MacDoel CA 96058

FCC Amateur Radio Licenses in Mad River

Call Sign: KE6VMV
Michael A Fraser
Mad River CA 95552

Call Sign: KF6EFP
Donna M Pollard Fraser
Mad River CA 95552

FCC Amateur Radio Licenses in Madeline

Call Sign: WD6EKP
Herbert V Corns
702 700 Brockman Rd
Madeline CA 96119

Call Sign: W0WJP
Tommy L May
182 Mudhen
Madeline CA 96119

FCC Amateur Radio Licenses in Manchester

Call Sign: KG6TOH
Gordon E Cady
43850 Acquistapace Rd
Manchester CA 95459

Call Sign: KG6PUC
Walt A Rush
43751 Cypress Pkwy
Manchester CA 95459

Call Sign: KI6KRI
Nicolas V Epanchin
15721 Forest View Rd
Manchester CA 95459

Call Sign: KG6PUD
Sarah J Riley
14901 Mallo Pass Dr
Manchester CA 95459

Call Sign: KF6FEC
Thomas W Craig
Manchester CA
954590033

Call Sign: KB2PBW
Roland A De Longoria
Manchester CA
954590144

Call Sign: KI6KRN
Glenn D Ohara
Manchester CA 95459

Call Sign: KG6IPU
Gerald Pesavento
Manchester CA 95459

Call Sign: N6OZP
David J Snow
Manchester CA 95459

FCC Amateur Radio Licenses in Manton

Call Sign: KD6LOF
Elizabeth A Marsh
Rt 1 Box 212
Manton CA 96059

Call Sign: WA6WDB
Jack I Winning
21660 Manton School Rd
Manton CA 96059

Call Sign: KD6KGN
Eric J Simpkins
31717 Rock Creek Rd
Manton CA 96059

Call Sign: KD6VXJ
Susan E Young
Manton CA 96059

Call Sign: WD6GYU

Gary L Young
Manton CA 960590455

FCC Amateur Radio Licenses in McArthur

Call Sign: AC6VC
Robert A Lewis
214 Irma Ln
McArthur CA 96056

Call Sign: KE6UDK
Rosalie J Lewis
214 Irma Ln
McArthur CA 96056

Call Sign: WB6GBY
Thomas K Powers
250 Lorenzen Ranch Dr
McArthur CA 96056

Call Sign: KE6EN
Lawrence A Ramil
44992 Old Brown Ranch
Rd
McArthur CA 96056

Call Sign: N6KQN
Courtland A Myers
Pine Shadow Rd
McArthur CA 96056

Call Sign: KB6SBS
Anna L Garner
45192 State Hwy 299 E
McArthur CA 96056

Call Sign: KB6ZAT
Donald R Garner Jr
45192 State Hwy 299 E
McArthur CA 96056

Call Sign: WB6TTW
Myron L Koehler
McArthur CA 96056

Call Sign: KF6VYF
Richard A Pope
McArthur CA 960560696

Call Sign: AE6DH
Richard A Pope
McArthur CA 960560696

Call Sign: KG6ZDY
Patricia K Pope
McArthur CA 96056

Call Sign: N6VBN
Neil E Simmons
McArthur CA 960560035

FCC Amateur Radio Licenses in McCloud

Call Sign: KD6CBV
Keith P Potts
837 Hennessey Way
McCloud CA 96057

Call Sign: N6EGN
Michael J Black Sr
925 North St
McCloud CA 96057

Call Sign: N6GW
Michael J Black Sr
925 North St
McCloud CA 96057

Call Sign: W6AMW
Robert L Dalleske
801 Oak St
McCloud CA 960570220

Call Sign: KB6HLT
Robert L Rowley
407 Quincy Ave
McCloud CA 96057

Call Sign: W3OES
Robert L Rowley
407 Quincy Ave
McCloud CA 96057

Call Sign: KI6GVN
Talon Baldwin
Shasta Ave
McCloud CA 96057

Call Sign: K6AWR
Hubert J Franklin
239 Shasta Pines Dr
McCloud CA 960571047

Call Sign: N6LJS
Orvin B Curley
2731 Squaw Valley Rd
McCloud CA 96057

Call Sign: WA6RIQ
Florence L Burke
2901 Squaw Vly Rd
McCloud CA 96057

Call Sign: KD6WGX
Kathryn E Curley
McCloud CA 96057

Call Sign: KE7QB
Bob E Turner
McCloud CA 96057

Call Sign: K6SDZ
Thomas B Watson
McCloud CA 96057

Call Sign: N6ONB
Ronald R Anderson
McCloud CA 960570808

Call Sign: KE6RBM
Claude F Barnes
McCloud CA 96057

Call Sign: KJ6AHT
Alan C Bodiford
McCloud CA 96057

Call Sign: KF6WCG
Greg W Carr
McCloud CA 96057

Call Sign: KD6LNH
Christine M Crocker
McCloud CA 96057

Call Sign: KI6UMI
Richard L Dexter Jr
McCloud CA 96057

Call Sign: KI6UMJ
Jerry Glynn
McCloud CA 96057

Call Sign: KG6ZDZ
Brian Parodi
McCloud CA 96057

Call Sign: KE6SXR
Randy L Prinz
McCloud CA 96057

Call Sign: KI6VZN
Ethan J Simpson
McCloud CA 96057

**FCC Amateur Radio
Licenses in McKinleyville**

Call Sign: KE6IBB
Janet L Marnell
2234 1st Rd
McKinleyville CA 95519

Call Sign: KJ6HGJ
Jason M Patton
1905 A Ave
McKinleyville CA 95519

Call Sign: KE6FDU
Robert D Webster
1825 Aspen Ct
McKinleyville CA 95521

Call Sign: KA6OKU
Willis C Trimmer
4651 Aster Ave
McKinleyville CA 95521

Call Sign: WA6EEB
Gregory W Kordes
1010 Azalea Ave
McKinleyville CA 95519

Call Sign: KG6EFB
Jon Freret
1670 Baird Rd
McKinleyville CA 95519

Call Sign: W6KOZ
Lawrence D Freret Jr
1670 Baird Rd
McKinleyville CA 95519

Call Sign: KF6FLD
William R Ramey
1760 Baird Rd
McKinleyville CA 95519

Call Sign: W6GD
Geraldine A Greer
3396 Barnett Ave
McKinleyville CA 95519

Call Sign: KF6ZVB
Vicki N Christian
1977 Bartow Rd
McKinleyville CA 95519

Call Sign: WA6KEB
David D Christian
1977 Bartow Rd
Mckinleyville CA
955194313

Call Sign: KE6ISM
Inge S Goetz Cordova
3175 Beau Pre Dr
McKinleyville CA 95521

Call Sign: KG6LNU
Donald L Dodd
1730 Bella Vista Rd
McKinleyville CA 95519

Call Sign: KF6WMS
Earl H Ward
1865 Bird
McKinleyville CA 95519

Call Sign: KJ6JVO
Cairn Stuart Maver
1670 Blackhawk Ln 38
McKinleyville CA 95519

Call Sign: W6CAI
Cairn Stuart Maver
1670 Blackhawk Ln 38
McKinleyville CA 95519

Call Sign: AF6YH
Wesley J Rishel
1975 Blake Rd
McKinleyville CA 95519

Call Sign: KF6PIO
Warren C Morton
2485 Bolier Ave
McKinleyville CA 95519

Call Sign: KJ6NZB
Kimberly Comet
3091 Bonanza St
McKinleyville CA 95519

Call Sign: N6YFA
David L Brown
1595 Bugenig Ave
McKinleyville CA 95519

Call Sign: KG6DZX
Boni M Brown
1595 Bugenig Ave
McKinleyville CA 95519

Call Sign: N6PFF
Laurence E Sebring
702 Burnt Stump Ln
Mckinleyville CA
955199701

Call Sign: N6PIY
Paula D Sebring
702 Burnt Stump Ln
Mckinleyville CA
955199701

Call Sign: WB6TRD
Thomas R Dager
1779 Catherine Ct
McKinleyville CA 95519

Call Sign: KJ6NNB
Robert S Lackey
2423 Central Ave
McKinleyville CA 95519

Call Sign: KG6JBO
Deborah L Flint
2580 Central Ave 53
McKinleyville CA 95519

Call Sign: KG6JBP
Douglas L Flint
2580 Central Ave 53
McKinleyville CA 95519

Call Sign: KJ6SYI
William A Wennerholm
1225 Central Ave Ste 2
McKinleyville CA 95519

Call Sign: KJ6PEP
Michael H Calkins

2580 Central Ave Ste 35
McKinleyville CA 95519

Call Sign: KM4KK
Robert E Martz
2580 Central Ave Ste 6
Mckinleyville CA
955193634

Call Sign: KJ6BDK
Eureka Stake Amateur
Radio Association
2720 Central Ave Ste E
McKinleyville CA 95519

Call Sign: KJ6NZC
Steve A Engle
4523 Chaffin Rd
McKinleyville CA 95519

Call Sign: KD6PCQ
John W Wolff
1195 Chance Ln C
McKinleyville CA 95519

Call Sign: KJ6EMY
Roger W Herick
1300 Clam Beach Rd
McKinleyville CA 95519

Call Sign: N6EXK
Don L Brubaker
2762 Clay Rd
McKinleyville CA 95519

Call Sign: KA6NNQ
Robert G Deja
2070 Crystal Way
McKinleyville CA 95519

Call Sign: KJ6NNA
Betty Marie Ruth
2583 Daffodil Ave
McKinleyville CA 95519

Call Sign: N6DBZ
Michel Ter Sarkissoff
2525 Daffodil Rd
McKinleyville CA 95519

Call Sign: KD6VAV
Rita L Ter Sarkissoff
2525 Daffodil Rd
McKinleyville CA 95519

Call Sign: KG6UUH
Harold B Reed
1849 Douglas Rd
Mckinleyville CA
955199466

Call Sign: AE6TC
Harold B Reed
1849 Douglas Rd
Mckinleyville CA
955199466

Call Sign: KE6FEH
Don H Hicks
3761 Dows Prairie Rd
McKinleyville CA 95521

Call Sign: KE6TMO
John H Ridlon II
4085 Dows Prairie Rd
McKinleyville CA 95519

Call Sign: N6IFN
Jeffrey W Arnold
4677 Dows Prairie Rd
McKinleyville CA 95519

Call Sign: W6EY
David A Smith
3082 Eagle Ln
McKinleyville CA 95521

Call Sign: WA6MKC
Gerald F Guilliams
1229 Fernwood Dr

McKinleyville CA 95521

Call Sign: KG6ZDV
Tristen M Joy
1640 Fischer Ave
McKinleyville CA 95519

Call Sign: WL7CTD
Keith A Witte
1046 Fritz Rd
McKinleyville CA 95519

Call Sign: KF6LZX
Stephen K Jackson
1081 Fritz Rd
McKinleyville CA 95519

Call Sign: KD6EWF
John B Croul
555 Hiller Rd
McKinleyville CA 95521

Call Sign: N6BOB
Linda G Milender
1715 Holly Dr
McKinleyville CA 95521

Call Sign: WD6GHO
Bill L Milender
1715 Holly Dr
McKinleyville CA 95521

Call Sign: KG6GKH
Dena R Price
1110 Joanna Ct
McKinleyville CA 95519

Call Sign: KA6ZAI
Steve J Halmo
1935 Juniper Ave
McKinleyville CA 95519

Call Sign: KE6YQR
Carolyn V Stemen
1940 Juniper Ave

McKinleyville CA 95519

Call Sign: KE6ZRS
Vicki M Hayler
1170 Katrina Ct
McKinleyville CA 95519

Call Sign: WA6PVS
Edward W Johnson
2681 Kelly Ave
McKinleyville CA 95519

Call Sign: KF6HQG
Thomas A Schallert
2682 Kelly Ave
McKinleyville CA 95519

Call Sign: KD6PCS
Shawn R Tauscher
1108 Killdeer Rd
McKinleyville CA 95519

Call Sign: N6KVV
Lillian F Robins
1121 Killdeer Rd
McKinleyville CA 95521

Call Sign: KI6IJE
Janet R Wickman
4590 Kjer Rd
McKinleyville CA 95519

Call Sign: KI6IKE
William S Wickman
4590 Kjer Rd
McKinleyville CA 95519

Call Sign: KG6OYB
Alecia R Mourin
1445 Larissa Cir C
McKinleyville CA 95519

Call Sign: KF6VSJ
Matthias Lehmann
1206 Liscom Hill Rd

McKinleyville CA 95519

Call Sign: KF6VSK
Thea M Lehmann
1206 Liscom Hill Rd
McKinleyville CA 95519

Call Sign: N6MBS
Frieda M Bradley
1450 Marty Ave
McKinleyville CA 95519

Call Sign: WA6KZJ
Charles D Bradley
1450 Marty Ave
McKinleyville CA 95519

Call Sign: N6URU
Harry A Marnell
1475A Murray Rd
Mckinleyville CA
955193516

Call Sign: KM6KMA
Harry A Marnell
1475A Murray Rd
Mckinleyville CA
955193516

Call Sign: N6URU
Harry A Marnell
1475A Murray Rd
Mckinleyville CA
955193516

Call Sign: KC2JVT
Francis S Bawden
1745 Noble Ct
McKinleyville CA 95519

Call Sign: KG6KG
Thomas G Morrissey
1750 Oakdale Dr
McKinleyville CA 95521

Call Sign: KF6MAC
Anthony R Karreman
1630 Ocean Dr
McKinleyville CA 95519

Call Sign: KG6PWX
George A Corbett
1801 Ocean Dr
McKinleyville CA 95519

Call Sign: N4RSM
Daniel J Scarr
1143 Railroad Dr
McKinleyville CA 95519

Call Sign: KJ6NYZ
John E Mccarthy
3011 Sand Pointe Dr
McKinleyville CA 95519

Call Sign: WA6HZT
Gary L Nixon
3017 Sand Pointe Dr
McKinleyville CA 95519

Call Sign: W6OFM
Oec Wireless Society
3017 Sand Pointe Dr
McKinleyville CA 95519

Call Sign: KF6LZU
Stephen H Brown Jr
689 School Rd
McKinleyville CA 95519

Call Sign: KE6BVL
Sherilyn A Munger
808 School Rd
McKinleyville CA 95519

Call Sign: AB6TR
Scott W Binder
2220 Silverbrook Ct
McKinleyville CA 95519

Call Sign: W6ZZK
Humboldt ARC
2220 Silverbrook Ct
Mckinleyville CA
955196516

Call Sign: KG6JBN
Caleb J Lesher
2993 Springer Dr
McKinleyville CA 95519

Call Sign: N6IIT
Susan C Schlosser
1979 St Mary Ln
McKinleyville CA 95519

Call Sign: W6BME
Roscoe E Peithman
2704 Sunny Grove Ave
McKinleyville CA 95519

Call Sign: WB6DUH
Arthur D Quigley
1700 Sutter Rd H
McKinleyville CA 95521

Call Sign: N6ZZO
Kai J Wagner
1825 Sycamore Ct
McKinleyville CA 95519

Call Sign: KF6FKV
Kour T Chau
1934 Sycamore Ct
McKinleyville CA 95519

Call Sign: KI6ZQT
David L Wooley
1611 Timothy Rd
McKinleyville CA 95519

Call Sign: KB6PIE
Eric R Hayes
1626 Timothy Rd
McKinleyville CA 95519

Call Sign: AA6EH
Eric R Hayes
1626 Timothy Rd
McKinleyville CA 95519

Call Sign: KJ6HGM
Ross G Mcdonald
2310 Tulip Ct
McKinleyville CA 95519

Call Sign: KE7EUV
Donald E Mckenzie
2070 Walker Ave
McKinleyville CA 95519

Call Sign: KF6LZT
Melvin R Brown
1770 Wild Canary St
McKinleyville CA 95519

Call Sign: KE6MY
Lynn W Johnson
1780 Wild Canary St
McKinleyville CA 95519

Call Sign: KF6ZUH
Harold A Horne
2285 Williams Ct
McKinleyville CA 95519

Call Sign: K6JFD
Thomas P Watson
1386 Winchester Ave
McKinleyville CA 95519

Call Sign: N6MUI
Gwen M Rust
1396 Winchester Ave
McKinleyville CA 95519

Call Sign: N6YLR
Clarence D Ashey Jr
McKinleyville CA 95519

Call Sign: WB6HWB
Beverly A Moyle
McKinleyville CA 95521

Call Sign: N6BQE
Robert G Bahneman
McKinleyville CA 95521

Call Sign: KF6OUQ
Karrie L Bosma
McKinleyville CA 95519

Call Sign: KE6PXJ
Gerald P Frederick
McKinleyville CA 95519

Call Sign: KF6UGG
Bruce W Hart
McKinleyville CA 95519

Call Sign: KG6ZGW
Tony R Mcalexander
McKinleyville CA 95519

Call Sign: KF6WMR
Carey L Morris
McKinleyville CA 95519

Call Sign: K1TTY
Eradea S Morwyntine
McKinleyville CA 95519

Call Sign: KQ6WV
Lennie J Moyle
McKinleyville CA 95519

Call Sign: KI6UIF
Norcal Qrp &
Mountaintopping Club
McKinleyville CA 95519

Call Sign: W2LAR
Norcal Qrp &
Mountaintopping Club
McKinleyville CA 95519

Call Sign: KI6QYJ
Adam M Wade
McKinleyville CA 95519

Call Sign: AD6VS
Paul V Williamson
McKinleyville CA 95519

FCC Amateur Radio Licenses in Mendocino

Call Sign: KC6EOM
William H Scott
45175 Fern Dr
Mendocino CA 95460

Call Sign: KJ6AQO
Arthur L Schiro
44270 Gordon Ln
Mendocino CA 95460

Call Sign: KD6VAQ
Torben Deirup
41908 Little Lake Rd
Mendocino CA 95460

Call Sign: KI6KRK
Michael J Petherick
45301 Overton Dr
Mendocino CA 95460

Call Sign: W6SXY
Norman F De Groot
14240 Pt Cabrillo Dr
Mendocino CA 95460

Call Sign: W6MHZ
Eugene B Abbett
Mendocino CA 95460

Call Sign: AA6EI
John B McFall
Mendocino CA 95460

Call Sign: KI6ZOH
Stanley M Fidler
Mendocino CA 95460

Call Sign: WB6GOX
Richard L Comen
Mendocino CA 95460

Call Sign: K6FOG
Pete Ball
Mendocino CA 95460

Call Sign: K6BCM
Willis B Foote
Mendocino CA 95460

Call Sign: KI6ISL
James R Hay
Mendocino CA 95460

Call Sign: KD6QQT
Kathleen M Ittel
Mendocino CA 95460

Call Sign: N7AGR
Peter E Kapp
Mendocino CA 95460

Call Sign: K6CTQ
Charles L King III
Mendocino CA 954601004

Call Sign: KI6CHD
Thomas D Lehman
Mendocino CA 95640

Call Sign: KJ6KET
Arthur A Reeves
Mendocino CA 95460

Call Sign: KI6RIY
Mary K Rosenthal
Mendocino CA 954601764

Call Sign: KB6BMS

Linn M Turner
Mendocino CA 954601240

Call Sign: KG6BKG
Kenneth M Wallich
Mendocino CA 95460

Call Sign: KA6GBQ
John E Wilder
Mendocino CA 954600008

Call Sign: K1TED
Ted R Williams
Mendocino CA 95460

Call Sign: KF6SKE
Mary G Williams
Mendocino CA 954600018

Call Sign: N0MOM
Mary G Williams
Mendocino CA 954600018

FCC Amateur Radio Licenses in Milford

Call Sign: K6INM
John K Helmbold
720 500 Deer Trl
Milford CA 96121

Call Sign: KJ6HHG
Ramona M Winegar
717 930 Desert Pine Trl
Milford CA 96121

Call Sign: KJ6HHI
William M Winegar
717 930 Desert Pine Trl
Milford CA 96121

Call Sign: K6YX
Donald R Gerue
718 000 Desert Pine Trl
Milford CA 96121

Call Sign: KF6QZJ
Barbara P Paulson
Milford CA 96121

Call Sign: K6GHD
Doyle E Rose
Milford CA 96121

FCC Amateur Radio Licenses in Mill Creek

Call Sign: KB6AXJ
George B Crockett
53 Cedar Way
Mill Creek CA 96061

FCC Amateur Radio Licenses in Millville

Call Sign: N6VLH
Ernest M Taylor
8807 Bass Pond Rd
Millville CA 96062

Call Sign: KJ6NVH
Steve M Sakoman
24991 Hwy 44
Millville CA 96062

Call Sign: KD6CVA
Laurelie R Abbey
9635 Sunnywood Dr
Millville CA 96062

Call Sign: N6IPL
Judy L Abbey
9657 Sunnywood Dr
Millville CA 96062

Call Sign: N6AVS
David E Abbey
9657 Sunnywood Dr
Millville CA 96062

Call Sign: KE6EB
Charles F Bailey
Millville CA 96062

Call Sign: KC6OQV
Raymond W Coffelt
Millville CA 96062

Call Sign: KI6UNP
Bill Bogenreif
Millville CA 960620279

Call Sign: KJ6VEW
Aaron P Smith
Millville CA 96062

FCC Amateur Radio Licenses in Mineral

Call Sign: WB6FDG
James R Spliethof
Mineral CA 96063

Call Sign: KI6MGK
Robert F Blank
Mineral CA 96063

Call Sign: AB7AK
Paul Walkewicz
Mineral CA 96063

FCC Amateur Radio Licenses in Miranda

Call Sign: KC6MBK
William D Bonillas
6450 Ave Of The Giants
Miranda CA 95553

Call Sign: W6CLG
Leland G Smith
911 Logan Rd
Miranda CA 95553

Call Sign: KD6EGJ

William D Smith
Miranda CA 95553

Call Sign: KE6GPQ
Michael H Shearer
Miranda CA 95553

Call Sign: KI6IUN
Angelita S Bonillas
Miranda CA 95553

Call Sign: KF6PZB
Nathan M Downey
Miranda CA 95553

Call Sign: KG6BQZ
Nicholas J Downey
Miranda CA 95553

Call Sign: KI6CQB
Marilyn L Foote
Miranda CA 95553

Call Sign: KG6BIJ
Robert G Harris
Miranda CA 95553

Call Sign: KI6PQX
Bambi Henderson
Miranda CA 95553

Call Sign: KG6FOJ
Brian C Sargent
Miranda CA 95553

Call Sign: KE6GQC
Larry M Smith
Miranda CA 95553

Call Sign: KI6PQV
Dustin J Stark
Miranda CA 95553

FCC Amateur Radio Licenses in Montague

Call Sign: KF6HCA
William D Golden
5821 Ager Rd
Montague CA 96064

Call Sign: KC6CGV
Dorman D Clark
7420 Agerbeswick Rd
Montague CA 96064

Call Sign: W6EZO
Malcolm W Brister
1015 Airport Rd
Montague CA 96064

Call Sign: W6AKI
Donald S Teague Jr
11106 Apache Rd
Montague CA 96064

Call Sign: KG6ZEH
Lynnette M Corliss
11032 Aztec Rd
Montague CA 96064

Call Sign: KF6HYD
James L Derra
5920 Big Springs Rd
Montague CA 96064

Call Sign: WB6WPZ
Richard L Smith
6230 Big Springs Rd
Montague CA 96064

Call Sign: KN6BH
Clarence G Mundt
6535 Big Springs Rd
Montague CA 96064

Call Sign: W4RLW
Ryan L Williams
8900 Colleen Cir Rd
Montague CA 96064

Call Sign: KB6EZA
Deana J Farrington
5904 Harry Cash Rd
Montague CA 96064

Call Sign: KI6QI
Larry L Farrington
5904 Harry Cash Rd
Montague CA 96064

Call Sign: KD6WZD
Gary L Crunk
10916 Hwy A12
Montague CA 96064

Call Sign: WA6WNK
Darryl D Solus
535 Lichen Rd
Montague CA 96064

Call Sign: KO6GJ
Don A Donnelly
9700 Little Bogus Creek
Rd
Montague CA 96064

Call Sign: N6HWY
Brian A Green
13109 Norman Dr
Montague CA 96064

Call Sign: KG6ZEE
David J Herfindahl
4515 Oberlin Rd
Montague CA 96064

Call Sign: KC6BAV
Michael E Varco
16139 Patrica Ave
Montague CA 96064

Call Sign: KC6IXD
Rexford D Thompson
16104 Patricia Ave

Montague CA 96064

Call Sign: KF6YKF
Robert L Allen
15029 Quail Rd
Montague CA 96064

Call Sign: KA6QYH
Curtis M Lobush Jr
14929 Shasta Ln
Montague CA 96064

Call Sign: N6SHU
Ann E Pope
460 W Scobie
Montague CA 96064

Call Sign: N6RQT
Lee N Pope
460 W Scobie St
Montague CA 96064

Call Sign: KI6MPY
Brian E Bachman
Montague CA 96064

Call Sign: KI6TNU
Julie Bachman
Montague CA 96064

Call Sign: K6JUL
Julie Bachman
Montague CA 96064

Call Sign: KG6CSM
Phil J Clancy
Montague CA 96064

Call Sign: KI6YIS
Danielle M Deppen
Montague CA 96064

Call Sign: W6ICM
Oswaldo Diaz
Montague CA 96064

Call Sign: KD6HVD
Ted A Harvell
Montague CA 96064

Call Sign: KJ6PZX
Alfred Lange
Montague CA 96064

Call Sign: KJ6NDH
Dennis E Lange
Montague CA 96064

Call Sign: AD6CF
Terry M Rood
Montague CA 96064

Call Sign: KI6VAG
Dave B Sumerlin II
Montague CA 96064

Call Sign: K6DBS
Dave B Sumerlin II
Montague CA 96064

Call Sign: KF6ERG
Catherine A Golden
5821 Ager Rd
Montegue CA 96094

**FCC Amateur Radio
Licenses in Montgomery
Creek**

Call Sign: KI6WAY
Mauro Oliveira
Montgomery Creek CA
96065

Call Sign: KG6RYD
Shasta County Amateur
Radio Emergency Service
Montgomery Creek CA
96065

Call Sign: N6DLL
Nicholas J Ciaramella
404 Adams Dr
Mount Shasta CA 96067

Call Sign: KJ6OXZ
Thomas E Wick
419 Alpine Dr
Mount Shasta CA 96067

Call Sign: WB6TNY
Eugene E Wood
1204 Audubon Rd
Mount Shasta CA 96067

Call Sign: KJ6PMH
Joseph Heller
406 Berry St
Mount Shasta CA 96067

Call Sign: KJ6PMI
Kathleen M Heller
406 Berry St
Mount Shasta CA 96067

Call Sign: WA2MJC
Prem Rajababa
509 Berry St
Mount Shasta CA 96067

Call Sign: KD6CBU
Gary L Hornbeck
612 Brush St
Mount Shasta CA 96067

Call Sign: K6JU
David H Rees
819 Butte Ave
Mount Shasta CA 96067

Call Sign: KG6WTO
Kyle C Zanni

805 Carmen Ave Apt C
Mount Shasta CA 96067

Call Sign: KE6EIB
George R Faithorn
802 Caroline Ave
Mount Shasta CA 96067

Call Sign: KF6WH
Robert L Stephen
402 Chester St
Mount Shasta CA 96067

Call Sign: KJ6TRA
Ronald E Sortor
1541 Davis Place Rd
Mount Shasta CA 96067

Call Sign: KJ6TMN
Thomas E Scovill
5808 Deer Creek Rd
Mount Shasta CA 96067

Call Sign: N6GXJ
Andrea M Nibecker
303 E Lake St
Mount Shasta CA 96067

Call Sign: WB6JHX
Guy Covert
1921 Eddy Cir
Mount Shasta CA 96067

Call Sign: W6VTJ
Larry J Marks
1635 Eddy Dr
Mount Shasta CA
960670317

Call Sign: K6PRN
Patio Radio Network
511 Freeman Ln
Mount Shasta CA 96067

Call Sign: KJ6RA

Richard A Zanni
511 Freeman Ln
Mount Shasta CA 96067

Call Sign: KA6YUM
James H Applegate
503 Glen Mar Dr
Mount Shasta CA 96067

Call Sign: N6KCT
John L Howarth
1504 Highland Dr
Mount Shasta CA 96067

Call Sign: W6WJR
Michael F Zanger
1938 Hill Rd
Mount Shasta CA 96067

Call Sign: WB6IDM
Charles F Moss
495 Jefferson Dr
Mount Shasta CA 96067

Call Sign: N6ZRF
Richard J Resh
545 Jefferson Dr
Mount Shasta CA 96067

Call Sign: KD6LIS
Howard Priddy
1600 Lombardi Rd
Mount Shasta CA 96067

Call Sign: W6YJG
H Carter O Brien
202 Magnolia St
Mount Shasta CA
960672350

Call Sign: W6OMR
Irving Astmann
205 McCloud Ave
Mount Shasta CA 96067

Call Sign: AF6TU
Dennis Engdahl
527 McCloud Ave
Mount Shasta CA 96067

Call Sign: NR6J
Dennis Engdahl
527 McCloud Ave
Mount Shasta CA 96067

Call Sign: KI6WJP
Martin J Nile
800 Michele Dr
Mount Shasta CA 96067

Call Sign: KJ6BNG
Peter J Nile
800 Michele Dr
Mount Shasta CA 96067

Call Sign: W6ZFW
Henry V Quinley Jr
110 N C St
Mount Shasta CA 96067

Call Sign: KD6PCF
Arlene L Gillespie
219 N Mt Shasta Blvd
Mount Shasta CA 96067

Call Sign: KJ6OXV
Marcus A Pilkenton
404 N Mt Shasta Blvd 101
Mount Shasta CA 96067

Call Sign: KJ6OXU
Daniel A Kealey
3609 N Old Stage Rd
Mount Shasta CA 96067

Call Sign: WB6ABF
Walter L Christenson
2601 N Old Stage Rd 9
Mount Shasta CA 96067

Call Sign: KD6YCL
Gary Zukav
200 N Washington Dr
Mount Shasta CA 96067

Call Sign: W6BML
Mount Shasta ARC
329 N Washington Dr
Mount Shasta CA 96067

Call Sign: W6LXK
Kerry D Mauro
220 Pack Trl
Mount Shasta CA 96067

Call Sign: KC6MSW
David G Mauro
2220 Pack Trl
Mount Shasta CA 96067

Call Sign: KO6PB
Joseph A Fornero
217 Perry St
Mount Shasta CA 96067

Call Sign: AB6MF
Eric C Petersen
1521 Pine Grove
Mount Shasta CA 96067

Call Sign: KJ6PMG
Jessie E Ayani
1431 Pine Grove Dr
Mount Shasta CA 96067

Call Sign: KE6HUJ
Duane L Dufault
1828 Pine Grove Dr
Mount Shasta CA 96067

Call Sign: KI6HDV
Glenn P Davis
2008 Pine Grove Dr
Mount Shasta CA 96067

Call Sign: WA6ICK
Robert G Marrs Jr
2205 Pine Grove Dr
Mount Shasta CA
960679046

Call Sign: KG6AUO
Pamela Y Fawcett-Moore
5121 Plum Ave
Mount Shasta CA 96067

Call Sign: K6AFT
Pamela Y Fawcett-Moore
5121 Plum Ave
Mount Shasta CA 96067

Call Sign: KG6AFA
William D Moore
5121 Plum Ave
Mount Shasta CA 96067

Call Sign: KI6VGB
Ben A Chandon
309 Pony Trl
Mount Shasta CA 96067

Call Sign: KE6SXM
Joanne L Steele
316 Pony Trl
Mount Shasta CA 96067

Call Sign: KE6SXN
Edward M Steele
316 Pony Trl
Mount Shasta CA 96067

Call Sign: N6BAC
William E Truby III
510 Quail Hill Dr
Mount Shasta CA 96067

Call Sign: KE6MZM
Pauline T McCoy
1002 Ream Ave
Mount Shasta CA 96067

Call Sign: KE6ZHI
Matthew D Ireland
812 Remour Ln
Mount Shasta CA 96067

Call Sign: KF6QVV
Nicholas R Ireland
812 Remour Ln
Mount Shasta CA 96067

Call Sign: KJ6OXY
Robert W Warren
301 S Mount Shasta Blvd
Mount Shasta CA
960679998

Call Sign: KF6ERI
Linda M Chandon
1112 S Mt Shasta Blvd
Mount Shasta CA 96067

Call Sign: WD8CCL
A Jonathan Webb
1124 S Mt Shasta Blvd
Mount Shasta CA
960670706

Call Sign: KE6JGH
Myron E Lysinger
2539 Sean Way
Mount Shasta CA 96067

Call Sign: KA6LOC
Gerald A Heikura
2701 Sean Way
Mount Shasta CA 96067

Call Sign: KD6DGX
Barbara Jea Graves
201 Shasta Ave
Mount Shasta CA 96067

Call Sign: WA6VBZ
John D Del Amico

309 Shasta Way
Mount Shasta CA 96067

Call Sign: KJ6OXS
John D Dell Amico
309 Shasta Way
Mount Shasta CA 96067

Call Sign: W6IBX
Mark A Healy
214 Sheldon Ave
Mount Shasta CA 96067

Call Sign: KE6SXP
Fred W Smith
309 Sheldon Ave
Mount Shasta CA 96067

Call Sign: KF6QBG
Paul B Melo
519 Spruce St
Mount Shasta CA 96067

Call Sign: KG6FBH
Atara Y Melo
519 Spruce St
Mount Shasta CA 96067

Call Sign: K6UCS
Atara Y Melo
519 Spruce St
Mount Shasta CA 96067

Call Sign: KI6TYU
Kathryn M Hansen
1332 Timber Hills Rd
Mount Shasta CA 96067

Call Sign: WB7EGG
Dennis Heikura
248 Villa Rd
Mount Shasta CA 96067

Call Sign: KD6WZE
James R Atchison

Mount Shasta CA 96067

Call Sign: KE6BFF
Robert B Ballering
Mount Shasta CA 96067

Call Sign: KK6XS
Carolyn L Ballering
Mount Shasta CA 96067

Call Sign: W6SDP
Robert D Caley
Mount Shasta CA 96067

Call Sign: W6QLB
James A Christianson
Mount Shasta CA 96067

Call Sign: N6SXB
Jonathan W Rees
Mount Shasta CA 96067

Call Sign: KD6YXO
Esther Sutton
Mount Shasta CA 96067

Call Sign: KB6MGR
James B Sutton III
Mount Shasta CA 96067

Call Sign: KJ6YS
Virginia A Williams
Mount Shasta CA 96067

Call Sign: KD6WZC
Wilma J Dibelka
Mount Shasta CA 96067

Call Sign: KF6ERH
Paul E Armantrout
Mount Shasta CA 96067

Call Sign: KE6MZR
Rick L Chandon
Mount Shasta CA 96067

Call Sign: KE6SXS
Todd R Cory
Mount Shasta CA 96067

Call Sign: KE6HUO
Karen K Faithorn
Mount Shasta CA 96067

Call Sign: WB6MBF
Dennis R Freeman
Mount Shasta CA 96067

Call Sign: KJ6YQ
Albert C Germann
Mount Shasta CA 96067

Call Sign: KB6ECC
Barbara J Harris
Mount Shasta CA 96067

Call Sign: KD6ZUI
Doreen K Healy
Mount Shasta CA 96067

Call Sign: WH6LZ
James D Healy
Mount Shasta CA 96067

Call Sign: KJ6OXT
Harry M Huffman
Mount Shasta CA 96067

Call Sign: KI6HUT
Marie D Mitchell
Mount Shasta CA
960670833

Call Sign: KG6TTB
Daniel L Parkin
Mount Shasta CA 96067

Call Sign: KF6OVZ
Prem Raja Baba

Mount Shasta CA
960671401

Call Sign: KJ6OXW
Touson Saryon
Mount Shasta CA 96067

Call Sign: KJ6OXX
Art J Scharf
Mount Shasta CA 96067

Call Sign: KF6PM
Gordon A Seese
Mount Shasta CA 96067

Call Sign: W6NQA
Edwin L Stockton
Mount Shasta CA 96067

Call Sign: N7YXK
Ralph Thomas
Mount Shasta CA
960670262

Call Sign: KJ6TMO
David M Webb
Mount Shasta CA 96067

**FCC Amateur Radio
Licenses in Myers Flat**

Call Sign: KF6AVY
Corinna I McDavitt
11527 Dyerville Loop Rd
Myers Flat CA 95554

Call Sign: KE6KKJ
Francis L Kinnebrew
70 Kinnebrew Ln
Myers Flat CA 95554

Call Sign: KE6VDE
Clifford B Banfill
Myers Flat CA 95554

Call Sign: KI6YDG
Wade S Connell
Myers Flat CA 95554

Call Sign: KQ6ET
William L Eastham
Myers Flat CA 95554

Call Sign: N6NWX
William G Thompson
Myers Flat CA 95554

**FCC Amateur Radio
Licenses in Navarro**

Call Sign: KF6CBL
Randy L Johnson
Navarro CA 954630308

**FCC Amateur Radio
Licenses in Oak Run**

Call Sign: KF6VFS
Lee M Crenshaw
27984 Bullskin Ridge Rd
Oak Run CA 960699504

Call Sign: KD6GHR
Steve Thorwaldson
30500 Houston Ln
Oak Run CA 960699500

Call Sign: K6ORF
Sue Ann Bogue
Oak Run CA 960690001

Call Sign: KN6ZB
Jim W Bogue
Oak Run CA 960690001

Call Sign: N7TD
Thomas R Diskin
Oak Run CA 960690171

Call Sign: KF6MSK

Patrick W Farrell
Oak Run CA 96069

FCC Amateur Radio Licenses in Ono

Call Sign: K6BZ
Gerald W Boyd
Ono CA 96047

Call Sign: K6BZJ
Jay Boyd
Ono CA 96047

Call Sign: KB6GJG
Brian M Boyd
Ono CA 96047

Call Sign: KB6GKK
Kevin S Boyd
Ono CA 96047

Call Sign: KF6UER
San Joaquin Contest Club
Ono CA 96047

FCC Amateur Radio Licenses in Orick

Call Sign: KJ6KAY
John R Vallett
Orick CA 95555

FCC Amateur Radio Licenses in Orleans

Call Sign: KF6VLZ
Bill R Beck
Orleans CA 95556

Call Sign: KG6BDW
Debra Beck
Orleans CA 95556

Call Sign: W6WRB

Bill R Beck
Orleans CA 95556

Call Sign: KJ6DDR
Michael J Derry
Orleans CA 95556

FCC Amateur Radio Licenses in Palo Cedro

Call Sign: KC6WTP
Katie L Fowler
21971 Berkeley Dr
Palo Cedro CA 96073

Call Sign: KE6KMR
Melanie K Fowler
21971 Berkeley Dr
Palo Cedro CA 96073

Call Sign: KE6FXC
Sheila R Freier
21971 Berkeley Dr
Palo Cedro CA 96073

Call Sign: N6PQV
Richard D Freier
21971 Berkeley Dr
Palo Cedro CA 96073

Call Sign: KC6UMQ
Scott D Thompson
21763 Beryl Dr
Palo Cedro CA 96073

Call Sign: KA6OZP
San L Cavin
21314 Boyle Rd
Palo Cedro CA 96073

Call Sign: KI6OWG
George R Galloway
22019 Brundage Rd
Palo Cedro CA 96073

Call Sign: KI6SUU
Robert J Grosch
10810 Cheshire Way
Palo Cedro CA 960739777

Call Sign: N6GEK
Richard E Truitt
9759 Cow Creek Dr
Palo Cedro CA 96073

Call Sign: KI6WAL
Sandy K Harrison
8635 Deschutes Rd
Palo Cedro CA 96073

Call Sign: KF6WSX
Franz J Hoffman
8635 Deschutes Rd
Palo Cedro CA 96073

Call Sign: KF6DCZ
Peter N Blue
10399 Deschutes Rd
Palo Cedro CA 96073

Call Sign: KC6NXF
Paul Westwind
9200 Deschutes Rd 4
Palo Cedro CA 96073

Call Sign: KE6KMS
Marie J Lyons
21910 Hillside Dr
Palo Cedro CA 96073

Call Sign: KG6RPH
Amy I Gibson
9829 Hillview Dr
Palo Cedro CA 96073

Call Sign: KD6WDZ
Naomi P Kratz
9829 Hillview Dr
Palo Cedro CA 96073

Call Sign: KX6Q
Leslie D Kratz
9829 Hillview Dr
Palo Cedro CA 96073

Call Sign: WA6QWB
Robb P Lightfoot
9951 Hillview Dr
Palo Cedro CA 96073

Call Sign: W6LEE
Evan L Fitzsimmons
22153 Lassen View Dr
Palo Cedro CA 96073

Call Sign: KI6PSE
William T East
8151 Oakcrest Pl
Palo Cedro CA 96073

Call Sign: KI6WAE
Edward J Berry Jr
9556 Quarter Horse Ln
Palo Cedro CA 96073

Call Sign: K6EIX
Donald D Churchill
21815 Shady Oak Ln
Palo Cedro CA 96073

Call Sign: KF6YNT
Amy M Morris
22653 Silverlode Ln
Palo Cedro CA 96073

Call Sign: AA6UB
Allison L Caldwell
Palo Cedro CA 96073

Call Sign: KD6LLY
James B Hawkins
Palo Cedro CA 96073

Call Sign: KD6UNK
Joseph M Case

Palo Cedro CA 96073

Call Sign: KJ6RFC
Michael L Damoth
Palo Cedro CA 96073

Call Sign: KJ6EYR
Allan Macho
Palo Cedro CA 96073

Call Sign: WB6FHN
Herbert Manoli
Palo Cedro CA 960730423

Call Sign: KJ6EYQ
Kelly O'Leary
Palo Cedro CA 96073

Call Sign: KR6AR
John R Skeete
Palo Cedro CA 96073

Call Sign: KD6FO
Lia V Subrecky
Palo Cedro CA 96073

Call Sign: KG6BU
James R Subrecky
Palo Cedro CA 96073

FCC Amateur Radio
Licenses in Paynes Creek

Call Sign: KJ6EOX
Bryan Dale
18931 Summit Rd
Paynes Creek CA 96075

Call Sign: KI6UZQ
Joshua J Dale
18931 Summit Rd
Paynes Creek CA 96075

Call Sign: K6JJD
Joshua J Dale

18931 Summit Rd
Paynes Creek CA 96075

FCC Amateur Radio
Licenses in Petrolia

Call Sign: KF6AAU
Randall P Stemler
36330 Mattole Rd
Petrolia CA 95558

Call Sign: WB6UMK
Leland W Hadley
41088 Mattole Rd
Petrolia CA 95558

Call Sign: KF6CMM
William A Selby
29131 Mattolerd
Petrolia CA 95558

Call Sign: KJ6BVJ
Joshua Free
Petrolia CA 95558

Call Sign: KJ6BVK
Chris M Gilda
Petrolia CA 95558

Call Sign: KI6BGL
James L Isaacson
Petrolia CA 95558

Call Sign: KJ6BVL
Brian S Jahnke
Petrolia CA 95558

Call Sign: KJ6BVM
Carson T Morgan
Petrolia CA 95558

Call Sign: KJ6BVN
Tammy L Picconi
Petrolia CA 95558

Call Sign: WA4SOP
Charles B Solo
Petrolia CA 95558

Call Sign: KJ6BVO
Leslie A Swafford
Petrolia CA 95558

FCC Amateur Radio Licenses in Phillipsville

Call Sign: KG6DZY
Neil D Logan
1325 Hwy 254
Phillipsville CA 95559

Call Sign: WD6AOJ
Daniel M Gribi
Phillipsville CA 95559

Call Sign: KG6FOL
Sally S Cambel
Phillipsville CA 95559

Call Sign: KG6UCF
David R Davidson
Phillipsville CA 95559

FCC Amateur Radio Licenses in Philo

Call Sign: WA6VMB
Nicki A Parsons
Philo CA 95466

Call Sign: KF6WCF
Carolyn L Brooks
Philo CA 95466

Call Sign: KE6JKA
Gary R Brooks
Philo CA 95466

Call Sign: KJ6HZX
Judy A Nelson

Philo CA 954660660

FCC Amateur Radio Licenses in Piercy

Call Sign: KE6DNA
Gene J Bernstein
77200 Hwy 271
Piercy CA 95587

Call Sign: N6TBC
Alan K Ebert
Piercy CA 95467

Call Sign: KE6DNB
Robert C Kirk
Piercy CA 95587

Call Sign: N6TOE
Bruce L Collins
Piercy CA 95467

Call Sign: KB6KFO
Robert D Porter
Piercy CA 95587

Call Sign: KF6IZF
Erica H Bernstein
Piercy CA 95587

Call Sign: KF6IZG
Joe E Bernstein
Piercy CA 95587

Call Sign: KG6BFR
Sidney E Hudson
Piercy CA 95587

Call Sign: WH6CUQ
Ralph H Penner
Piercy CA 95587

Call Sign: KG6RHL
Edward R Ryan
Piercy CA 95587

FCC Amateur Radio Licenses in Platina

Call Sign: KF6QAT
Sheila A Taylor
3530 Harrison Gulch Rd
Platina CA 960760011

Call Sign: WB6WWH
James C White
Platina CA 96076

Call Sign: KF6WCE
Paul A Taylor Jr
Platina CA 96076

FCC Amateur Radio Licenses in Point Arena

Call Sign: N3ZF
Alexander F Kovach
43700 Creekside Spur
Point Arena CA 95468

Call Sign: KF6CBJ
Patricia D Lambert
42685 Hataway Xing
Point Arena CA
954688809

Call Sign: KF6AII
Nicholas L Scanlon Hill
42515 Hathaway Xing
Point Arena CA
954688809

Call Sign: KE6DZC
Janice L Haverty
46051 Iversen Rd
Point Arena CA 95468

Call Sign: W1HUW
John F Haverty
46051 Iversen Rd

Point Arena CA
954680649

Call Sign: K1JRW
Janice L Haverty
46051 Iversen Rd
Point Arena CA 95468

Call Sign: K3FIV
John F Haverty
46051 Iversen Rd
Point Arena CA
954680649

Call Sign: KI6KRM
Lewis S Sternberg
46331 Iverson Dr
Point Arena CA 95468

Call Sign: KG6FPO
Jeffrey B Gunning
125 Mill St
Point Arena CA
954681089

Call Sign: KE6CQG
Scott Ignacio
210 School St
Point Arena CA
954680606

Call Sign: KD6TEI
David G Danchuk
Point Arena CA 95468

Call Sign: KD6MEZ
Dale C Ice
Point Arena CA 95468

Call Sign: KG6PUA
John D Bastian
Point Arena CA 95468

Call Sign: KG6FPQ
Linda J Bostwick

Point Arena CA 95468

Call Sign: KG6PUB
Frances I Buentjen
Point Arena CA 95468

Call Sign: AF6MQ
Scott A Gasparian
Point Arena CA 95468

Call Sign: KF6PLT
Chistopher K Jentoft
Point Arena CA
954680832

Call Sign: KG6YLZ
Darlene G Johnson
Point Arena CA 95468

Call Sign: KI6EKX
Alexander F Kovach
Point Arena CA 95468

Call Sign: KG6YLY
Karl J Mellander
Point Arena CA 95468

Call Sign: KG6OHM
Mary Jacquetta Nisbet
Point Arena CA 95468

Call Sign: W6FMZ
Laurence G Riddle
Point Arena CA 95468

Call Sign: KG6FPL
Melvin L Smith
Point Arena CA 95468

Call Sign: KG6PTZ
Michelle Staples
Point Arena CA 95468

**FCC Amateur Radio
Licenses in Potter Valley**

Call Sign: KF6JNP
Marianne Gerssing
9181 East Rd
Potter Valley CA 95469

Call Sign: KG6PBP
Shelly D Campbell
10781 East Rd
Potter Valley CA
954699707

Call Sign: KF6JNT
Nina J Curtis
10901 East Rd
Potter Valley CA 95469

Call Sign: KF6JHW
Gary A Pierachini
10901 East Rd
Potter Valley CA 95469

Call Sign: KF6JHU
Richard A Knox
11501 East Rd
Potter Valley CA 95469

Call Sign: KI6URS
Robert Feltman
13951 N Busch Ln
Potter Valley CA 95469

Call Sign: K6BPK
Robert Feltman
13951 N Busch Ln
Potter Valley CA
954699794

Call Sign: KF6QAS
Lura E Smith
13501 N Busch Rd
Potter Valley CA
954699722

Call Sign: KF6KNZ

Paul P Pollock
8055 Old Wagon Rd
Potter Valley CA 95469

Call Sign: KF6JOA
Linda C Pollock
8055 Old Wagon Rd
Potter Valley CA
954699718

Call Sign: WA6CWL
Rose M Siemer
11100 Pine Ave
Potter Valley CA 95469

Call Sign: WA6HSR
Quenten C Siemer
11100 Pine Ave
Potter Valley CA 95469

Call Sign: KD6SAY
Theresa A Reichert
12746 Pine Ave
Potter Valley CA
954699708

Call Sign: KE6SPM
Katrina A Reichert
12746 Pine Ave
Potter Valley CA
954699708

Call Sign: KN6GQ
Curtis R Reichert
12746 Pine Ave
Potter Valley CA
954699708

Call Sign: KF6QAP
Karen A Zimmerman
13125 Pine Ave
Potter Valley CA
954699708

Call Sign: KI6IDY

Yvonne L Bell
12605 Powerhouse Rd
Potter Valley CA 95469

Call Sign: KF6UVI
Peter S Davis
13451 Powerhouse Rd
Potter Valley CA 95469

Call Sign: KF6TJT
Christine L McCord
9900 Spring Valley Rd
Potter Valley CA 95469

Call Sign: KA6BIN
George M Wood III
11920 Westside Rd
Potter Valley CA 95469

Call Sign: KF6JHR
Mary E Collins
Potter Valley CA 95469

Call Sign: KC6ZCB
Henry B Graham
Potter Valley CA
954690502

Call Sign: KF6TCI
Laura L Oberfeld
Potter Valley CA
954690021

Call Sign: KG6NXP
Claudia J Pollock
Potter Valley CA
954690155

FCC Amateur Radio Licenses in Pumpkin Center

Call Sign: KG6BBE
Mario Cerna
Pumpkin Center CA 93383

Call Sign: KG6BBH
Rigoberto Sanchez
Pumpkin Center CA 93383

FCC Amateur Radio Licenses in Ravendale

Call Sign: KJ6JFR
Samuel P Sagan
512 450 Hwy 395
Ravendale CA 96123

Call Sign: AF6YI
Samuel P Sagan
512 450 Hwy 395
Ravendale CA 96123

Call Sign: K6NBY
Samuel P Sagan
512 450 Hwy 395
Ravendale CA 96123

Call Sign: KJ6LPF
Elisa M Mehl
Ravendale CA 96123

FCC Amateur Radio Licenses in Red Bluff

Call Sign: KI6IFI
Louis T Dudley
200 Aqua Verdi Dr
Red Bluff CA 96080

Call Sign: AA6TE
David L Kersey
13499 Arch St
Red Bluff CA 96080

Call Sign: KC6DWR
Dorothy L Kersey
13499 Arch St
Red Bluff CA 96080

Call Sign: KC6EJE
Daniel L Kersey
13499 Arch St
Red Bluff CA 96080

Call Sign: KD6VXE
David L Kersey
13499 Arch St
Red Bluff CA 96080

Call Sign: KD6KYS
Daniel C Cumpton
13553 Arch St
Red Bluff CA 96080

Call Sign: KC6SDJ
Rodney D Sparks
13560 Arch St
Red Bluff CA 96080

Call Sign: KI6WAG
William E Cox
645 Armstrong Ct
Red Bluff CA 96080

Call Sign: WA6PRG
Rick M Madrid
15764 Ash Ln
Red Bluff CA 960809304

Call Sign: WA6LEF
Arne W Hansen
12680 Ashland Ave
Red Bluff CA 96080

Call Sign: KF6EMN
David W Smith
720 Ashmount Ave
Red Bluff CA 96080

Call Sign: KN6UB
Johnny E Tanner
21795 Bend Ferry Rd 17
Red Bluff CA 96080

Call Sign: KB6EF
Lawrence R Cilk
158 Beverley Ave
Red Bluff CA 96080

Call Sign: K6AAW
Larry D Murdoch
14370 Brian Rd
Red Bluff CA 96080

Call Sign: K6WWV
Alice I Murdoch
14370 Brian Rd
Red Bluff CA 96080

Call Sign: WA6AGO
Bert D Murdoch
14370 Brian Rd
Red Bluff CA 96080

Call Sign: K6KHZ
Tehama County Amat Rad
Club
14370 Brian Rd
Red Bluff CA 96080

Call Sign: KJ6DMT
Frank S Clyne
1220 Britt Ln
Red Bluff CA 96080

Call Sign: KA6BVU
Everett E Rury Sr
57 Byron Ave
Red Bluff CA 96808

Call Sign: N6CVF
Bradford R Williams
14585 Carriage Ln
Red Bluff CA 96080

Call Sign: WD6AAM
Kenneth M Kees
69 Casa Grande Dr
Red Bluff CA 96080

Call Sign: KD6HBX
Jean D Youngs
106 Casa Grande Dr
Red Bluff CA 96080

Call Sign: W6BLM
Doyle L Youngs
106 Casa Grande Dr
Red Bluff CA 96080

Call Sign: KC6BRH
Kenneth J Johnson
14420 Center Fork
Red Bluff CA 96080

Call Sign: W6SYY
Andrew E McClure
95 Chestnut Ave
Red Bluff CA 96080

Call Sign: AB6VT
Robert H Ochs
15480 China Rapids Dr
Red Bluff CA 96080

Call Sign: KD6LGU
McKenzie A Smith
23580 Cone Grove Rd
Red Bluff CA 96080

Call Sign: KJ6IOF
Rupert H Jung
14395 Del Oro Ct
Red Bluff CA 96080

Call Sign: N6DNU
John F Lorentz
14900 Diamond Star Rd
Red Bluff CA 96080

Call Sign: KJ6TYB
Nicholas R Dohmen
21100 Doe Run Way
Red Bluff CA 96080

Call Sign: WA6KUP
Richard J Brown
1420 Donita
Red Bluff CA 96080

Call Sign: KF6TK
Theodore L Polster
5 Dunvin Ct
Red Bluff CA 96080

Call Sign: N6HFQ
Barbara J Polster
5 Dunvin Ct
Red Bluff CA 96080

Call Sign: K6UEE
Jack L Kraft
1540 El Cerrito Dr
Red Bluff CA 96080

Call Sign: KB6XP
Gerald L Rasmussen
1650 Elcerrito Ct
Red Bluff CA 96080

Call Sign: WA6VRZ
Dewey A Blankenship
24275 Electric Ave
Red Bluff CA 96080

Call Sign: WA6ZMU
Muriel A Blankenship
24275 Electric Ave
Red Bluff CA 96080

Call Sign: KC6BRL
John R Lively
1040 Franzel Rd
Red Bluff CA 96080

Call Sign: KC6CDA
Donna J Lively
1040 Franzel Rd
Red Bluff CA 96080

Call Sign: KG6KUN
Ralph J Berti
1215 Franzel Rd
Red Bluff CA 960804157

Call Sign: KC6BRK
Walter L Wilson
21 Gamay Ct Apt 26E
Red Bluff CA 96080

Call Sign: KD6TWF
Donn H Kelley
130 Gillmore Rd
Red Bluff CA 96080

Call Sign: KD6IRP
Robert C Carpenter
130 Gilmore Rd 59
Red Bluff CA 96080

Call Sign: KA7IGP
Fred V Arrasmith
23099 Greene St
Red Bluff CA 96080

Call Sign: N6LOR
Florence M Arrasmith
23099 Greene St
Red Bluff CA 96080

Call Sign: K7KUS
William M Caldwell
145 Gurnsey Ave
Red Bluff CA 96080

Call Sign: KE6GLJ
Robert L Whatley
22295 Harness Ln
Red Bluff CA 96080

Call Sign: KN6JY
Arthur E Dowell III
2710 Highland Bluffs Dr
Red Bluff CA 96080

Call Sign: KG6PSE
Froozandeh Waits
2740 Highland Bluffs Dr
Red Bluff CA 96080

Call Sign: KG6ORA
Kevin A Waits
2740 Highland Bluffs Dr
Red Bluff CA 96080

Call Sign: KJ6DMP
Michael D Paisley
20775 Highland Ct
Red Bluff CA 96080

Call Sign: KJ6NTL
Jerry D Barr
29650 Hwy 36E
Red Bluff CA 96080

Call Sign: KJ6RPE
Jerry D Barr
29650 Hwy 36E
Red Bluff CA 96080

Call Sign: AB6Y
Mark D Tieman
19799 Hwy 36W
Red Bluff CA 960807919

Call Sign: KG6FSY
Lori D Smith
539 Jackson St
Red Bluff CA 96080

Call Sign: KJ6AIC
Michelle A Wiggley
381 James Ave
Red Bluff CA 96080

Call Sign: KI6WAS
Randy D Hunt
915 Johnson St
Red Bluff CA 96080

Call Sign: KB6UCS
Thomas T Sheen
1056 Johnson St
Red Bluff CA 96080

Call Sign: KC6EOI
Kevin A Leddy
160 Mary Ln
Red Bluff CA 96080

Call Sign: KG6WYK
Denise Bline
655 Palmer Ave
Red Bluff CA 960804717

Call Sign: KC6PSF
Brent N Dawson
22665 Juanita Ct
Red Bluff CA 96080

Call Sign: KM6UA
Dan C Albertson
16160 Matlock Loop
Red Bluff CA 96080

Call Sign: KG6WYJ
Harold F Bline
655 Palmer Ave
Red Bluff CA 960804717

Call Sign: N6OHH
Fred Lowndes
320 Kaer Ave
Red Bluff CA 96080

Call Sign: W6TJG
Russell C Myer
14460 Molluc Dr
Red Bluff CA 96080

Call Sign: KD6IRO
Billie W Mendenhall
675 Palmer Dr
Red Bluff CA 96080

Call Sign: K6OEZ
Albert E Henderson Jr
14500 Kenney Ave
Red Bluff CA 96080

Call Sign: WA6CGX
Brent S Simons
13090 Montecito Rd
Red Bluff CA 96080

Call Sign: WB6LPZ
Michael S Edwards
21935 Parkway Dr
Red Bluff CA 96080

Call Sign: KD6SLL
Danene R Mercill Casey
1357 Kirsten Ct
Red Bluff CA 96080

Call Sign: KE6TAR
Patrick A McCauley
100 Mulberry St
Red Bluff CA 96080

Call Sign: WB6RCC
Eugene H Ono
21935 Parkway Dr
Red Bluff CA 96080

Call Sign: N6LUY
Wallace L Stillwell
411 Lincoln St
Red Bluff CA 96080

Call Sign: WB6KOE
Harry A Johnson
14110 Noble Oaks Dr
Red Bluff CA 96080

Call Sign: KG6WYM
Ernie F Sandberg
13531 Patricie St
Red Bluff CA 96080

Call Sign: W6RTS
Randy J Thomas
20065 Live Oak Rd
Red Bluff CA 96080

Call Sign: WA6CKI
Alvin L Small
14225 Noble Oaks Dr
Red Bluff CA 96080

Call Sign: KG6WYN
Virginia L Sandberg
13531 Patricie St
Red Bluff CA 96080

Call Sign: K6RW
George E Fiedler
233 Manzanita Ave
Red Bluff CA 96080

Call Sign: WA6PSW
Butch R Stehno
21650 Noblecrest Ct
Red Bluff CA 96080

Call Sign: K6AAA
Tyler R Christensen
23595 Patterson Rd
Red Bluff CA 96080

Call Sign: KF6KDD
Jacob M Hickok
239 Manzanita Ave
Red Bluff CA 96080

Call Sign: WD6FEH
Sarah K Pellersels
24365 Oklahoma Ave
Red Bluff CA 96080

Call Sign: WB6USH
Jack D Sharp
14810 Peppertree Ln
Red Bluff CA 96080

Call Sign: KF6ZJD
Daniel B Ryant
11336 Rawson Rd
Red Bluff CA 96080

Call Sign: KJ6BSU
Riki M Holliday
72 Rio Vista Ln
Red Bluff CA 96080

Call Sign: KE6BPQ
Kenneth G Burton
215 Sherman Dr
Red Bluff CA 96080

Call Sign: KJ6FOB
Frank V Caltabiano
19920 Red Bank Rd
Red Bluff CA 96080

Call Sign: KM6JJ
Donald G Fereira
13380 Roadrunner Loop
Red Bluff CA 96080

Call Sign: KI6YNI
Frank L Debenedetti
551 Spyglass Dr
Red Bluff CA 96080

Call Sign: N6NNR
Cal G Chamberlain
18930 Reeds Creek Rd
Red Bluff CA 96080

Call Sign: KG6PEE
Donald E Waits
1436 Robinson Dr
Red Bluff CA 96080

Call Sign: KI6YNS
Pam K Debenedetti
551 Spyglass Dr
Red Bluff CA 96080

Call Sign: KF6AYU
Michael T Nellums
19875 Reeds Creek Rd
Red Bluff CA 96080

Call Sign: KC6RJI
Ben H Steel
1476 Robinson Dr
Red Bluff CA 96080

Call Sign: KE6LPS
Leo N Thurston
635 Spyglass Dr
Red Bluff CA 96080

Call Sign: WB6VLD
Robert J Friday
Reeds Creek Rd
Red Bluff CA 96080

Call Sign: KD6TWG
Randy J Thomas
14496 Ryan Ln
Red Bluff CA 96080

Call Sign: KJ6AHZ
Casey J Hickok
14025 Trinity Ave
Red Bluff CA 96080

Call Sign: KF6YDN
Mike K Lewis
41 Rio Vista Ln
Red Bluff CA 96080

Call Sign: KG6EON
Christina A Ryant
21610 Sacramento Ave
Red Bluff CA 96080

Call Sign: KD6YXK
Donna L Kersey
838 Union St 2
Red Bluff CA 96080

Call Sign: KI6UZR
Edward O Holliday
72 Rio Vista Ln
Red Bluff CA 96080

Call Sign: KG6EOO
Michael P Ryant
21610 Sacramento Ave
Red Bluff CA 96080

Call Sign: N6UGY
Dennis J Flora
3630 Via Hermosa
Red Bluff CA 96080

Call Sign: N6EOH
Edward O Holliday
72 Rio Vista Ln
Red Bluff CA 96080

Call Sign: KF6JG
John S Benka
710 Sacramento Ave 4
Red Bluff CA 960804141

Call Sign: KD6TRT
John C Wilburn
1514 Walbridge St
Red Bluff CA 96080

Call Sign: KJ6PUZ
Justin S Holliday
72 Rio Vista Ln
Red Bluff CA 96080

Call Sign: WB6LHP
Frederick J Lourence
22495 Saron Rd
Red Bluff CA 96080

Call Sign: WB6TMA
Allan C Gossett
1440 Walnut St
Red Bluff CA 96080

Call Sign: KE6ADE
John W Cornelison
Red Bluff CA 96080

Call Sign: W6RFC
Albert H Davidson
Red Bluff CA 96080

Call Sign: WA6GPI
Thomas M Wulfert
Red Bluff CA 96080

Call Sign: KB6MLK
Andre A Maurel
Red Bluff CA 96080

Call Sign: W6COB
Donald R Custer
Red Bluff CA 960800816

Call Sign: KE6PMT
Russell W Doughty
Red Bluff CA 96080

Call Sign: N6DUK
Clarence Gunsolus
Red Bluff CA 96080

Call Sign: KR6CY
Jeffrey H Kelly
Red Bluff CA 96080

Call Sign: WA6GXQ
Jeffrey H Kelly
Red Bluff CA 960800043

Call Sign: KD6TRS
Sandy C Thomas
Red Bluff CA 96080

Call Sign: N6RTS
Randy J Thomas
Red Bluff CA 96080

Call Sign: KF6ZGY
Richard D White
Red Bluff CA 96080

Call Sign: N6UXA
Daniel T Polster
5 Dunvin Ct
Red Buff CA 96080

Call Sign: KF6IBV
Arthur C McChesney
1240 S Pointe
Red Buff CA 96080

**FCC Amateur Radio
Licenses in Redcrest**

Call Sign: KF6RLR
Julie A Wills
Redcrest CA 955690273

**FCC Amateur Radio
Licenses in Redding**

Call Sign: KC6QKM
Lester S Miller
3305 Adams Ln
Redding CA 96002

Call Sign: KF6GXT
Micah A Seth
4364 Agnes May Dr
Redding CA 96002

Call Sign: KD6RGG
Ingrid T Potts
4393 Agnes May Dr
Redding CA 96002

Call Sign: WA6PEO
John H Potts
4393 Agnes May Dr
Redding CA 96002

Call Sign: KK6JP

John H Potts
4393 Agnes May Dr
Redding CA 96002

Call Sign: WA6SZO
Bobbie R Hill
6101 Airport Rd
Redding CA 96002

Call Sign: KI6WAO
Anthony J Huff
8761 Airport Rd Ste B
Redding CA 96002

Call Sign: KI6WAP
Tracie R Huff
8761 Airport Rd Ste B
Redding CA 96002

Call Sign: AB6JA
Martin I Fitzsimmons
2124 Airstrip Rd
Redding CA 96003

Call Sign: KF6GJY
Mollie I Fitzsimmons
2124 Airstrip Rd
Redding CA 96003

Call Sign: W6TWC
Douglas G Remington
440 Alamine Dr
Redding CA 96003

Call Sign: KA6LIE
Charlene L Pohrman
3635 Alma Ave
Redding CA 96002

Call Sign: KD6FML
Kristel L Pohrman
3635 Alma Ave
Redding CA 96002

Call Sign: N6DTL

Garry J Pohrman
3635 Alma Ave
Redding CA 96002

Call Sign: K6LYT
Kenneth H Nudson
3643 Alma Ave
Redding CA 96002

Call Sign: KI6LY
Charlotte A Nudson
3643 Alma Ave
Redding CA 96002

Call Sign: WA6DGS
John M Ashcraft
3808 Alma Ave
Redding CA 96002

Call Sign: KI6PRY
Peter H Westler
3824 Alma Ave
Redding CA 960023216

Call Sign: KG6ZSH
Richard W Karpinen
3936 Alma Ave
Redding CA 96002

Call Sign: K6LJC
Richard W Karpinen
3936 Alma Ave
Redding CA 96002

Call Sign: N7MYU
Sandy M Elmore
12281 Alpha Ln
Redding CA 960039570

Call Sign: WA6UAG
Noel C Benner
4832 Alta Camino Dr
Redding CA 96002

Call Sign: WA6MUU

Gary G Self
4350 Alta Campo Dr
Redding CA 96002

Call Sign: KE6ALC
Tom R Hodges
4320 Alta Mesa
Redding CA 96002

Call Sign: KE6ALD
Carole A Hodges
4320 Alta Mesa
Redding CA 96002

Call Sign: KA6MYP
Charlie G Kondrath Jr
3640 Altura Dr
Redding CA 96001

Call Sign: AC6ED
Mark D McGowan
2414 Annette Dr
Redding CA 96001

Call Sign: KD6DUZ
Donna L McGowan
2414 Annette Dr
Redding CA 96001

Call Sign: KC6OMJ
Eric R Waits
464 Arbor Pl
Redding CA 96001

Call Sign: W6FWJ
Donald L Oestreicher
493 Arbor Pl
Redding CA 96001

Call Sign: KD6OMT
Gary M Corum
2281 Athens Ave
Redding CA 96001

Call Sign: WA6SQP

B M Perry
2192 Athens St
Redding CA 960010923

Call Sign: KG6QGH
Evan M Goldstein
947 Bahama Ct
Redding CA 96003

Call Sign: KJ6RGL
Richard A Wilkinson Jr
3187 Barrel Ct
Redding CA 96001

Call Sign: KF6PMI
Jason A Duncan
22181 Basin Way
Redding CA 960037706

Call Sign: KI6WAC
Harold C Ascherman III
13638 Bear Mtn Rd
Redding CA 96003

Call Sign: KJ6RGJ
Valerie A Winterberg
14216 Bear Mtn Rd
Redding CA 96003

Call Sign: W6QJY
Charles F Denny
1922 Bechelli Ln
Redding CA 960020128

Call Sign: KI6ZE
Jack S Roberts
1972 Bechelli Ln
Redding CA 96002

Call Sign: WA6ZNW
William F Nicol
3678 Bechelli Ln
Redding CA 96002

Call Sign: W7BFH

William A Weathers
3874 Bechelli Ln
Redding CA 96002

Call Sign: W6NTD
William A Weathers
3874 Bechelli Ln
Redding CA 96002

Call Sign: AF6PB
Chris Cassata
3521 Bechelli Ln Unit B
Redding CA 96002

Call Sign: KK6EL
Richard F Somers
1039 Belcrest Dr
Redding CA 96003

Call Sign: KG6EPT
Josh M Pavlovich
2420 Belladonna St
Redding CA 96002

Call Sign: KI6OMX
Vernon E Lee Jr
990 Beltline Rd
Redding CA 96003

Call Sign: KI6UZT
Joseph E Cutshaw
1865 Benton Dr 4
Redding CA 96003

Call Sign: N0WSU
Robert S Hamilton
20992 Bernard Way
Redding CA 96003

Call Sign: KD6QAZ
Steven G Lovely
3175 Blue Bell Dr
Redding CA 96001

Call Sign: KE6JUN

Jason P Melfa
20481 Blue Mountain Rd
Redding CA 96003

Call Sign: N6GST
Joseph A Louzao
4205 Boston Ave
Redding CA 96001

Call Sign: KI7RQ
Michael H Schaub
4250 Boston Ave
Redding CA 96001

Call Sign: N7PDF
Karl C Schaub
4250 Boston Ave
Redding CA 96001

Call Sign: KE6OUB
James D Larkin
2505 Botte St
Redding CA 96001

Call Sign: N6QKD
Jim G Wiley
510 Bottlebrush
Redding CA 96003

Call Sign: KI6OMW
Sandra L Kotch
20858 Boyle Rd
Redding CA 96003

Call Sign: KB6SJP
Dwane I Olson
120 Branstetter Ln
Redding CA 96001

Call Sign: KG6VYL
Stephanie A Renfer
1918 Breckenwood Dr
Redding CA 96002

Call Sign: KD6YXH

Dennis E Burts
3481 Bridger Dr
Redding CA 96002

Call Sign: N7YWX
Richard H Guglielmino
4172 Brittany Dr
Redding CA 96002

Call Sign: KD6VZP
James A Johnson
4465 Brittany Dr
Redding CA 96002

Call Sign: KF6ZUP
Ted Pella
4485 Brittany Dr
Redding CA 96002

Call Sign: N7YWY
Carolyn M Guglielmino
4172 Brittany Dr
Redding CA 96002

Call Sign: KI6UNM
Ronald N Grider
14359 Bryan Way
Redding CA 96003

Call Sign: KE6NYH
Terry G Fifield
330 Buckeye Ter
Redding CA 96003

Call Sign: AL7QR
Daniel R Spliethof
10987 Bud Ln
Redding CA 96001

Call Sign: KI6RTZ
Bolton M Allred
1165 Burton Dr Apt C
Redding CA 96003

Call Sign: KJ6BWO

Michelle I Allred
1165 Burton Dr Apt C
Redding CA 96003

Call Sign: KG6NEO
Robert R Lenk
3641 Cal Ore Dr
Redding CA 96001

Call Sign: KA6YPV
Gerald E Halgreen
11075 Campers Ct 89
Redding CA 96007

Call Sign: KE6CGA
Deems T Taylor
2761 Camulos Way
Redding CA 96002

Call Sign: N6LOP
Charles E Humphrey
2789 Camulos Way
Redding CA 96002

Call Sign: KC6IWI
Richard D Schneck
2871 Camulos Way
Redding CA 96002

Call Sign: WA6ZIV
Kenneth C Browning
1582 Canyon Rd
Redding CA 96001

Call Sign: KI6EBK
William E Siemer
10255 Carrousel
Redding CA 96001

Call Sign: KQ6LT
John L Garland
3015 Carson Dr 2
Redding CA 96003

Call Sign: AA6OS

Leonard G Fletcher
1433 Carter Way
Redding CA 96002

Call Sign: KB6NFC
La Rocque A Creighton
1645 Cascade Ln
Redding CA 96002

Call Sign: K6AAN
Larry M Stromberg
1652 Cascade Ln
Redding CA 960020827

Call Sign: W6BVC
Thomas R Miller
536 Castenda Dr
Redding CA 960036602

Call Sign: KC6ZEJ
Kenneth T Merz Mr
7870 Castle View Ln
Redding CA 96001

Call Sign: KF6FEI
Paul E Peterson
2378 Castlewood Dr
Redding CA 96002

Call Sign: KG6FSX
Douglas J Held
2499 Castlewood Dr
Redding CA 96002

Call Sign: K6LSN
John M Hewitt
5921 Cedars Rd
Redding CA 96001

Call Sign: KF6IBW
James T Stark
1833 Cedarwood Dr
Redding CA 96002

Call Sign: KE6QBP

Kenneth J Payne
2521 Center Waverly Ave
Redding CA 96001

Call Sign: KE4UEJ
Diane L East
9021 Chaparral Dr
Redding CA 96001

Call Sign: N6QG
Clark T Ballard Jr
1001 Chardonnay Walk
Redding CA 96001

Call Sign: KI6SUM
Brenda L Belongie
20251 Charlanne Dr
Redding CA 96002

Call Sign: KI6SUN
Robert M Belongie
20251 Charlanne Dr
Redding CA 96002

Call Sign: KF6DDB
Marshall S Blaisdell
3647 Cherrywood Dr
Redding CA 96002

Call Sign: N6CHH
Don E Nead
3844 Cheryl Dr
Redding CA 96002

Call Sign: KI6LNQ
Cameron H Mooney
20985 Chicken Springs Rd
Redding CA 96003

Call Sign: KC6IWQ
David S Funk
1769 Chicory Ct
Redding CA 96002

Call Sign: WA6GUT

William M Wyatt
4501 Chippewa Ln
Redding CA 96003

Call Sign: KF6GXS
Ryan M Hibbs
2257 Christian Ave
Redding CA 96002

Call Sign: KN4ID
Robert E Kelly III
14378 Christian Way
Redding CA 96003

Call Sign: W6HXQ
Clarence A Roen
815 Christine Ave
Redding CA 96003

Call Sign: KE6CRF
Peggy A Clapper
3716 Churn Creek Rd Apt
D
Redding CA 960022903

Call Sign: KH6JRC
James D Clapper
3716 Churn Creek Rd Apt
D
Redding CA 960022903

Call Sign: KC6FGW
James D Clapper
3716 Churn Creek Rd Apt
D
Redding CA 960022903

Call Sign: KH6JRC
James D Clapper
3716 Churn Creek Rd Apt
D
Redding CA 960022903

Call Sign: W6BYT
Robert E Rice

2262 Cilantro Dr
Redding CA 96003

Call Sign: KI6WBM
Ian I Stufkosky
1952 Cirrus St
Redding CA 96002

Call Sign: KJ6BSW
John W Stufkosky
1952 Cirrus St
Redding CA 96002

Call Sign: N6ZFI
Carl A Bechtle
4485 Clark River Dr
Redding CA 96002

Call Sign: KI6UNS
Kathleen M Schweitzer
4087 Cloverway Dr
Redding CA 96002

Call Sign: K3JKW
Stanley A Clark
1017 Coggins St
Redding CA 96003

Call Sign: KD6W
Frank H Beardsley
694 Collyer Dr
Redding CA 96003

Call Sign: KD6DUX
Glenn D West
57 Cooper Dr
Redding CA 96001

Call Sign: KI6SUV
Pegg P Parker-Lagrange
4687 Corita Pl
Redding CA 96001

Call Sign: KI6WAN
Thomas E Henthorn

3129 Corto St
Redding CA 96001

Call Sign: NC6I
ARC Anderson
3165 Corto St
Redding CA 96001

Call Sign: W6MAC
Emmett L McCulley
3165 Corto St
Redding CA 96001

Call Sign: W6STF
Stephanie M McCulley
3165 Corto St
Redding CA 96001

Call Sign: KI6SUW
Debbie E Pranausk
591 Country Oak Dr
Redding CA 96003

Call Sign: KJ6PVA
Louis A Polcari
2948 Cove Point Ct
Redding CA 96001

Call Sign: KE6GVA
Ken F Shaw
2948 Cove Point Ct
Redding CA 96001

Call Sign: WA6IZO
Elayne J Smith
1263 Crag Walk
Redding CA 96003

Call Sign: KB6DOW
R Lyle Van Norman
6624 Creekside St
Redding CA 960011552

Call Sign: W6OBU
Bruce A Roth

2510 Crescent Moon Ct
Redding CA 96001

15981 Delano
Redding CA 96001

1347 E Cypress Ave
Redding CA 96002

Call Sign: KC7CGM
Chuck D Creighton
2278 Crescent Moon Dr
Redding CA 96001

Call Sign: W6CMV
Carl E Bretzke
1865 Dellwood Dr
Redding CA 96003

Call Sign: KJ6DMO
Mark E Kent
1347 E Cypress Ave
Redding CA 96002

Call Sign: KB6UGU
Fred C Schweizer
4504 Crimsonwood Dr
Redding CA 96001

Call Sign: KC7OCE
Jack H Yerkes
2569 Dewberry Dr
Redding CA 96003

Call Sign: K6GJQ
James W Eddy
1221 E Cypress Ave 307
Redding CA 96002

Call Sign: KJ6EYP
Shirlyn L Pappas
4546 Crimsonwood Dr
Redding CA 96001

Call Sign: KF6ZVU
Morgan J Hannaford
7965 Dorenda Ln
Redding CA 96001

Call Sign: KI6PRW
Debra L Lupeika
3933 Eagle Parkway
Redding CA 96001

Call Sign: KC6VSL
Stephen E Biechman
4676 Dandelion Dr
Redding CA 96002

Call Sign: KI6WBK
Gary L Schultz
3078 Dove St
Redding CA 96001

Call Sign: KC6FZZ
David L Sims
1080 Eaglenest Rd
Redding CA 96003

Call Sign: KC6IWN
Brett D Hamilton
4810 Dandelion Dr
Redding CA 96002

Call Sign: KI6PRX
Ian Carton
3549 Dune St
Redding CA 96002

Call Sign: KB6UYO
Edith M Wilson
1080 Eaglenest Rd
Redding CA 96003

Call Sign: KA6GXV
Walter R Williams Jr
5032 Dapple Gray Dr
Redding CA 96002

Call Sign: WB6UCC
Mark A Lourenco
400 E 12 St 20
Redding CA 96001

Call Sign: AD6MA
Matthew R Gowan
11366 Easy St
Redding CA 96003

Call Sign: WB6CEJ
Leo Guichard
5015 Debbie Ln
Redding CA 96002

Call Sign: KF6IKB
Tom C Pottorff
4401 E Bonnyview Rd
Redding CA 96001

Call Sign: KD6HVH
Leslie J Faires
1113 Echo Rd
Redding CA 96002

Call Sign: KE6GVE
Lester D Jensen
5095 Debbie Ln
Redding CA 96002

Call Sign: KF6YTE
Clifford D Piazza
5561 E Bonnyview Rd
Redding CA 96001

Call Sign: KF6KGC
Dennis H Price
1194 Echo Rd
Redding CA 96002

Call Sign: KE6UBT
George A Copeland

Call Sign: KJ6EYL
Lynda R Kent

Call Sign: KG6JZM
Michael V Neel

11424 Eden Dr
Redding CA 96003

Call Sign: KF6BMZ
David R Hoodenpyle
1303 Edgewood Dr
Redding CA 96003

Call Sign: AC6KX
William D Johnson
1352 Edgewood Dr
Redding CA 96003

Call Sign: W6KZW
George N McGarvey
1755 El Verano St
Redding CA 960024038

Call Sign: KJ6JZV
Ethan D Van Gent
2499 El Verano St
Redding CA 96002

Call Sign: KJ6JXZ
Matthew G Van Gent
2499 El Verano St
Redding CA 96002

Call Sign: KG6QGF
Steven G Van Gent
2499 El Verano St
Redding CA 960023702

Call Sign: KE6LGP
Todd A Holbrook
1603 Eldorado Way
Redding CA 96002

Call Sign: K6DOT
Todd A Holbrook
1603 Eldorado Way
Redding CA 96002

Call Sign: W6DY
Lawrence H Fleming

22690 Elk Trail E
Redding CA 96003

Call Sign: KD6NOL
Lyle W Breese
22925 Elk Trail E
Redding CA 96003

Call Sign: KD6KYA
Bennie R Jackson
21745 Elk Trl W
Redding CA 96003

Call Sign: KE7IB
Dan E Salisbury
20077 Elteda Ln
Redding CA 96003

Call Sign: WD6EYO
Neva M Drake
20924 Elvina Way
Redding CA 96003

Call Sign: WD6EYP
Robert E Drake
20924 Elvina Way
Redding CA 96003

Call Sign: NX6H
Richard R Rouse
580 Estate St
Redding CA 96002

Call Sign: KG6HPT
Erich A Zoellmer
11943 Fawn Dr
Redding CA 96003

Call Sign: KG6JDW
Joann Zoellmer
11943 Fawn Dr
Redding CA 96003

Call Sign: KG6RPG
Steven T Hill

7518 Fiesta Way
Redding CA 96002

Call Sign: KF6JAR
Ralph E Stephenson
20747 Fig Tree Ln
Redding CA 96002

Call Sign: KJ6NUZ
Michael L Kennedy
1640 Filaree Dr
Redding CA 96002

Call Sign: N6DMN
Michael L Kennedy
1640 Filaree Dr
Redding CA 96002

Call Sign: W1RCT
Robert A Hagensen
3133 Forest Hills Dr
Redding CA 96002

Call Sign: KB6WNG
Philip F Heckenberg
3295 Forest Hills Dr
Redding CA 96002

Call Sign: KJ6VEV
Audra W Curtis
786 Fountain Cir
Redding CA 96003

Call Sign: K2ZLT
Stuart R Wagner
2807 Foxglove Ln
Redding CA 96001

Call Sign: K6SRW
Stuart R Wagner
2807 Foxglove Ln
Redding CA 96001

Call Sign: WA6LTJ
Junior H Shoemate

1552 French Lace Ln
Redding CA 96003

6055 Gleneagles Ct
Redding CA 96003

20345 Greenview Dr
Redding CA 960029635

Call Sign: KF6CCB
Butch M Garrity
3789 Fujiyama Way
Redding CA 96001

Call Sign: KD6EFL
Hugh J Collis
1961 Glenrose Dr
Redding CA 96001

Call Sign: K6PJF
Joseph H Alcox
1020 Grissom Ct
Redding CA 96002

Call Sign: KF6AYW
Eugene L Wahl
3798 Fujiyama Way
Redding CA 960012963

Call Sign: W7RAY
Raymond H Bovee Jr
2025 Glenrose Dr
Redding CA 960014942

Call Sign: WB6PKP
Euderah E Stuck
696 Grove St C
Redding CA 96002

Call Sign: KJ6DMV
Kent S Hiemforth
1918 Galaxy Way
Redding CA 96002

Call Sign: WN6G
Karl Hoyer
12715 Glide Way
Redding CA 96003

Call Sign: KE6SLX
Stanford W Smith Sr
4651 Hardwood Blvd
Redding CA 96003

Call Sign: KJ6EOZ
Edward R Wilhelm Jr
18536 Gingeral Ave
Redding CA 96003

Call Sign: N6MVM
Catherine E Hoyer
12715 Glideway
Redding CA 96003

Call Sign: N6WBX
Everitt O Knott
2226 Harley Leighton Rd
Redding CA 96003

Call Sign: W6WJD
Edward R Wilhelm Jr
18536 Gingeral Ave
Redding CA 96003

Call Sign: KG6PED
Erik G Noll
1810 Grant St
Redding CA 96001

Call Sign: KF6MCZ
David O Smith
9911 Harley Leighton Rd
Redding CA 96003

Call Sign: WA6GSX
Roger E Decker
8771 Glendive Ln
Redding CA 96001

Call Sign: N6OQE
Everett H Prewett
19287 Green Acres W
Redding CA 96002

Call Sign: KF6DCX
Matthew J Gordon
10034 Harley Leighton Rd
Redding CA 96003

Call Sign: KI6SUT
Kenneth W Frowd
6055 Gleneagles Ct
Redding CA 96003

Call Sign: KG6FDW
Nathaniel Burger
10546 Green Oaks Ln
Redding CA 960039287

Call Sign: KJ6AIB
Carl R Weitkamp
2471 Hartnell Ave
Redding CA 96002

Call Sign: AF6QV
Kenneth W Frowd
6055 Gleneagles Ct
Redding CA 96003

Call Sign: K6NHB
Nathaniel Burger
10546 Green Oaks Ln
Redding CA 960039287

Call Sign: KI6PFS
Jesse R Gililland
85 Harvest Walk
Redding CA 96003

Call Sign: KJ6EOW
Patricia J Frowd

Call Sign: W6OMG
Benjamin H Westphal

Call Sign: W6ZVE
William F Gwin

11421 Hawley Rd
Redding CA 96003

Call Sign: KF6IKC
Stanley R Clewett
11487 Hawley Rd
Redding CA 96003

Call Sign: KC6IWO
Tyson C Long
2247 Hawn Ave
Redding CA 96002

Call Sign: KC6TRP
Joshua R Smith
2895 Hawn Ave
Redding CA 96002

Call Sign: KE6JUL
Jessee R Smith
2895 Hawn Ave
Redding CA 96002

Call Sign: KC6WRG
Marshall E Saunders
1285 Hawthorne
Redding CA 96002

Call Sign: WB7NQW
Lewis J Bornmann Phd
2025 Hedgerow Ave
Redding CA 96003

Call Sign: KE6SZU
Donna R Swim
1945 Herbscenta
Redding CA 96003

Call Sign: KE6OUD
Charles H Swim
1945 Herbscenta Ln
Redding CA 96003

Call Sign: KI6LMO
David J Swim

1945 Herbscenta Ln
Redding CA 96003

Call Sign: KJ6NVE
Nicole J Swim
1945 Herbscenta Ln
Redding CA 96003

Call Sign: N6KKI
Nicole J Swim
1945 Herbscenta Ln
Redding CA 96003

Call Sign: KI6OXK
James S Williams Jr
2205 Hilltop Dr 1026
Redding CA 96002

Call Sign: KG6BBU
Sandra B Woods Sperling
2205 Hilltop Dr 186
Redding CA 96002

Call Sign: KB6WIJ
Joseph T Melvin
1095 Hilltop Dr 228
Redding CA 96003

Call Sign: W6TCS
Donald L Rendahl
1095 Hilltop Dr 319
Redding CA 96003

Call Sign: KA6UUS
Francyse E Elliott
451 Hilltop Dr Apt 143
Redding CA 960033758

Call Sign: WA6TBT
Joseph J Mannina
451 Hilltop Dr Apt 143
Redding CA 960033758

Call Sign: W7IUL
Adolph G Myhre

130 3780 Hole In One Dr
Redding CA 96001

Call Sign: W7IUM
Wilma A Myhre
130 3780 Hole In One Dr
Redding CA 96001

Call Sign: K6AKF
Harry A Downard
50350 Hole In One Dr Sp
107
Redding CA 96002

Call Sign: KE6ZWO
Robert W Blohm
20350 Hole In One Dr Sp
111
Redding CA 96002

Call Sign: W6DZE
Franklyn A Glassow
19434 Hollow Ln
Redding CA 96003

Call Sign: WA6NCK
William M Vine
11613 Homestead Ln
Redding CA 96003

Call Sign: K6HSV
Philip G Marquis
11707 Homestead Ln
Redding CA 96003

Call Sign: WA6GCZ
Clarence G Smith
4454 Honey Comb Way
Redding CA 96003

Call Sign: WA6DFG
Albert E Pantalone
2173 Hope Ln
Redding CA 960038631

Call Sign: AF6P
Albert E Pantalone
2173 Hope Ln
Redding CA 960038631

Call Sign: WB6JOT
Carl F Alger
1560 Jay St
Redding CA 96001

Call Sign: WA6PQG
Geraldine A Schmiedl
19342 Kinene Ct
Redding CA 96003

Call Sign: KE6ALB
Chester C Wright
2760 Howard Dr
Redding CA 96001

Call Sign: KI6SVA
Lambert W Stead
13598 Jeep Trl
Redding CA 96003

Call Sign: WA6RGV
Ernst Schmiedl
19342 Kinene Ct
Redding CA 96003

Call Sign: KE6OUA
James A Bremer
2919 Inez
Redding CA 96002

Call Sign: KE6POW
Nancy L Seguin
2105 Jessica
Redding CA 96002

Call Sign: KJ6HJO
Nancy A Geer
864 Kite Ln
Redding CA 96001

Call Sign: KK6MM
James A Bremer
2919 Inez
Redding CA 96002

Call Sign: N6TWU
Kelley D Clark
606 Julian St
Redding CA 96003

Call Sign: KF6DCY
Anthony E Sterk
1520 Lacey Ln
Redding CA 96003

Call Sign: N1GAK
Scott L Statton
11085 Iron Mountain Rd
Redding CA 96007

Call Sign: KC6RTE
Mark E Eminger
1162 Kellinger St
Redding CA 96003

Call Sign: KG6HYM
Ruth A Clary
1610 Lacey Ln
Redding CA 96003

Call Sign: KG6WNT
Bryan N Frerichs
6979 Irving Rd
Redding CA 96001

Call Sign: KD6VDU
John P Labutski
12141 Kern Dr
Redding CA 960037558

Call Sign: W6RAC
Ruth A Clary
1610 Lacey Ln
Redding CA 96003

Call Sign: W6BNF
Bryan N Frerichs
6979 Irving Rd
Redding CA 96001

Call Sign: WD6DKY
William R Wright
2352 Kerry Ave
Redding CA 96002

Call Sign: KG6AAU
Esther Lay
834 Lake Blvd
Redding CA 96003

Call Sign: W6FNU
Thomas H Blankenship
2865 Irwin Rd
Redding CA 960021219

Call Sign: W6OHX
William R Campbell
2049 Kildare
Redding CA 96001

Call Sign: KG6CYJ
Nikolai A Navarro Pena
834 Lake Blvd
Redding CA 96003

Call Sign: KJ6CRY
Mary J Blankenship
2865 Irwin Rd
Redding CA 96002

Call Sign: KI6OMS
Jason N Schuler
1695 Kildare Dr
Redding CA 96001

Call Sign: KQ6YW
Al Pena
834 Lake Blvd
Redding CA 960030778

Call Sign: KD6GBW
Matthew R Gowan
12538 Lake Blvd
Redding CA 96003

Call Sign: KJ6DMU
Alveno M Pelonio
215 Lake Blvd 538
Redding CA 96003

Call Sign: KF6WGV
Joseph E Hickerson
1747 Lakeside Dr
Redding CA 96001

Call Sign: KK6JOE
Joseph E Hickerson
1747 Lakeside Dr
Redding CA 96001

Call Sign: KD6EVN
Benjamin H Phillips
2880 Lakewood Dr
Redding CA 96001

Call Sign: KB6SMF
John F O Neill
3154 Lakewood Dr
Redding CA 96001

Call Sign: KE6POS
Charles R Hardy
1185 Lancers Ln Apt A
Redding CA 96003

Call Sign: KF6EMO
Linda A Barnes
20623 Lassen View Ln
Redding CA 96002

Call Sign: WA6BSA
John W Barnes
20623 Lassen View Ln
Redding CA 96002

Call Sign: KG6NHS
Clayton R Bartlett
20646 Lassenview Ln
Redding CA 96002

Call Sign: KG6AXB
Gary J Vaughan II
1544 Lavender Way
Redding CA 96003

Call Sign: AF6EH
Donald J Buckley III
1747 Lazelle Ct
Redding CA 96002

Call Sign: KF6QMU
Chris D Rudolph
1774 Lazelle Ct
Redding CA 96002

Call Sign: KG6SHE
Donald J Buckley III
1786 Lazelle Ct
Redding CA 96002

Call Sign: KI6JGY
Donald J Buckley III
1786 Lazelle Ct
Redding CA 96002

Call Sign: KJ6NWP
Thomas M Simpson
79 Leisha Ln
Redding CA 96001

Call Sign: KJ6EYT
Criselda Rodriguez-
Simpson
879 Leisha Ln
Redding CA 96001

Call Sign: KC6OMP
Duane Tomei
1154 Lema Rd
Redding CA 96003

Call Sign: WB6JOM
Donald Hascall II
20278 Leon Ln
Redding CA 96003

Call Sign: KE6GVD
James S Kennedy
620 Lincoln St
Redding CA 96001

Call Sign: WB6NPN
Robert Wilson
19992 Lois Ln
Redding CA 96003

Call Sign: KA7OXN
Alf G Speaker
885 Loma St Apt 1
Redding CA 96003

Call Sign: KF6IKA
Neil R Moore
1715 Lori Ln
Redding CA 96002

Call Sign: W6NCE
Donald C Popp
1028 Lorraine
Redding CA 96001

Call Sign: KE6ALE
Terry J Antrim
12883 Los Osos St
Redding CA 96003

Call Sign: KG6CRZ
William W Stuart
20038 Lowry Ln
Redding CA 96003

Call Sign: W6BEG
Robert W Adams
6597 Lucerne Ct
Redding CA 96001

Call Sign: W6DKC
George B Hood
4451 1 Lynbrook Loop
Redding CA 96003

Call Sign: W6ON
Stanley R Clewett
4327 Lynbrook Loop 1
Redding CA 96003

Call Sign: KG6FOI
Kenneth L Stephens
11671 Mae Ln
Redding CA 96003

Call Sign: KG6BPO
Steven A Mena
3778 Magnums Way
Redding CA 96003

Call Sign: N6SPU
Harry E Starr
3370 Magnums Way 2
Redding CA 960032261

Call Sign: K6TUG
James K Samuels
592 Mammoth Path
Redding CA 96003

Call Sign: KD6KQY
Genevieve A Finneran
1251 Manatowa Ct
Redding CA 960025060

Call Sign: KF7RA
Michael F Burton
12277 Manzanoaks Dr
Redding CA 96003

Call Sign: KJ6HJT
Edward J Puchalski
4696 Maple Trl
Redding CA 96003

Call Sign: KB6VPX
Steven R Thomas
2306 Marilyn Ave
Redding CA 96002

Call Sign: KA6OWS
Donald G Showalter
2405 Marion Ct
Redding CA 96001

Call Sign: KE6EIG
Robert D Wells
1488 Mariposa Ct
Redding CA 96003

Call Sign: KB6CHY
Peter H Baar
566 Markwood Dr
Redding CA 960021911

Call Sign: N6UAF
Richard B Brimhall
1700 Marlene Ave
Redding CA 96002

Call Sign: WB6CUX
William M Hendricks
2041 Marlene Ave
Redding CA 96002

Call Sign: W6WMH
William M Hendricks
2041 Marlene Ave
Redding CA 96002

Call Sign: K6KHS
Robert F Chambers
21065 Mars Ln
Redding CA 96003

Call Sign: K6LLS
Dorotha E Chambers
21065 Mars Ln
Redding CA 96003

Call Sign: KF6KJL
Nancy Cardoza
2133 Martian Way
Redding CA 96002

Call Sign: N6HDC
Lawrence E Cardoza
2133 Martian Way
Redding CA 96002

Call Sign: KI6OSC
Christopher E Cardoza
2133 Martian Way
Redding CA 96002

Call Sign: KF6RAG
Kenny C Crall
597 Martinique Cir
Redding CA 96003

Call Sign: KG6AIA
Andrew B Witham
7022 Marvin Trl
Redding CA 96001

Call Sign: KC7KUU
Nancy J Quirus
1950 Mary Lake Dr
Redding CA 960015618

Call Sign: KF6ICH
Michael A Garland
4464 Mayvane Dr
Redding CA 96001

Call Sign: KJ6DMQ
Dale E Hackney
22139 Meadow Vista Way
Redding CA 96003

Call Sign: KI6WAH
Jerald M Fikes
1900 Meadowbrrok Dr
Redding CA 96001

Call Sign: WA6RGF
L Gene Davidson
11442 Menlo Way
Redding CA 96003

Call Sign: N6VSO
John Juul
11442 Menlo Way
Redding CA 96003

Call Sign: KI6OMY
Lavaughn Bishop
2077 Merle Dr
Redding CA 96001

Call Sign: N6OEQ
Arthur R Nelson
1450 Mesa St
Redding CA 96001

Call Sign: KE6IXF
Debbie E Widmer
830 Middle St
Redding CA 960032229

Call Sign: KE6IXE
Owen K Widmer
830 Middle St
Redding CA 960032229

Call Sign: KJ6DMN
John P Greaves Jr
15742 Middletown Park
Redding CA 96001

Call Sign: KI6GFU
Jay F Helms
15090 Middletown Park
Dr
Redding CA 96001

Call Sign: W6HHT
Jay F Helms

15090 Middletown Park
Dr
Redding CA 96001

Call Sign: KB6VPH
Howard C Holcomb
2163 Miller St
Redding CA 96001

Call Sign: KF6CCE
Janet E Peterson
3213 Miramar Way
Redding CA 96001

Call Sign: KF6DDE
Chris E Peterson
3213 Miramar Way
Redding CA 96001

Call Sign: K6PTT
Paul E Peterson
3213 Miramar Way
Redding CA 960015849

Call Sign: KE6QMX
Troy E Nicolls
22300 Mirror Valley Ln
Redding CA 96003

Call Sign: KC6IWL
Joel D Lockwood
999 Mission De Oro
Redding CA 96003

Call Sign: K7CVC
Chris Cassata
690 Monardas Dr
Redding CA 96002

Call Sign: KI6SUP
Chris Cassata
690 Monardas Dr
Redding CA 96002

Call Sign: WB6NDL

David R McCusker
429 Moonstone Way
Redding CA 96003

Call Sign: KI6OMU
Gary D Sanda
279 Mora Ct
Redding CA 96003

Call Sign: KG6ZSG
Ronnie D Gregory
1046 Mountain Shadows
Blvd
Redding CA 96003

Call Sign: KJ6NVA
Patricia A Heinsohn
15270 Mountain Shadows
Dr
Redding CA 96001

Call Sign: KQ6KM
Shaun P Garland
4464 Moyvane Dr
Redding CA 96001

Call Sign: WB6ILF
Gary J Reitemeyer
1871 N Bechelli Ln
Redding CA 96002

Call Sign: KF6KJM
Mark C Allen
4575 Nantucket Dr
Redding CA 96001

Call Sign: K6MCA
Mark C Allen
4575 Nantucket Dr
Redding CA 96001

Call Sign: KI6WAW
Douglas B Mcmullin
15849 Nauvoo Trl
Redding CA 96001

Call Sign: KI6WAJ
Stephanie K Halpenny
15849 Nauvoo Trl
Redding CA 96001

Call Sign: WA6WLT
Larry R Hansen
3633 Navajo Ct
Redding CA 96001

Call Sign: KF6YGB
John T Vestal III
3652 Navajo Ct
Redding CA 96001

Call Sign: KE6EIE
Ellen J Schjoth
2269 Nebula St
Redding CA 96002

Call Sign: KC6TRR
Jeremy D Hollyman
2442 Nebula St
Redding CA 96002

Call Sign: KI6WBA
Linda M Pickenpaugh
2066 Neptune Terr
Redding CA 96002

Call Sign: KG6ORF
Leslie H Morgan
294 Newport Dr
Redding CA 96001

Call Sign: KJ6EYS
Stephen W Dean Sr
16335 North St
Redding CA 96001

Call Sign: KC6SNT
Richard L Hazen
201 Northpoint Dr Apt 4
Redding CA 96003

Call Sign: W6LTL
George G Zoll
830 Northridge Dr
Redding CA 96001

Call Sign: KE6FJN
Robert H Mercer
1869 O Conner Ave
Redding CA 96001

Call Sign: WD9EHY
Louis E Sommerville
2084 O Conner Ave
Redding CA 96001

Call Sign: KF6BNA
Michael W Diefenderfer
3328 Oak Haven Ct
Redding CA 96002

Call Sign: W6GAT
Edward Gilbert
2101 Oak Leaf Land
Redding CA 96001

Call Sign: WA7MOA
Phyllis A Whitman
12098 Oak Leaf Ln
Redding CA 96003

Call Sign: KG6YNT
Curtis N Christensen
12106 Oak Leaf Ln
Redding CA 96003

Call Sign: N6ECB
Kathryn A Getzinger
1760 Oak Mesa Ln
Redding CA 96003

Call Sign: N6LKQ
Daniel J Getzinger
1760 Oak Mesa Ln
Redding CA 96003

Call Sign: KE6JUP
Terry P Healey
1524 Oakdale Ln
Redding CA 96002

Call Sign: KC5CZL
Allen D Irwin
995 Oakmont Dr
Redding CA 960039027

Call Sign: KD6TYC
Raymond L Dean
3390 Old Lantern Dr
Redding CA 96003

Call Sign: KE6QNH
Tom P Templeton
9811 Old Oregon Tr
Redding CA 96003

Call Sign: WA6OUU
Ben D Jones
13553 Old Oregon Trl
Redding CA 96003

Call Sign: KJ6EYO
Terry R Politi
8963 Onley Park Dr
Redding CA 96001

Call Sign: KI6WAD
David H Avery
19900 Orfino Ln
Redding CA 96003

Call Sign: KF6BMY
Donald C Campbell
3600 Oro St
Redding CA 96001

Call Sign: WD6FAP
Billy J Clayborn
3815 Oro St
Redding CA 96001

Call Sign: N6IKP
Virginia L Wulff
3880 Oro St
Redding CA 96001

Call Sign: KA6D
Earl G Wulff Jr
3880 Oro St
Redding CA 960012940

Call Sign: KI6WAZ
Timothy M Persinger
3235 Panorama Dr
Redding CA 96003

Call Sign: KA6TEZ
Maureen C Murphy
2155 Park Marina Dr 37
Redding CA 96001

Call Sign: N6RBM
Norma G Seeley
569 Parsons Dr
Redding CA 96002

Call Sign: N6TEU
Sterling L Seeley
569 Parsons Dr
Redding CA 96002

Call Sign: N6URS
Pamela D Sheridan
4241 Pasatiempo Ct
Redding CA 96002

Call Sign: N6BBL
David W Sheridan
4241 Pasatiempo Ct
Redding CA 96002

Call Sign: KF6VIT
Robert A Brink
6528 Paso Dr
Redding CA 96001

Call Sign: KC6IWJ
Joseph M Paramo
3744 Pegasus
Redding CA 96002

Call Sign: KA6WGS
Peggy D Moore
2066 Penn Dr
Redding CA 96002

Call Sign: KD6MSK
Kent A Beams
2548 Phil Ct
Redding CA 96002

Call Sign: KD6OSH
Donna M Beams
2548 Phil Ct
Redding CA 96002

Call Sign: W6HWC
John B Gramyk
3143 Pinehaven Ct
Redding CA 96003

Call Sign: W7DBZ
David J Bradley
4344 Pintail Dr
Redding CA 96001

Call Sign: KC6CLK
David J Bradley
4344 Pintail Dr
Redding CA 96001

Call Sign: K4VGE
Willis C Lynch Jr
7043 Pit Rd
Redding CA 96001

Call Sign: KI6WBF
Michael S Rainey
16077 Plateau Cir
Redding CA 96001

Call Sign: KI6WBE
Marcene J Rainey
16077 Plateau Cir
Redding CA 96001

Call Sign: KE6EFW
Laurence Waugh
7599 Platinum Way
Redding CA 96001

Call Sign: KF6FPI
Wayne G Rathe
8390 Potosi Rd
Redding CA 96001

Call Sign: KF6HFI
Laura K Rathe
8390 Potosi Rd
Redding CA 96001

Call Sign: WB6JXJ
Michael M George
20546 Prairie Ln
Redding CA 96002

Call Sign: KF6EMM
Luke Marvin G Smith
20634 Prairie Ln
Redding CA 96002

Call Sign: KB6WEC
Paul H Stein
15299 Prospect Dr
Redding CA 96001

Call Sign: W6PHS
Paul H Stein
15299 Prospect Dr
Redding CA 96001

Call Sign: WA6FYP
Michael J Turner
15537 Prospect Dr
Redding CA 96001

Call Sign: KJ6NVF
Michael E Swim
11478 Quartz Hill Rd
Redding CA 96003

Call Sign: KE6MNO
Fred L Millard
12114 Quartz Hill Rd
Redding CA 96003

Call Sign: WA6TWW
Kenneth F Camozzi
2614 Queens Way
Redding CA 96001

Call Sign: WB6WCU
Elizabeth R Cosca
21027 Rae Ln
Redding CA 96003

Call Sign: KI6PSD
Mark A Crumpton
21194 Rae Ln
Redding CA 96003

Call Sign: KF6CCA
Holly L Ware
21195 Rae Ln
Redding CA 96003

Call Sign: KO6HS
Gerald J Ware
21195 Rae Ln
Redding CA 96003

Call Sign: KF6DWE
Danner T Hodgson
2688 Rainbow Ln
Redding CA 96002

Call Sign: W6HSN
Grant E Bohm
15701 Ranchland Dr
Redding CA 96001

Call Sign: KF6QMW
Al J Jensen
5373 Rancho Vista Way
Redding CA 96002

Call Sign: KF6YER
Joann M Jensen
5373 Rancho Vista Way
Redding CA 96002

Call Sign: W6HEH
Vern A Gerboth
14817 Ravine Rd
Redding CA 96003

Call Sign: KD6LOM
William D Rowe
1759 Record Ln
Redding CA 96001

Call Sign: KD6HVW
Evelyn N Phillips
8441 Redbank Rd
Redding CA 96001

Call Sign: KN6WB
Frank E Phillips
8441 Redbank Rd
Redding CA 96001

Call Sign: N0CIE
Bernard E Northrup
861 Redwood Blvd
Redding CA 96003

Call Sign: KC6GFR
Larry J Kent
701 Redwood Blvd 46
Redding CA 96003

Call Sign: W6BJH
Theodore C Davis
11595 Ridgewood Rd
Redding CA 96003

Call Sign: K6SDX
Shasta Dx And Contest
Club
11595 Ridgewood Rd
Redding CA 96003

Call Sign: KI6YVR
Larry J Smith
867 Rincon Way
Redding CA 96003

Call Sign: KJ6RFG
John B Maich
395 Rio St
Redding CA 96001

Call Sign: KJ6RFF
Rudy W Maich
395 Rio St
Redding CA 96001

Call Sign: KD6IKL
Thomas F Riley
4375 Rising Mist Cir
Redding CA 96001

Call Sign: KE6NWD
Rodney N Pedersen
4890 Rising River Ct
Redding CA 96002

Call Sign: K6KAV
Kristyanna Free
6870 Riverland Dr 67
Redding CA 96002

Call Sign: KI6MOZ
Muriel J Locke
6934 Riverland Dr 9
Redding CA 96002

Call Sign: KI6UNQ
Nicole J Bonkrude
6940 Riverside Dr

Redding CA 96001

Call Sign: K6VVY
William K Rogers
3800 Riverview Dr
Redding CA 960013928

Call Sign: KB6YFS
Bruce G Winship
3800 Riverview Dr
Redding CA 96001

Call Sign: KE6YZA
Mark L Perreault
1266 Riviera Dr
Redding CA 96001

Call Sign: WB6QNJ
Melvin L Riffel
1513 Riviera Dr
Redding CA 96001

Call Sign: KF6VSB
Mark L Kendall
7380 Robles Dr
Redding CA 96002

Call Sign: KD6KOV
Millie M Webb
5481 Rosswood Ln
Redding CA 96001

Call Sign: KG6FSZ
Kenneth E Bird
3744 Rushmore Dr
Redding CA 96001

Call Sign: KD6TWE
Laura L West
2715 Russell St
Redding CA 96001

Call Sign: KI6WBQ
Susan R Whitaker
3080 Sacramento Dr

Redding CA 96001

Call Sign: KE6HUN
Dee E Wintle
3150 Sacramento Dr
Redding CA 96001

Call Sign: KC6GEP
Mark S Krauska
3171 Sacramento Dr
Redding CA 96001

Call Sign: KF6UFG
Christopher N Fryer
4015 Saffron Way
Redding CA 96002

Call Sign: KE6QNA
Chester E Randall
637 Saint Marks St
Redding CA 960031835

Call Sign: KE6GVB
Robert H Pugh
1635 Santa Fe Ave
Redding CA 96003

Call Sign: WB6PEN
Robert E Lee
3435 Santa Rosa Way Apt
1
Redding CA 96003

Call Sign: KD6MTV
Michael W Bonner
4148 Saratoga Dr
Redding CA 96002

Call Sign: KC6RTA
Daniel K Davis
4643 Saratoga Dr
Redding CA 96002

Call Sign: KD6SW
Richard C Trautmann

19518 Scenic Rail Dr
Redding CA 96003

Call Sign: KI6WAI
Lisa K Garren
3194 School St
Redding CA 96002

Call Sign: KK6WD
James H Goodman
2955 Shasta St
Redding CA 96001

Call Sign: WA7YQA
Jerold D Aaronson
2810 Shasta St
Redding CA 96001

Call Sign: KI6KPE
Richard L Lenz
2551 Shasta View Dr
Redding CA 960021538

Call Sign: K1KPE
Richard L Lenz
2551 Shasta View Dr
Redding CA 960021538

Call Sign: WA6QJM
Thomas M Carlson
3317 Sherman Way
Redding CA 960031718

Call Sign: W6GQT
Ralph W Miller
2172 Solar Way
Redding CA 96002

Call Sign: KK6VB
Jo Anne M Last
1748 Somerset Ct
Redding CA 96002

Call Sign: W6GSQ
Albert G Last Sr

1748 Somerset Ct
Redding CA 96002

14673 Spring Branch Rd
Redding CA 96003

2826 Starlight Blvd
Redding CA 96001

Call Sign: KI6ONO
Janice L Galloway
4328 Songbird Way
Redding CA 96001

Call Sign: W6HUK
Joseph C Cosca
821 St Marks St 1
Redding CA 96003

Call Sign: KI6SUO
Karen Bronson
951 State St
Redding CA 96001

Call Sign: KI6OMV
Diana L Stockwell
4328 Songbird Way
Redding CA 96001

Call Sign: K6RQC
Elizabeth R Cosca
821 St Marks St 1
Redding CA 96003

Call Sign: KI6IRB
Mick A Waligorski
4255 Stonewalk Ct C
Redding CA 96003

Call Sign: KD6OMS
Kenneth O Kirby
2172 Sophy Pl
Redding CA 96003

Call Sign: W6RAE
Elizabeth R Cosca
821 St Marks St 1
Redding CA 96003

Call Sign: N6ATE
Donald F Lafferty
11410 Suggie Ln
Redding CA 96003

Call Sign: WA6BKN
Kenneth C Bower
4325 Sounding Brook Ct
Redding CA 96001

Call Sign: N6CPH
Douglas L Guy
768 St Thomas Pky
Redding CA 96003

Call Sign: KC6GEO
Barbara A Hild
3510 Summit Dr
Redding CA 96001

Call Sign: KI6OUZ
Tyler I Tillson
905 South St
Redding CA 96001

Call Sign: KJ6EZI
Herbant S Mahal
3353 Stanford Dr
Redding CA 96003

Call Sign: WA6KOQ
Timothy A Brock
19757 Sunbeam Cir
Redding CA 96003

Call Sign: W6ZQD
Robert L Howland
14673 Spring Branch Rd
Redding CA 96003

Call Sign: N6RNL
Hugh R Tenney
2380 Star Dr
Redding CA 96001

Call Sign: WA6PXT
Clifford D Brock
19757 Sunbeam Cir
Redding CA 96003

Call Sign: KI6WAQ
Edna L Huff
14673 Spring Branch Rd
Redding CA 96003

Call Sign: KD6JJI
Robert D Terrell
2975 Starburst Dr
Redding CA 96001

Call Sign: KI6TRM
Donald F Lafferty
1052 Sunriver Ln
Redding CA 96001

Call Sign: KI6WAR
William J Huff
14673 Spring Branch Rd
Redding CA 96003

Call Sign: KD6JJJ
Donna S Terrell
2975 Starburst Dr
Redding CA 96001

Call Sign: WA6IEO
James R McKeown
3834 Sunwood Dr
Redding CA 960024902

Call Sign: N6WAR
William J Huff

Call Sign: KI6PRU
Venicia D Cuara-Shelton

Call Sign: WA6IO
James R McKeown

3834 Sunwood Dr
Redding CA 960024902

Call Sign: KG6GAJ
Northern Amateur Satellite
Association
3834 Sunwood Dr
Redding CA 960024902

Call Sign: NA0SA
Northern Amateur Satellite
Association
3834 Sunwood Dr
Redding CA 960024902

Call Sign: KE6WKC
Shasta Cascade Amateur
Radio Society
3834 Sunwood Dr
Redding CA 96002

Call Sign: NC6SV
Shasta Cascade Amateur
Radio Society
3834 Sunwood Dr
Redding CA 96002

Call Sign: KE6CHO
Western Amateur Radio
Repeater And Echolink
Association
3834 Sunwood Dr
Redding CA 96002

Call Sign: KD6MTU
Guy S Lemke
4486 Swallowtail Ct
Redding CA 96003

Call Sign: KI6QBS
Western Amateur Radio
Repeater And Echolink
Association
4486 Swallowtail Ct
Redding CA 96003

Call Sign: KG6TYQ
Daniel J Lemke
4486 Swallowtail Ct
Redding CA 96003

Call Sign: W3FF
Budd L Drummond
2390 Templeton Dr
Redding CA 96002

Call Sign: KG6NVM
Chris D Drummond
2390 Templeton Dr
Redding CA 96002

Call Sign: KF6YIT
Robert J Wilson
7597 Terra Linda Way
Redding CA 96003

Call Sign: KB6IPP
David A Snary
7392 Terralinda Way
Redding CA 96003

Call Sign: KB6NOS
Nicholas J Webb
16314 Texas Springs Rd
Redding CA 96001

Call Sign: KI6WBP
Taylor M Webb
16314 Texas Springs Rd
Redding CA 96001

Call Sign: KD6QBA
Lee A Sherman
13698 Thunder Dr
Redding CA 96003

Call Sign: KG6CUR
James M Yates
1914 Tiburon Dr
Redding CA 96003

Call Sign: N6DGC
Ronald D Thompson
13330 Tierra Heights
Redding CA 96003

Call Sign: KA6RON
Ronald D Thompson
13330 Tierra Heights
Redding CA 96003

Call Sign: KD6EUL
Richard A Villacres Jr
13220 Tierra Heights Rd
Redding CA 96003

Call Sign: KE6GPG
Gary D Sasenbery
3421 Topaz Ct
Redding CA 96001

Call Sign: KE6VSH
Sharon D Gilmore
3375 Toro Way
Redding CA 96002

Call Sign: KD6SNM
Shirley A Schroeder
3471 Toro Way
Redding CA 96002

Call Sign: KD6SNO
Ralph L Schroeder Jr
3471 Toro Way
Redding CA 96002

Call Sign: KJ6HJQ
Richard D Yoder
1874 Trailwood Ct
Redding CA 960032175

Call Sign: KI6OVA
Ryan Perez
2937 Tropicana Ct
Redding CA 96003

Call Sign: KD6IRQ
Tommy R Stinson
1912 Trumpet Dr
Redding CA 96003

Call Sign: KE6VFP
Raymond L Chilton
1922 Trumpet Dr
Redding CA 96003

Call Sign: W6HWQ
Lillian H Ray
481 Twin View Blvd Sp
48
Redding CA 96003

Call Sign: N0HHO
Judy D Perry
4672 Underwood
Redding CA 96003

Call Sign: KG6G
James T Hull Sr
4617 Underwood Dr
Redding CA 96003

Call Sign: KF6YGA
David A Hudson
1857 Vale Dr
Redding CA 96002

Call Sign: KA6JBG
David E Homewood
1040 Valli Ct
Redding CA 96003

Call Sign: KS8CTR
Kenneth E Swanson
560 Vansicklen Way
Redding CA 96049

Call Sign: KF6MSL
Harvey T Wetterstrom III
2007 Vega St

Redding CA 96002

Call Sign: KC6IWM
Jason W Wilburn
2463 Venus Way
Redding CA 96002

Call Sign: WB6HNF
John E Schlenz
1713 Veracruz Trl
Redding CA 96003

Call Sign: KF6CCD
Philip E Hernandez
20076 Veruita Dr
Redding CA 96003

Call Sign: KI6PRZ
Jeffery A Nelson
2773 Victor Av
Redding CA 96002

Call Sign: W6AEK
Ronald B Greenberg
2741 Victor Ave
Redding CA 960021431

Call Sign: KJ6BSV
Garnet G Reinhardt
1640 Victor Ave 48
Redding CA 96003

Call Sign: KJ6AID
Jeromy S Reinhardt
1640 Victor Ave 48
Redding CA 96003

Call Sign: KJ6HJS
Robert D Epperson
430 Viewpoint Dr
Redding CA 96003

Call Sign: N6VYU
Melissa K Epperson
430 Viewpoint Rd

Redding CA 96003

Call Sign: WW6AA
James T Hull Sr
1700 Vinson Dr
Redding CA 96003

Call Sign: KI6WBI
Gordon L Robbins
327 Vintage Path
Redding CA 96003

Call Sign: KB6OHP
William N Johnson
340 Vintage Path
Redding CA 96003

Call Sign: KI6PRS
Denise R Rowlett
2225 Vista Ave
Redding CA 96001

Call Sign: WB9EEK
Paul B Kelley
18118 Vista Pine Ln
Redding CA 96003

Call Sign: KE6DOD
Kenneth R Ely
19003 W Niles Ln
Redding CA 96002

Call Sign: KJ6NVC
Garland W Dirks
11519 Wales Ct
Redding CA 96003

Call Sign: KF6KJO
Arthur R Steinbach Jr
17616 Walker Mine Rd
Redding CA 96003

Call Sign: WA6BXF
Haney Pack
17857 Walker Mine Rd

Redding CA 960030167

Call Sign: KD6TVD
Douglas R Hampton
2045 Walnut Ave
Redding CA 96001

Call Sign: KC6OMC
Kenneth B Williams
12039 Wanda Ln
Redding CA 96003

Call Sign: KF6WXH
Silas S Warner
17648 Warwick Pl
Redding CA 96099

Call Sign: KF4LPK
Adam B Short
3791 Westgate Ave
Redding CA 96001

Call Sign: KF6AYV
John T Vestal II
4410 Westside Rd 55
Redding CA 96001

Call Sign: WB6NTU
John R Ahlf
10620 Whistleberry Way
Redding CA 96003

Call Sign: W6CE
John R Ahlf
10620 Whistleberry Way
Redding CA 96003

Call Sign: KF6VAN
David L Grossman
1606 Whistling Dr
Redding CA 96003

Call Sign: KG6ZCE
Elaine L Grossman
1606 Whistling Dr

Redding CA 96003

Call Sign: KE6BEF
William J Corum
1664 Whistling Dr
Redding CA 96003

Call Sign: KI6UNO
Vicki D Bayster
4474 White River Dr
Redding CA 96003

Call Sign: KA6UNG
Robert P Brooks
2098 Wilder Dr
Redding CA 96001

Call Sign: K6MIA
Henry C Woodrum
200 Wilshire Dr
Redding CA 96001

Call Sign: WR6TV
Redding Repeater And Atv
Society
3289 Wilshire Dr
Redding CA 96002

Call Sign: W6QWN
Charles M Seevers Jr
3289 Wilshire Dr
Redding CA 96002

Call Sign: K6ICZ
Harold C Moore
3336 Wilshire Dr
Redding CA 96002

Call Sign: KD6GBV
Kenneth R McKinzie
2831 Wilson Ave
Redding CA 96002

Call Sign: KG6LEG
John P Zubro

2740 Wilson Ave 2
Redding CA 96002

Call Sign: WA6KZS
John P Zubro
2740 Wilson Ave 2
Redding CA 96002

Call Sign: WA6LCT
Kathleen K Lockhart
3050 Winding Way
Redding CA 96003

Call Sign: NT6E
Reva J Bromwell
3110 Winding Way
Redding CA 96003

Call Sign: K6BCK
Janet M Belluso
1575 Wisconsin Ave
Redding CA 96001

Call Sign: WR6ED
Edward F Belluso
1575 Wisconsin Ave
Redding CA 96001

Call Sign: NN6AA
Edward F Belluso
1575 Wisconsin Ave
Redding CA 96001

Call Sign: WA6ED
Edward F Belluso
1575 Wisconsin Ave
Redding CA 96001

Call Sign: KT6LA
Edward F Belluso
1575 Wisconsin Ave
Redding CA 96001

Call Sign: NT6NT
Edward F Belluso

1575 Wisconsin Ave
Redding CA 96001

Call Sign: N6BCK
Edward F Belluso
1575 Wisconsin Ave
Redding CA 96001

Call Sign: NN6AA
Edward F Belluso
1575 Wisconsin Ave
Redding CA 96001

Call Sign: WA6JAN
Janet M Belluso
1575 Wisconsin Ave
Redding CA 96001

Call Sign: KV6AMP
Janet M Belluso
1575 Wisconsin Ave
Redding CA 96001

Call Sign: WA6JAN
Janet M Belluso
1575 Wisconsin Ave
Redding CA 96001

Call Sign: WS6IX
Oldtimers On Six
1575 Wisconsin Ave
Redding CA 96001

Call Sign: KR7CR
Oldtimers On Six
1575 Wisconsin Ave
Redding CA 96001

Call Sign: WT6OT
Oldtimers On Six
1575 Wisconsin Ave
Redding CA 96001

Call Sign: KJ6QYD
Shasta Bally ARC

1575 Wisconsin Ave
Redding CA 96001

Call Sign: KR7CR
Shasta Bally ARC
1575 Wisconsin Ave
Redding CA 96001

Call Sign: KG6TJK
Shasta Bally Amateur
Radio System
1575 Wisconsin Ave
Redding CA 96001

Call Sign: WS6BRS
Shasta Bally Amateur
Radio System
1575 Wisconsin Ave
Redding CA 96001

Call Sign: KR7CR
Shasta Bally Amateur
Radio System
1575 Wisconsin Ave
Redding CA 96001

Call Sign: W6FZI
Everett G Ackerman
1715 Wisconsin Ave
Redding CA 96001

Call Sign: KI6OWH
David R Guglielmetti
263 Woodhill Dr
Redding CA 96003

Call Sign: AC6LF
Claudia D Yerion
2891 Wyndham Ln
Redding CA 96001

Call Sign: KI6IAP
Claudia L Yerion
2891 Wyndham Ln
Redding CA 96001

Call Sign: AC6LF
Claudia L Yerion
2891 Wyndham Ln
Redding CA 96001

Call Sign: KI6OWI
Stephen A Williams
2935 Wyndham Ln
Redding CA 96001

Call Sign: KI6PSA
Brian E Connolly
1857 Yahi Ln
Redding CA 96002

Call Sign: KF6HBX
John E Draper
2518 Yana Ave
Redding CA 96002

Call Sign: WA6ASQ
Jack E Ehrlich
4362 Yellowstone Dr
Redding CA 96002

Call Sign: KD6DVA
Robert E Gley Sr
Redding CA 96049

Call Sign: WB5YDH
James B Holder
Redding CA 96099

Call Sign: KD6QAY
Kevin A Palm
Redding CA 96099

Call Sign: KA4VZZ
Roger C Van Arsdell
Redding CA 96099

Call Sign: N4FTZ
Marcia N Van Arsdell
Redding CA 96099

Call Sign: KA6LMJ
Patricia A Clayborn
Redding CA 96049

Call Sign: KG6URZ
Christopher J Capron
Redding CA 960990721

Call Sign: KJ6EZH
Rudolph L Carver
Redding CA 960493498

Call Sign: KG6VCT
Daniel L Clark
Redding CA 960990721

Call Sign: KI6WEX
George H Durfee Jr
Redding CA 960992276

Call Sign: KI6YVS
George H Durfee Jr
Redding CA 960992276

Call Sign: WR6F
George H Durfee Jr
Redding CA 960992276

Call Sign: K6KAF
Kristyanna Free
Redding CA 960990761

Call Sign: N6TWK
Edward L Huey Jr
Redding CA 960991062

Call Sign: KG6TYO
Joanna M Krieg
Redding CA 96099

Call Sign: K6KSS
Steven E Mosconi
Redding CA 960997333

Call Sign: KJ6BPG
Janel E Mosconi
Redding CA 96099

Call Sign: N6JEM
Janel E Mosconi
Redding CA 96099

Call Sign: K6KS
Steven E Mosconi
Redding CA 960997333

Call Sign: KG6ORC
William G Payne
Redding CA 96099

Call Sign: AE6LP
William G Payne
Redding CA 96099

Call Sign: WO7P
William G Payne
Redding CA 96099

Call Sign: KF6ZUO
Tom Pella
Redding CA 96099

Call Sign: KI6WBG
Gregor G Rill
Redding CA 96049

Call Sign: N6NEQ
Wilbur A Rouse
Redding CA 960493834

Call Sign: KJ6AIA
Joshua M Sanderson
Redding CA 960990457

Call Sign: N7LMV
Jeryl E Steinhardt
Redding CA 96001

Call Sign: WA6UWT

Harold A Stephens
Redding CA 96049

Call Sign: N2IFT
William C Stevens
Redding CA 960491897

Call Sign: KJ6EYM
Kenneth E Swanson
Redding CA 96049

Call Sign: KI6OMR
Bradford T Tillson
Redding CA 96049

Call Sign: KJ6FOE
Alexander T Turner
Redding CA 96099

Call Sign: KG6WGK
Jackie T Turner
Redding CA 96099

Call Sign: N6BOO
Jackie T Turner
Redding CA 96099

Call Sign: KG6WGD
Laureen Turner
Redding CA 96099

Call Sign: WE6ONE
Laureen Turner
Redding CA 96099

Call Sign: KD6SNH
Stephen K Wopschall
Redding CA 96049

FCC Amateur Radio Licenses in Redway

Call Sign: WA6GHI
Bernard D Hammer
5594 Briceland Thorn Rd

Redway CA 95560

Call Sign: KE6KKG
Gerald E Myers
Elk Ridge Rd
Redway CA 95560

Call Sign: KB6LAC
Mara J Rogers
1600 Miller Creek Rd
Redway CA 95560

Call Sign: N6STZ
William E Shoemaker
Redway CA 95560

Call Sign: KF6CYN
Bob J Howard
Redway CA 95560

Call Sign: KG6UCD
Peter Ryce
Redway CA 95560

Call Sign: KF6WLJ
Benjamin M Anderson
Redway CA 95560

Call Sign: KG6SXN
Victor B Anderson
Redway CA 95560

Call Sign: KF6LTU
Margaret Andrews
Redway CA 95560

Call Sign: KJ6KZN
Keith M Brooks
Redway CA 95560

Call Sign: KE6QQT
Bonnie K Burgess
Redway CA 95560

Call Sign: KI6IUL

Michael D Bynum
Redway CA 95560

Call Sign: KF6FQH
Iris R Carpenter
Redway CA 95560

Call Sign: KE6PAL
Fred D Davis
Redway CA 95560

Call Sign: KE6PAN
Deborah S Davis
Redway CA 95560

Call Sign: KE6VDD
Scott M Elliott
Redway CA 95560

Call Sign: KI6PHF
Marie A Etherton
Redway CA 95560

Call Sign: KJ6SSK
Milo Federico
Redway CA 95560

Call Sign: KE6VDB
Estelle R Fennell
Redway CA 95560

Call Sign: KG6BFS
Richard Fitzsimmons
Redway CA 95560

Call Sign: KE6KKH
Simon Frech
Redway CA 95560

Call Sign: KE6VDC
James F Fulton
Redway CA 95560

Call Sign: KE6QQU
Darin B George

Redway CA 95560

Call Sign: KF6WLK
Douglas C George
Redway CA 955600908

Call Sign: KF6KBU
Teresa L Green
Redway CA 95560

Call Sign: KF6KBV
Randy S Green
Redway CA 95560

Call Sign: KG6BJB
Patricia A Green
Redway CA 95560

Call Sign: KF6IZK
Michael C Grosser
Redway CA 95560

Call Sign: KI6DGX
John D Hardin
Redway CA 95560

Call Sign: KF6IBQ
Florian T Hass
Redway CA 95560

Call Sign: KI6IUP
Joe Hiney
Redway CA 95560

Call Sign: KG6FOE
David L Hudson
Redway CA 95560

Call Sign: AE6LJ
David L Hudson
Redway CA 95560

Call Sign: KI6IUM
Rena Kay
Redway CA 95560

Call Sign: KE6VDF
Philip A Kreider
Redway CA 95560

Call Sign: N6KIT
Jakie E Kreider
Redway CA 95560

Call Sign: KE6MLW
Rex L Leonard
Redway CA 95560

Call Sign: KI6IUQ
Theodore I Madsen
Redway CA 95560

Call Sign: KF6WLI
Jerry J Miller Jr
Redway CA 95560

Call Sign: KJ6HGB
John L Moore
Redway CA 95560

Call Sign: KE6MLV
Kevin C Muller
Redway CA 95560

Call Sign: KG6UCE
Michael J Nicklin
Redway CA 95560

Call Sign: KE6VDA
Fritz Oppliger
Redway CA 95560

Call Sign: KF6YAD
Mary Orazem
Redway CA 95560

Call Sign: KI6CQA
Donald J Orazem
Redway CA 95560

Call Sign: KJ6HGC
David R Ordonez
Redway CA 95560

Call Sign: KE6VDH
Arthur B Philpott
Redway CA 95560

Call Sign: KF6KBS
Leo J Power
Redway CA 95560

Call Sign: KI6IUR
Patricia Rae
Redway CA 95560

Call Sign: WB6ZYK
Samuel T Rappold
Redway CA 95560

Call Sign: KG6FOH
Rick G Silva
Redway CA 95560

Call Sign: KG6USG
Edward H Smith Jr
Redway CA 95560

Call Sign: KG6UCO
Southern Humboldt ARC
Redway CA 95560

Call Sign: W6HUM
Southern Humboldt ARC
Redway CA 95560

Call Sign: KI6ZQX
Isaac C Stafslien
Redway CA 95560

Call Sign: KJ6HGD
Malcolm Stebbins
Redway CA 95560

Call Sign: KJ6UPE

Danon S Taylor
Redway CA 95560

Call Sign: KF6IZI
Diana R Totten
Redway CA 95560

Call Sign: KF6YAE
Jonathan Vito
Redway CA 955601916

FCC Amateur Radio Licenses in Redwood Valley

Call Sign: KE6WGQ
Nathaniel Z Barre
7110 Black Bart Trl
Redwood Valley CA
95470

Call Sign: KE6UZR
Georgann Barre
7110 Black Bart Trl
Redwood Valley CA
954709409

Call Sign: KI6RJC
Theresa C Hanson
2300 Blackbart Ter
Redwood Valley CA
954706226

Call Sign: KD6CJU
Frank R Bednar
8951 Colony Dr
Redwood Valley CA
954709504

Call Sign: KF6QAQ
Phil A Saye
9500 Colony Dr
Redwood Valley CA
954709703

Call Sign: KE6CQI
Thomas W Applebee
3400 Colony Dr B
Redwood Valley CA
95470

Call Sign: KE6TIZ
Betty Budrow
7601 East Rd
Redwood Valley CA
95470

Call Sign: KF6LUV
Robert T Marsh
11301 East Rd
Redwood Valley CA
95470

Call Sign: KI6JTI
Nathan E Armstrong
431 Ellen Lynn Rd
Redwood Valley CA
95470

Call Sign: K6UMW
Terence S Kirk
5701 Kirk Dr
Redwood Valley CA
95470

Call Sign: KB6EJM
Doak McWilliams
9150 Laughlin Way
Redwood Valley CA
95470

Call Sign: KA6RKK
Elizabeth Marsden
1921 Mohawk Trl
Redwood Valley CA
954709547

Call Sign: WN6AOH
Albert L Marsden
1921 Mohawk Trl

Redwood Valley CA
954709753

Call Sign: KA6CXM
Robert R Rowe
1000 Rd A
Redwood Valley CA
95470

Call Sign: KA6EQT
Barbara J Rowe
1000 Rd A
Redwood Valley CA
95470

Call Sign: WA6HIS
David G Johnson
2350 Rd B
Redwood Valley CA
95470

Call Sign: KB6UWZ
Roger B Butler
2440 Rd B
Redwood Valley CA
95470

Call Sign: KI6HBC
Eddie T Alexander
2301 Rd E
Redwood Valley CA
95470

Call Sign: AF6AZ
Eddie T Alexander
2301 Rd E
Redwood Valley CA
95470

Call Sign: KI6ISD
Onnie S Alexander
2301 Rd E
Redwood Valley CA
95470

Call Sign: KG6GOC
Mary V Miller
2340 Rd E
Redwood Valley CA
954709517

Call Sign: KJ6IAF
Marybeth Kelly
2791 Rd E
Redwood Valley CA
954706325

Call Sign: KE6PEQ
Norman L R Hutchings
1101 Skyloah Way
Redwood Valley CA
95470

Call Sign: WA6L
Frank Le Port
1101 Skyloah Way
Redwood Valley CA
95470

Call Sign: KE6ZZI
Saundra J Leport
1101 Skyloah Way
Redwood Valley CA
95470

Call Sign: N7AZU
Paul C Shefchek
235 Terra Verde Ct
Redwood Valley CA
954709427

Call Sign: KD6IBE
Tracy L Oster
13500 Tomki Rd
Redwood Valley CA
95470

Call Sign: KD6BSQ
June B Oster
13501 Tomki Rd

Redwood Valley CA
95470

Call Sign: N6VZW
Wayne H Oster
13501 Tomki Rd
Redwood Valley CA
95470

Call Sign: KF6OWN
Michael J Donovan
15990 Tomki Rd
Redwood Valley CA
95470

Call Sign: KI6IDP
Bobbie R Tilley
9001 West Rd
Redwood Valley CA
95470

Call Sign: KI6IDO
John W Tilley
9001 West Rd
Redwood Valley CA
95470

Call Sign: KE6ACZ
Charles F Blake
9801 West Rd
Redwood Valley CA
95470

Call Sign: W6YBZ
Robert J Fetzer
11000 West Rd
Redwood Valley CA
95470

Call Sign: WB0USR
Bonnie Lee Andrews
Harriott
Redwood Valley CA
95470

Call Sign: KF6LUT
David A Ford
Redwood Valley CA
95470

Call Sign: KF6LUU
Russell D Ford
Redwood Valley CA
954700363

Call Sign: KF6QAU
Ina D Ford
Redwood Valley CA
954700363

Call Sign: KC6RCM
Douglas C Gomez
Redwood Valley CA
95470

Call Sign: KG6CTL
Terry P Montgomery
Redwood Valley CA
954700750

Call Sign: KE6CQK
John Ragland
Redwood Valley CA
954700143

Call Sign: KJ6IBP
John Ragland
Redwood Valley CA
954700143

Call Sign: WA6JBK
Alan L Spivak
Redwood Valley CA
954700831

Call Sign: WA6IGI
Larry A Steppe
Redwood Valley CA
95470

Call Sign: KN6ZW
Donald G Conness
351 1st Ave
Rio Dell CA 95562

Call Sign: KE6YLV
Bryan P Murphy
201 Center St 7
Rio Dell CA 95562

Call Sign: WB6MYF
Richard H Sweet
394 Cherry Ln
Rio Dell CA 95562

Call Sign: KF6KGB
Steven J Walstrom
762 Rigby Ave
Rio Dell CA 95562

Call Sign: KI6KEC
Dennis J Marks
1264 Riverside Dr
Rio Dell CA 95562

Call Sign: KI6KED
Matthew C Marks
1264 Riverside Dr
Rio Dell CA 95562

Call Sign: W6HPZ
Edward Obenchain
441 Second Ave
Rio Dell CA 95562

Call Sign: KF6LZR
Timothy R Marks
560 View Ave
Rio Dell CA 95562

Call Sign: KF6LZS
Seth A Marks

560 View Ave
Rio Dell CA 95562

Call Sign: KD6IFP
Stuart R Cox
Rio Dell CA 95562

Call Sign: WA6WPO
Herbert M Andersen
Rio Dell CA 95562

FCC Amateur Radio Licenses in Round Mountain

Call Sign: KC6ECF
Herschel A Reed
29650 Round Mountain Rd
Round Mountain CA 96084

Call Sign: WA6YEV
Lloyd H Cooper
Round Mountain CA 96084

Call Sign: KI6LNR
Richard K Everett
Round Mountain CA 96084

Call Sign: KJ6OAX
Girard F Klapatch
Round Mountain CA 96084

Call Sign: KF6MQQ
Tracey A Licerio
Round Mountain CA 96084

FCC Amateur Radio Licenses in Ruth

Call Sign: WA7TTE

Shirley A Parker
19320 Lower Mad River Rd
Ruth CA 95526

Call Sign: K6IOG
Thomas M Oczkewecz
1 Oskey Ln
Ruth CA 95526

Call Sign: KD6VZK
Carol J Oczkewecz
Ruth CA 95526

Call Sign: KF6BGP
David B Simon
Ruth CA 95526

FCC Amateur Radio Licenses in Salyer

Call Sign: WG0O
Gene L Albert
Salyer CA 95563

Call Sign: K6SBI
Curtis A Knight
Salyer CA 95563

Call Sign: WA6OJI
Pearl M Knight
Salyer CA 95563

Call Sign: WB6LCN
David A Peck
Salyer CA 95563

FCC Amateur Radio Licenses in Samoa

Call Sign: KE6SLU
Anthony L Keeling
2328 Lindstrom Ave
Samoa CA 95564

FCC Amateur Radio Licenses in Scotia

Call Sign: KD6DCQ
Bruce D Sweet
807 7th
Scotia CA 95565

Call Sign: KJ6HGK
Robert D Close
682 Stafford Rd
Scotia CA 95565

Call Sign: WB6MYH
Don J Thompson
Scotia CA 95565

Call Sign: KI6QYE
Allen M Gillespie
Scotia CA 95565

Call Sign: KJ6AUL
Deanna S Toczyl
Scotia CA 95565

FCC Amateur Radio Licenses in Scott Bar

Call Sign: KD6WZB
Robert L Mitchell
27141 Scott River Rd
Scott Bar CA 96085

Call Sign: KC7QIG
Yvonne J Chase
Scott Bar CA 960850009

Call Sign: N7LRV
Jack C Chase
Scott Bar CA 960850009

FCC Amateur Radio Licenses in Seiad Center

Call Sign: N7ZZG

Charles E McCormick
Seiad Valley CA 96086

Call Sign: K6ZJY
Ronald E Baggs
Seiad Valley CA 96086

Call Sign: WA6TGK
Anna M Baggs
Seiad Valley CA 96086

Call Sign: WA6ONS
William C Hetherington
Seiad Valley CA 96086

Call Sign: W6GXF
Edward M Prather
Seiad Valley CA 96086

Call Sign: KJ6UQJ
Claudia J Ross Mcleish
Seiad Valley CA 96086

FCC Amateur Radio Licenses in Shasta

Call Sign: KE6OUC
Lewis N Hawks
Granit Dr
Shasta CA 96087

Call Sign: AK6TP
Tom C Pottorff
15244 Iola Dr
Shasta CA 96087

Call Sign: WA6YNG
Theodore R Spliethof
11035 Stardust Ln
Shasta CA 96087

Call Sign: KR6EY
Theodore R Spliethof
11035 Stardust Ln
Shasta CA 96087

Call Sign: WA6YNG
Theodore R Spliethof
11035 Stardust Ln
Shasta CA 96087

Call Sign: W7LGA
Tom C Pottorff
Shasta CA 96087

Call Sign: N6XEO
Allen M Slinkard
Shasta CA 96087

Call Sign: KF6QCF
Jerry C Gilbert
Shasta CA 96087

Call Sign: KB6KY
William H Hoogstad
Shasta CA 96087

Call Sign: KJ6RFE
Helen M Hoogstad
Shasta CA 96087

Call Sign: KI6OMZ
Harold R Horner Jr
Shasta CA 96087

Call Sign: KD6BPS
David Horvitz
Shasta CA 96087

Call Sign: AG6HT
David Horvitz
Shasta CA 96087

Call Sign: KI6WBB
Carson L Pottorff
Shasta CA 96087

Call Sign: AK6U
Tom C Pottorff
Shasta CA 96087

Call Sign: KJ6NUY
Saedra A Wederbrook
Shasta CA 96087

Call Sign: KE6EIH
Richard M Wilde
Shasta CA 96087

Call Sign: W7RMW
Richard M Wilde
Shasta CA 96087

Call Sign: KB6RBR
Ronald C Williamson
Shasta CA 96087

FCC Amateur Radio Licenses in Shasta Lake

Call Sign: KA6AIF
Robert E Henry Mr.
3382 Avington Way
Shasta Lake CA 96019

Call Sign: WA6LYJ
Paul E Wargo
3169 Avington Wy
Shasta Lake CA 96019

Call Sign: KC6KZX
Eric A Cassano
4512 Boca St
Shasta Lake CA 96019

Call Sign: KD6GBU
Betty A Cassano
4512 Boca St
Shasta Lake CA 96019

Call Sign: KF6GJZ
Roger W Pelser
4740 Chico St
Shasta Lake CA 96019

Call Sign: KJ6NVI
Randal M Sloan Sr
5020 Chico St Shasta Lake
Shasta Lake CA 96019

Call Sign: KJ6HJK
David W Sheridan
3872 Coeur D Alene Ave
Shasta Lake CA 96019

Call Sign: KJ6HJL
Pamela D Sheridan
3872 Coeur D Alene Ave
Shasta Lake CA 96019

Call Sign: KM6WT
Mont H Pierce
3834 Craftsman Ave
Shasta Lake CA 96019

Call Sign: KG6AIB
Paul E Brown
1935 Deer Creek Rd
Shasta Lake CA 96019

Call Sign: K6KTK
Richard E Klee
4345 Epping Ct
Shasta Lake CA 96019

Call Sign: KC7CDS
Bobby E Cort
4366 Impression Way
Shasta Lake CA
960192201

Call Sign: KO6PC
Herbert A Hall
1432 Lassen Ave
Shasta Lake CA 96019

Call Sign: K4EQY
Jacob P Swartzendruber
4620 Orkney Pl
Shasta Lake CA 96019

Call Sign: AF6IR
Joseph F Polen
1533 Pine Flat
Shasta Lake CA 96019

Call Sign: W6ILD
John W Cokeley
18197 Ranchera Rd
Shasta Lake CA 96019

Call Sign: KG6KLT
Michael P Bennett
5033 Red Bluff Ave
Shasta Lake CA 96019

Call Sign: KJ6NUV
Edward S Larmour
4265 Shasta Dam Blvd
Shasta Lake CA 96019

Call Sign: WB6TOW
Terry E Huber
3304 Shasta Dam Blvd 171
Shasta Lake CA 96019

Call Sign: N6TDT
Daniel H Ellis
3304 Shasta Dam Blvd Sp
28
Shasta Lake CA 96019

Call Sign: KI6UNR
Gloria J Newton
1325 Washington Ave
Shasta Lake CA 96019

Call Sign: KF6LCN
Kent S Roberts
3826 Wellington Pl
Shasta Lake CA 96019

Call Sign: KB6EMC
James I Dyer Jr
3164 Westminster Ct

Shasta Lake CA 96019

Call Sign: KD6GBX
Donald E Mills
17591 Yellow Pine Rd
Shasta Lake CA 96019

Call Sign: WA6CEC
David C Ashcraft
Shasta Lake CA 96019

Call Sign: KA6GLJ
Kenneth R Blevins
Shasta Lake CA
960190263

Call Sign: WD6BFC
Charles E Dahlen
Shasta Lake CA
960791083

Call Sign: KI6CPS
Chris L Kobe
Shasta Lake CA 96019

Call Sign: KI6CPT
Bonnie Y Martin
Shasta Lake CA 96079

Call Sign: KE6HLU
Nancy S Street
Shasta Lake CA 96089

Call Sign: KE6KMD
James A Street
Shasta Lake CA 96089

Call Sign: KI6WBN
Anna L Taylor
Shasta Lake CA 96019

Call Sign: KI6WBO
Mary S Taylor
Shasta Lake CA 96019

FCC Amateur Radio Licenses in Shasta Lake City

Call Sign: KG6LXG
Vicki L Bennett
4145 Chico St
Shasta Lake City CA 96019

Call Sign: KJ6NUW
James N Stapp
4912 Vallecito St
Shasta Lake City CA 96019

Call Sign: KF4LPV
Robert A Herrick
4060 Willow St
Shasta Lake City CA 96019

FCC Amateur Radio Licenses in Shelter Cove

Call Sign: KI6PHE
Cheryl A Anthony
575 Ridge Rd
Shelter Cove CA 95589

Call Sign: KF6IZJ
Diana S Cistaro
21 Sea Crest Rd
Shelter Cove CA 95589

Call Sign: W6UGZ
Eugene P Beauchamp
156 Shaker Rd
Shelter Cove CA 955899112

FCC Amateur Radio Licenses in Shingletown

Call Sign: AC6DK

Carl L Weidert Jr
30646 100 Rd
Shingletown CA 96088

Call Sign: KG6QHS
Gary R Powell
8277 Amberwoods Pl
Shingletown CA 96088

Call Sign: WA6SEU
Philip E Richardson
30826 Bambi Dr
Shingletown CA 96088

Call Sign: N6BMN
Franklin H Woodruff
30917 Bambi Dr
Shingletown CA 96088

Call Sign: KG6MQJ
Donald R White
27600 Camino Real
Shingletown CA 96088

Call Sign: WB6AZK
Robert A Ashurst
7352 Cedar Meadows Ln
Shingletown CA 96088

Call Sign: WA6CUQ
Raymond E Leutwiler
7384 Chip N Dale
Shingletown CA 96088

Call Sign: WB6YJQ
Frank E Otterstein
7271 Clarabelle Ln
Shingletown CA
960889615

Call Sign: KJ6EOY
Michael D Dennis
27373 Colley Ln
Shingletown CA 96088

Call Sign: KE6IPN
Cynthia L Lovely
7546 Creekside Mobile Cir 11
Shingletown CA 96088

Call Sign: KI6YVQ
Christen Hansen
27672 Dersch Rd
Shingletown CA 96088

Call Sign: KJ6JHI
Deborah A Zaech
27765 Dersch Rd
Shingletown CA 96088

Call Sign: N6DAZ
Deborah A Zaech
27765 Dersch Rd
Shingletown CA 96088

Call Sign: KJ6JHJ
Robert M Zaech
27765 Dersch Rd
Shingletown CA 96088

Call Sign: N6RMZ
Robert M Zaech
27765 Dersch Rd
Shingletown CA 96088

Call Sign: KF6JBC
Hugh G Hunt
7208 Dogwood Dr
Shingletown CA 96088

Call Sign: KF6ED
Robert L Lyon
7208 Dogwood Dr
Shingletown CA 96088

Call Sign: KF6TTL
Denise G Gardner
7795 Eastmoore Rd
Shingletown CA 96088

Call Sign: KD6HVE
Daniel F Ugbinada Sr
27054 Hobart Rd
Shingletown CA 96088

Call Sign: KE6TJG
Donald J Hatten
28622 Hwy 44
Shingletown CA 96088

Call Sign: KE6JUQ
Val J Brown
29633 Hwy 44
Shingletown CA 96088

Call Sign: KE6UBS
Laura B Brown
29633 Hwy 44
Shingletown CA 96088

Call Sign: N7SEA
Val J Brown
29633 Hwy 44
Shingletown CA 96088

Call Sign: KG6VNW
Kelley J McKelvey
29897 Hwy 44
Shingletown CA 96088

Call Sign: KE6DOA
Stephen L Miner
29897 Hwy 44
Shingletown CA 96088

Call Sign: KJ6NVG
Onna M Perkins
36272 Hwy 44
Shingletown CA 96088

Call Sign: KB6QDF
Walter C Wright Sr
7564 Joda Rd
Shingletown CA 96088

Call Sign: KJ6C
Carl L Seguin
7712 Joda Rd
Shingletown CA 96088

Call Sign: KG6TXL
Shasta Tehama County
Ares
7712 Joda Rd
Shingletown CA 96088

Call Sign: W6STA
Shasta Tehama County
Ares
7712 Joda Rd
Shingletown CA 96088

Call Sign: KE6IUB
Jerry A Dickinson
27436 Lack Creek Dr
Shingletown CA 96088

Call Sign: W6SEH
Philip G Graham
8200 Lake McCumber Rd
Shingletown CA 96088

Call Sign: WA6YRF
Gisela E Graham
8200 Lake McCumber Rd
Shingletown CA 96088

Call Sign: KJ6AHY
Tamara T Martinez
7638 Linda Rd
Shingletown CA 96088

Call Sign: KF6EMQ
Arthur W Peaslee
33791 Meteorite Way
Shingletown CA 96088

Call Sign: KC6NJZ
Emery H Sunday
33795 Meteorite Way
Shingletown CA 96088

Call Sign: KI6PRT
Scott E Fraser
9453 Mountain Meadow
Rd
Shingletown CA 96088

Call Sign: KI6PRV
Tami J Fraser
9453 Mountain Meadow
Rd
Shingletown CA 96088

Call Sign: KE6DHO
William K Maloy
10294 Ritts Mill Rd
Shingletown CA 96088

Call Sign: WA6ZFP
Jerry E Wallace
8141 Shadee Lake Dr
Shingletown CA 96088

Call Sign: KF6VIR
Robert U Braithwaite
7169 Shasta Forest Dr
Shingletown CA 96088

Call Sign: KA6VFZ
James L Pope
7186 Shasta Forest Dr
Shingletown CA 96088

Call Sign: KB6BZL
Donald R Nichols
7377 Shasta Forest Dr
Shingletown CA 96088

Call Sign: KE6PCR
Margaret Y Nichols
7377 Shasta Forest Dr
Shingletown CA 96088

Call Sign: KE6RZW
Clifford L Kinzy
7472 Shasta Forest Dr
Shingletown CA 96088

Call Sign: KE6RZX
Jacquelyn A Kinzy
7472 Shasta Forest Dr
Shingletown CA 96088

Call Sign: KE6WDG
Darcie M Goldsmith
7494 Shasta Forest Dr
Shingletown CA 96088

Call Sign: KQ6DU
Ted G Goldsmith
7494 Shasta Forest Dr
Shingletown CA 96088

Call Sign: KB6APB
Floyd L Stacy Sr
35424 Shenandoah Dr
Shingletown CA 96088

Call Sign: WB6CAN
Phillip M Stacy
35432 Shenandoah Dr
Shingletown CA 96088

Call Sign: KE6HUM
Neil M Severtson
35482 Shenandoah Dr
Shingletown CA 96088

Call Sign: KN6Q
Raymond Bruun
30578 Sleepy Hollow Dr
Shingletown CA 96088

Call Sign: KI6NPN
Steven G Bruun
30578 Sleepy Hollow Dr
Shingletown CA 96088

Call Sign: K6SEV
Steven G Bruun
30578 Sleepy Hollow Dr
Shingletown CA 96088

Call Sign: KJ6QED
Scott G Buechel
8117 Star Trek Dr
Shingletown CA 96088

Call Sign: KF6LCM
Chris L Peaslee
8003 Starlite Pines Rd
Shingletown CA 96088

Call Sign: KF6ZUQ
Robert L Smith
8126 Starlite Pines Rd
Shingletown CA 96088

Call Sign: KJ6NVB
James G Perkins
36272 State Hwy 44
Shingletown CA 96088

Call Sign: KK6LI
Edward M Stack
7288 Tahoe Ln
Shingletown CA 96088

Call Sign: WO6P
Richard V Cloyd
9309 Thatcher Mill Rd
Shingletown CA 96088

Call Sign: KF6JAQ
Marlene K Macomber
32602 Three Oaks Ct
Shingletown CA 96088

Call Sign: KO6VM
Bennie D Macomber
32602 Three Oaks Ct
Shingletown CA 96088

Call Sign: W6BEN
Bennie D Macomber
32602 Three Oaks Ct
Shingletown CA 96088

Call Sign: KE6QMH
Stuart A Bailey
30575 Thumper Dr
Shingletown CA 96088

Call Sign: WA6MXH
Dar M Walker
30877 Thumper Dr
Shingletown CA
960889422

Call Sign: W6IO
Dar M Walker
30877 Thumper Dr
Shingletown CA
960889422

Call Sign: KJ6DMR
Jeremiah Mantooth
34531 Twin Cedars
Shingletown CA 96088

Call Sign: WB6JOX
Elroy L Smith
Shingletown CA 96088

Call Sign: KJ6FOC
Chris Atkinson
Shingletown CA 96088

Call Sign: KJ6NVD
Bruce D Ballard
Shingletown CA 96088

Call Sign: WB6CSH
Michael A Hamann
Shingletown CA 96088

Call Sign: W6JIL
Marshall P Kilrain

Shingletown CA 96088

Call Sign: KI6WAU
Charles L Knight II
Shingletown CA 96088

Call Sign: KE6POV
Peggy A Lynch
Shingletown CA 96088

Call Sign: KQ6CS
Steven A Lynch
Shingletown CA 96088

Call Sign: KI6KPF
James L Phillips
Shingletown CA 96088

Call Sign: N6FYP
Dennis J Pool
Shingletown CA 96088

Call Sign: KF6IJZ
David A Shelby
Shingletown CA 96088

Call Sign: N6PCL
Carlton M Tanner
Shingletown CA 96088

Call Sign: KG6FKM
Sarah R Williamson
Shingletown CA 96088

Call Sign: WK6U
Paul V Williamson
Shingletown CA 96088

Call Sign: WA6DSV
Anthony Zydycrn
Shingletown CA 96088

**FCC Amateur Radio
Licenses in Smith River**

Call Sign: KF6AAN
Fred L Morrison
100 Blue Jay Ct
Smith River CA 95567

Call Sign: KO6MK
Dorothy G Morrison
100 Blue Jay Ct
Smith River CA 95567

Call Sign: KJ6UOX
Kimbly L Craddock
12400 Hwy 101 N Sp 932
Smith River CA 95567

Call Sign: KA6PKX
Eugene A Earickson
285 N Bradford Ave
Smith River CA
955679521

Call Sign: K6ELH
Robert W Edmonds
333 Ocean Heights Way
Smith River CA 95567

Call Sign: WA6IBT
A Ilene Gale
12123 Ocean View Dr
Smith River CA 95567

Call Sign: N6CZZ
Bob L Douglas
14125 Ocean View Dr
Smith River CA 95567

Call Sign: KJ6ATR
Chelsey H Cornelis
13107 S Indian Rd
Smith River CA 95567

Call Sign: KA6MCN
Allen H Snethen
12400 US Hwy 101 966
Smith River CA 95567

Call Sign: K6JSI
Jeffrey A Stouffer
9465 US Hwy 101 N
Smith River CA 95567

Call Sign: K6SLS
Susan L Stouffer
9465 US Hwy 101 N
Smith River CA 95567

Call Sign: KE6LTR
Erick L Snider
165 Wilson Ln
Smith River CA 95567

Call Sign: KJ6ATV
Darrell L Moorehead
Smith River CA 95567

Call Sign: KJ6JKL
Jaime A Yarbrough
Smith River CA 95567

**FCC Amateur Radio
Licenses in Standish**

Call Sign: N6TUO
Shane A Rickett
719 100 Boda Ln
Standish CA 96128

Call Sign: KD6SVP
Dean M Canavan
Standish CA 96128

Call Sign: KF6YKS
Mary J Cobb
Standish CA 96128

Call Sign: N6MRC
Mary J Cobb
Standish CA 96128

Call Sign: KC6YTQ

Thomas N Rabelos
Standish CA 96128

Call Sign: K6TNR
Thomas N Rabelos
Standish CA 96128

Call Sign: KI6QHO
Michelle A Sader
Standish CA 96128

**FCC Amateur Radio
Licenses in Susanville**

Call Sign: WA6GUB
Andrew T Nielsen
1911 1st St
Susanville CA 96130

Call Sign: KA6UEZ
Edward J Kimble
1740 3rd St
Susanville CA 96130

Call Sign: KI6NWR
Nathan T Duerksen
1601 5th St
Susanville CA 96130

Call Sign: KF6UQU
Eric L Duerksen
1601 5th St
Susanville CA 96130

Call Sign: KI6NWW
Marcus D Pacheco
472 915 Adele Ct
Susanville CA 96130

Call Sign: KI6NWO
Robert R Feller
365 Adelle St
Susanville CA 96130

Call Sign: KJ6BQJ

Lisa M Cammer
478 280 Alta Dr
Susanville CA 96130

Call Sign: KJ6QDU
Joseph D Watkins
478 285 Alta Dr
Susanville CA 96130

Call Sign: KB6ZOG
Richard L Ray
470 220 Amesbury Dr
Susanville CA 961305882

Call Sign: KI6QKJ
Mathew R Levine
470 825 Amesbury Dr
Susanville CA 96130

Call Sign: W6BIK
Albert S Feller
1209 Arnold St
Susanville CA 96130

Call Sign: KG6KPP
Karron S White
715 Ash St
Susanville CA 96130

Call Sign: W6AMU
Karron S White
715 Ash St
Susanville CA 96130

Call Sign: KG6AMU
Earl R White Jr
715 Ash St
Susanville CA 96130

Call Sign: K6AMU
Earl R White Jr
715 Ash St
Susanville CA 96130

Call Sign: KD6IUJ

David B Meserve
1235 Barbara St
Susanville CA 96130

Call Sign: KD4CEJ
Mari Ann Hanks
1105 Cameron Way
Susanville CA 96130

Call Sign: KE6NDG
Arlington J Pecore
1105 Cameron Way
Susanville CA 96130

Call Sign: KE6TXN
Michelle N Pecore
1105 Cameron Way
Susanville CA 96130

Call Sign: KI6VKG
Randy J Moore
430 Carroll St Apt A
Susanville CA 96130

Call Sign: KF6DJX
Vivian J Hasek
691 275 Cedar Way
Susanville CA 96130

Call Sign: K6VJH
Vivian J Hasek
691 275 Cedar Way
Susanville CA 96130

Call Sign: K6VIV
Vivian J Hasek
691 275 Cedar Way
Susanville CA 96130

Call Sign: KE6NOS
Bruce A Rhymes
760 Cherry Terr
Susanville CA 961303610

Call Sign: KA6UBN

Carol O Leo
472 305 Debi Dr
Susanville CA 96130

Call Sign: KI6VKH
Charlotte W Nebeker
471 875 Diamond Crest Rd
Susanville CA 96130

Call Sign: KI6NWU
Gabor Szovati Jr
620 Gem Dr
Susanville CA 96130

Call Sign: KS6R
Harry Sella Jr
698 200 Gold Run
Susanville CA 96130

Call Sign: KJ6MQV
Bethany A Duvarney
697 500 Gold Run Rd
Susanville CA 96130

Call Sign: KG6SHF
Janet V Corey
697 980 Gold Run Rd
Susanville CA 96130

Call Sign: K6JNT
Janet V Corey
697 980 Gold Run Rd
Susanville CA 96130

Call Sign: K6JKC
Alan G Corey
697 980 Gold Run Rd
Susanville CA 96130

Call Sign: KB6QNO
Yoshiko H Gifford
687 725 Hazel Way
Susanville CA 96130

Call Sign: N6TVU

Irene M Bailey
687 725 Hazel Wy
Susanville CA 961309636

Call Sign: KI6NIB
David R Beckwith
575 Hospital Ln
Susanville CA 96130

Call Sign: K6DQZ
Ford W Cox
691 580 Janet Way
Susanville CA 96130

Call Sign: KC6LVP
Marvin A Seaward
473 815 Johnstonville Rd
N
Susanville CA 96130

Call Sign: KJ6B
Robert J Leo
705 605 Jordanna Ln
Susanville CA 96130

Call Sign: KI6NWT
Steven J Shelley
474 850 Ladybug Ln
Susanville CA 96130

Call Sign: KI6NWS
Mary Lee Shelley
474 850 Ladybug Ln
Susanville CA 96130

Call Sign: KJ6MQW
Debra Lindsey
715 310 Lake Leavitt Rd
Susanville CA 96130

Call Sign: WD6BOM
Ray A Craig
691 290 Lassen Way
Susanville CA 96130

Call Sign: WD6BON
Ann M Craig
691 290 Lassen Way
Susanville CA 96130

Call Sign: KI6NWY
Mike J Martinez
2850 Main St Ste 12 141
Susanville CA 96130

Call Sign: WB6OSE
Michael C Madigan
288 Maple
Susanville CA 96130

Call Sign: KN6AG
Thomas L Page
572 Meadow View Dr
Susanville CA 96130

Call Sign: W6EXP
Ralph S Blake
1002 Modoc St
Susanville CA 96130

Call Sign: KC6ZDM
Leonard J Potter
157 Mountain View Pkwy
Susanville CA 96130

Call Sign: KJ6ESW
Amy S Smith
177 Mountain View Pkwy
Susanville CA 96130

Call Sign: KD6YVG
Orrin J Hoffman
225 N Gilman
Susanville CA 96130

Call Sign: KE6JCQ
John J Kluft
205 N Mesa 904
Susanville CA 96130

Call Sign: KE6OSL
John W Hamilton
375 N Sacramento
Susanville CA 96130

Call Sign: KS6Q
Alison Shelley
835 Plumas St
Susanville CA 96130

Call Sign: KJ6MQX
Nicholas B Mcbride
2309 River St
Susanville CA 96130

Call Sign: KF6QOU
Linda L Ross
455 N Spring St
Susanville CA 96130

Call Sign: KI6BDO
Kelley E Shelley
835 Plumas St
Susanville CA 961304861

Call Sign: KC6M
Jerry C Buberl
151 S Fairfield
Susanville CA 96130

Call Sign: KJ6BQH
Marlo Britt
1355 North St
Susanville CA 96130

Call Sign: KS6Z
Kelley E Shelley
835 Plumas St
Susanville CA 961304861

Call Sign: KF6ZWK
Aaron A Duerksen
139 S Fairfield Ave
Susanville CA 96130

Call Sign: KG6UGF
Harry K White
699 500 Oak Mountain Dr
Susanville CA 96130

Call Sign: KJ6MD
Benny B Morrow
745 Randolph Way
Susanville CA 96130

Call Sign: KG6WOG
Misty J Duerksen
139 S Fairfield Ave
Susanville CA 96130

Call Sign: KF6DAM
Dario Sezzi
15 Oakridge
Susanville CA 96130

Call Sign: KM6YL
Janis E Morrow
745 Randolph Way
Susanville CA 961306035

Call Sign: KJ6MQU
Austin Duerksen
139 S Fairfield Ave
Susanville CA 96130

Call Sign: N6GEU
Ernest E Wilson
1270 Orlo Dr
Susanville CA 96130

Call Sign: KJ6MQY
Christi S Myers
701 305 Richmond Rd
Susanville CA 96130

Call Sign: WA6VWS
Frederick W Zuehlke
110 S Gay St
Susanville CA 96130

Call Sign: KB9THD
James D Glowinski
1155 Overlook Dr
Susanville CA 96130

Call Sign: KJ6MQS
Leon C E Myers
701 305 Richmond Rd
Susanville CA 96130

Call Sign: KJ6BQF
Cheryl L Damm
250 S Gay St
Susanville CA 96130

Call Sign: W6MCE
Louie J Bengoa
362 Pardee Ave
Susanville CA 96130

Call Sign: KF6EKT
Susan A Taylor
701 670 Richmond Rd
Susanville CA 96130

Call Sign: KA6VKE
Melody A Anderson
145 S Gilman St
Susanville CA 96130

Call Sign: KI6MOS
Alison Shelley
835 Plumas St
Susanville CA 96130

Call Sign: KE6ILQ
Cliff R Bannister
701 670 Richmond Rd E
Susanville CA 96130

Call Sign: W6DZW
Rolland R Wakeman
370 S Lassen
Susanville CA 96130

Call Sign: KG6OAB
Janice L Salsbery
235 S Pine St
Susanville CA 961303843

Call Sign: KF6TQG
Alexander W Salsbery
235 S Pine St
Susanville CA 96130

Call Sign: WB6FGC
Clarence W Tweddell
35 S Weatherlow St
Susanville CA 96130

Call Sign: KI6VKF
Tom P Brown
699 895 Sierra Rd
Susanville CA 96130

Call Sign: KE6CQA
Brent L Baxter
691 460 Tara Way
Susanville CA 96130

Call Sign: KI6VKE
Ruth Ann Nielson
610 Willow St
Susanville CA 96130

Call Sign: KJ6OHD
Wayne Curtis
849 Willow St
Susanville CA 96130

Call Sign: KI6NWX
Tiffany K Joscelyn
470 070 Wingfield Rd 12
Susanville CA 96130

Call Sign: K6TKJ
Tiffany K Joscelyn
470 070 Wingfield Rd 12
Susanville CA 96130

Call Sign: KI6BZM
Jon R Joscelyn
470 070 Winnfield Rd 12
Susanville CA 96130

Call Sign: K6JRJ
Jon R Joscelyn
470 070 Winnfield Rd 12
Susanville CA 96130

Call Sign: KI6NWV
Arthur B Anderson
Susanville CA 96130

Call Sign: N6XSC
Judith E Ashbaugh
Susanville CA 96130

Call Sign: WA6YPL
James R Ashbaugh
Susanville CA 96130

Call Sign: KI6LSZ
Emily A Giddings
Susanville CA 96130

Call Sign: KI6LSY
Michael C Giddings
Susanville CA 96130

Call Sign: KE6LCN
Rose M Hansen
Susanville CA 961300217

Call Sign: KE6LTB
Floyd D Hansen
Susanville CA 961300217

Call Sign: KE6REA
Victor F Hasek
Susanville CA 96130

Call Sign: KE6QAU
R Cindy Kramer
Susanville CA 96127

Call Sign: KJ6MQQ
Judith S Oliver
Susanville CA 96130

Call Sign: KF6DVQ
Joel P Smath
Susanville CA 96130

Call Sign: N0JIW
Ralph D Wagnitz
Susanville CA 96127

Call Sign: KG6GGE
Russell A White
Susanville CA 96130

Call Sign: KG6GNH
Colleen K White
Susanville CA 96130

Call Sign: WN1Z
Orrin C Winton
Susanville CA 96130

**FCC Amateur Radio
Licenses in Talmage**

Call Sign: KF6JHS
Morgan C Gibson
Talmage CA 95481

Call Sign: KE6TIU
Sherwin C Lim
Talmage CA 95481

**FCC Amateur Radio
Licenses in Trinidad**

Call Sign: KB6SIR
Fred L Snapp
290 6th Ave
Trinidad CA 95570

Call Sign: K6AHA

James H Popenoe
263 Driftwood Ln
Trinidad CA 95570

Call Sign: KF6PIP
Michael A Bruce
828 Edwards St
Trinidad CA 95570

Call Sign: KF6JBV
Donald J Verwayen
800 Fox Farm Rd
Trinidad CA 95570

Call Sign: KG6IEF
Derek J Bond
11 Moonstone Beach Rd
Trinidad CA 95570

Call Sign: K7DRK
Derek J Bond
11 Moonstone Beach Rd
Trinidad CA 95570

Call Sign: K6ZXK
Derek J Bond
11 Moonstone Beach Rd
Trinidad CA 95570

Call Sign: KJ6NZD
Richard H Kieselhorst
673 N Westhaven Dr
Trinidad CA 95570

Call Sign: KA6CLO
Willis E Garrett
3512 Patricks Point Dr
Trinidad CA 95570

Call Sign: KG6JIP
John Reininghaus
3134 Patricks Point Dr
Trinidad CA 95570

Call Sign: AA6LZ

Edmund T Wright
150 Scenic Dr
Trinidad CA 95570

Call Sign: W6JSH
Charles C Kidder
1395 Scenic Dr
Trinidad CA 95570

Call Sign: KF6JBP
Eric L Stackpole
Trinidad CA 95570

Call Sign: KD6JKS
James H Baker
Trinidad CA 955700834

Call Sign: WR6I
Kenneth M Bechtol
Trinidad CA 95570

Call Sign: W6JRU
Richard T Kidder
Trinidad CA 95570

Call Sign: KI6JAW
Samuel S Linderman
Trinidad CA 95570

Call Sign: KG6NAO
Beverly Nachem
Trinidad CA 95570

Call Sign: W6CCW
Larry A Netz
Trinidad CA 95570

Call Sign: KJ6HGL
Stefan M Rheinschmidt
Trinidad CA 95570

Call Sign: KI6TMU
Nicole S Ross
Trinidad CA 95570

**FCC Amateur Radio
Licenses in Trinity
Center**

Call Sign: KF6AAS
Jerry A Van Gieson
Hc 2 Box 3955
Trinity Center CA 96091

Call Sign: K6CXF
Donald L Mullen
300 Cedar Rd
Trinity Center CA 96091

Call Sign: AE6DZ
Laurence J Fitzsimons
1364 Eagle Creek Loop
Trinity Center CA 96091

Call Sign: KH6IR
Harry C Bush
Trinity Center CA 96091

Call Sign: KC6KTW
Marjorie D Lauerman
Trinity Center CA 96091

Call Sign: KE6AOZ
Anne Molina
Trinity Center CA 96091

Call Sign: WB0NTP
Robert E Plumb
Trinity Center CA 96091

Call Sign: N6SVW
Elizabeth M Bush
Trinity Center CA 96091

Call Sign: AB6ML
Kenneth E Plowman
Trinity Center CA 96091

Call Sign: KD6GTG
Christine Plowman

Trinity Center CA 96091

Tulelake CA 96134

Ukiah CA 95482

Call Sign: KA6AWW
Jonathan D Pulliam
Trinity Center CA 96091

Call Sign: KI6UZP
John H Razzeto
Trinity Center CA 96091

Call Sign: KE6SAL
Steven H Renten Mr.
Trinity Center CA 96091

Call Sign: K6XB
David P Krizo
7890 Co Rd 120
Tulelake CA 96134

Call Sign: WA7SID
Corbyn R Pomeroy Jr
270 CR 173
Tulelake CA 96134

Call Sign: KI6IDU
Carla J Kinion
170 Antoni Ln
Ukiah CA 95482

Call Sign: KB6AEH
Dana C Howell
235 Antoni Ln
Ukiah CA 95482

FCC Amateur Radio Licenses in Tulelake

Call Sign: K6TLL
James E Havlina
Bently Rd
Tulelake CA 96134

Call Sign: KC6WML
Robert R Stern
Rt 2 Box 29A
Tulelake CA 96134

Call Sign: KD6HBP
Lela M Schey
Rt 2 Box 56
Tulelake CA 96134

Call Sign: KD6HBQ
Wendell A Schey
Rt 2 Box 56
Tulelake CA 96134

Call Sign: KC6SKU
Ira J Krizo
Rt 2 Box 81A
Tulelake CA 96134

Call Sign: WB6BWH
Jacqueline D Krizo
Rt 2 Box 81A

Call Sign: WB6QEN
Lindle R Willey
501 Main St
Tulelake CA 961340947

Call Sign: KB6IQQ
Marianne F Abraria
4611 S County Rd 111
Tulelake CA 96134

Call Sign: N6MRH
Robert G Abraria
4611 S CR111
Tulelake CA 96134

Call Sign: K7MAL
Joe F Yoerger
Tulelake CA 96134

Call Sign: KF6PIM
Richard H Davis
Tulelake CA 961340214

Call Sign: WB6MVH
Richard H Davis
Tulelake CA 961340214

FCC Amateur Radio Licenses in Ukiah

Call Sign: WO6A
Dennis L Thygesen
1901 Antler Rd

Call Sign: KD6BQP
Robert L Sharpe
2400 Appolinaris Dr
Ukiah CA 954824189

Call Sign: KD6LSW
Peggy J Sharpe
2400 Appolinaris Dr
Ukiah CA 954824189

Call Sign: KI6ISO
David B Jordan
41 Betty St
Ukiah CA 95482

Call Sign: WB6SRM
Larry R Shore
1361 Burgundy Dr
Ukiah CA 95482

Call Sign: KI6URO
Donald Pfleger
527 Capps Ln
Ukiah CA 95482

Call Sign: KJ6IAH
Don Rowe
531 Capps Ln 64
Ukiah CA 954827254

Call Sign: KE6UMT
Jerry D Hellman
313 Clara Ave

Ukiah CA 95482

Call Sign: KC6MLJ
John E Nitchman
143 Clara Aveune
Ukiah CA 95482

Call Sign: KD6JHM
Charles D Maddox
320 Crestview Dr
Ukiah CA 95482

Call Sign: KA6IAP
James W Scott
404 Cypress Ave
Ukiah CA 95482

Call Sign: KI6IDW
Kevin T Cotroneo
1730 Deerwood Dr
Ukiah CA 95482

Call Sign: N6GCE
Brooke J Clarke
3425 Deerwood Dr
Ukiah CA 954827541

Call Sign: KJ6TEI
Wesley B Stevens
1600 Despina Dr
Ukiah CA 95482

Call Sign: KD6OPK
Jaylon A Bromley
564 Donner Ln
Ukiah CA 95482

Call Sign: KD6DNF
Bruno Teichman
875 Doolan Canyon Dr
Ukiah CA 95482

Call Sign: W6KGM
Harry W Allen
425 E Gobbi St 17

Ukiah CA 95482

Call Sign: KD6FDI
Daniel H Alley
182 E Gobbi St F
Ukiah CA 954824944

Call Sign: KF6DAA
Thomas E Bunting II
3501 Eastside Calpella Rd
Ukiah CA 954829462

Call Sign: KE6SPA
Mary C Booth
3551 Eastside Calpella Rd
Ukiah CA 954829462

Call Sign: KE6SPB
Tyler W Booth
3551 Eastside Calpella Rd
Ukiah CA 954829462

Call Sign: KF6CZZ
Jack W Booth
3551 Eastside Calpella Rd
Ukiah CA 954829462

Call Sign: KI6KBN
Jason G Amoss
4040 Eastside Calpella Rd
Ukiah CA 954829555

Call Sign: KD6SBB
Robert W Collett
4267 Eastside Calpella Rd
Ukiah CA 95482

Call Sign: KE6AWY
David J White
4267 Eastside Calpella Rd
Ukiah CA 95482

Call Sign: KE6BEH
Debra A White
4267 Eastside Calpella Rd

Ukiah CA 95482

Call Sign: WA6STW
Glendon C Glass Jr
4354 Eastside Calpella Rd
Ukiah CA 95482

Call Sign: KG6CFL
Barbara Mason
5100 Eastside Calpella Rd
Ukiah CA 95482

Call Sign: KI6LUU
Larry C Cubberly
6300 Eastside Calpella Rd
Ukiah CA 954829483

Call Sign: K6PRQ
Kay R Schultz
5055 El Roble Rd
Ukiah CA 95482

Call Sign: KD6SBE
Sherry L Glavich
545 Empire Dr
Ukiah CA 95482

Call Sign: WA6RQX
Greg M Glavich
545 Empire Dr
Ukiah CA 95482

Call Sign: KE6UZT
Valley E Sawyer
545 Empire Dr
Ukiah CA 954827206

Call Sign: KA6FNS
Walter J Robinson
275 Fairview Ct
Ukiah CA 95482

Call Sign: KI6RIX
Carolyn E Ruddock
204 Faull Ave

Ukiah CA 954826540

Call Sign: KI6RJD
Natalie J Guster
8200 Feliz Creek Rd
Ukiah CA 954829359

Call Sign: KI6RJF
Linda G Edgington
8670 Feliz Creek Rd
Ukiah CA 954829361

Call Sign: WD6FKJ
Daniel J Grebil
1455 Fir Ter Dr
Ukiah CA 954827906

Call Sign: KI6URN
Marvin L Boss
135 Foothill Blvd
Ukiah CA 95482

Call Sign: N6VDE
Joseph D Landry
204 Freitas Ave
Ukiah CA 95482

Call Sign: N6RCD
John B McLeod
1540 Gamay Pl
Ukiah CA 95482

Call Sign: KI6OCO
Charles K Heath
3800 Goat Rock Rd
Ukiah CA 954829337

Call Sign: K6ZIZ
Charles K Heath
3800 Goat Rock Rd
Ukiah CA 954829337

Call Sign: KI6RJA
Elizabeth K Phillips
3800 Goat Rock Rd

Ukiah CA 954829337

Call Sign: K6OKO
Elizabeth K Phillips
3800 Goat Rock Rd
Ukiah CA 954829337

Call Sign: KI6ISQ
Jimmy N Lacy
932 Helen Ave
Ukiah CA 95482

Call Sign: N6CQH
Bill G Voreis
1161 Helen Ave
Ukiah CA 95482

Call Sign: W6CQH
Bill G Voreis
1161 Helen Ave
Ukiah CA 95482

Call Sign: KF6ZQS
Deborah L Grilli
1090 Hops Estates Ln
Ukiah CA 95482

Call Sign: KI6ISI
Anne R Dent
275 Hospital Dr
Ukiah CA 95482

Call Sign: KB6NWI
Sandra J Armfield
1120 Incline Dr
Ukiah CA 95482

Call Sign: KD6RBL
James E Armfield III
1120 Incline Dr
Ukiah CA 95482

Call Sign: KA6HDB
Lawrence A Ames
254 Irvington Dr

Ukiah CA 95482

Call Sign: KF6GWQ
Julie A Judd
860 Isola Way
Ukiah CA 95482

Call Sign: N6VUD
Alan K Judd
860 Isola Way
Ukiah CA 95482

Call Sign: KI6URJ
Jackson K Judd
860 Isola Way
Ukiah CA 95482

Call Sign: W6QGT
Allan E Ward
509 Jones St
Ukiah CA 95482

Call Sign: WA6GEI
Orian O Carpenter
605 Jones St
Ukiah CA 95482

Call Sign: KI6ISF
Diane J Cline
438 Kennwood Dr
Ukiah CA 95482

Call Sign: W6JRC
Jimmy R Cline
438 Kennwood Dr
Ukiah CA 95482

Call Sign: KG6YJM
Kenneth E Wood
1021 Lake Mendocino Dr
Ukiah CA 95482

Call Sign: K6UPZ
Darrell D McKibbin
4500 Lakeridge Dr

Ukiah CA 95482

Ukiah CA 954823734

Ukiah CA 95482

Call Sign: KE6FBN
Albert J McQueary
660 Leslie St Spc 45
Ukiah CA 95482

Call Sign: KJ6EIF
Stephen H Turner
498 Luce Ave
Ukiah CA 954825631

Call Sign: KI6ITA
Robin A Lampson
4020 McNab Ranch Rd
Ukiah CA 95482

Call Sign: WA6QXV
Lawerence G Von Schriltz
9 Lorraine St
Ukiah CA 95482

Call Sign: KD6VAP
Ernest H Bean
1425 Madrone Dr
Ukiah CA 95482

Call Sign: WA6PSP
Robin A Lampson
4020 McNab Ranch Rd
Ukiah CA 95482

Call Sign: KE6SPD
Dennis A Cooper
12 Lorraine St
Ukiah CA 954825919

Call Sign: KJ6TKM
Carlton E Jacobson
1659 Madrone Dr
Ukiah CA 95482

Call Sign: KB6FFA
William A Elliott
420 McPeak St
Ukiah CA 95482

Call Sign: WA6KIM
Lloyd A Carman
47 Lorraine St
Ukiah CA 95482

Call Sign: KJ6TKN
Kyle W Jacobson
1659 Madrone Dr
Ukiah CA 95482

Call Sign: WA6DIG
Howard O Marsh
2309 Mill Creek Rd
Ukiah CA 95482

Call Sign: KF6ZU
John Golder
1 Louise Ct 3
Ukiah CA 954825740

Call Sign: KG6VHA
Erika T Nosera
600 Marshall St
Ukiah CA 95482

Call Sign: KI6IDM
Candice L Welsh
1140 Mulberry 5
Ukiah CA 95482

Call Sign: K7BUG
John Golder
1 Louise Ct 3
Ukiah CA 954825740

Call Sign: KG6PUF
James C Nosera
600 Marshall St
Ukiah CA 95482

Call Sign: N6UMS
Billie M Morgan
621 N Bush St
Ukiah CA 95482

Call Sign: KF6DAB
Keith J Feigin
810 Lovers Ln
Ukiah CA 954823105

Call Sign: KA6FDU
Lowell E Tidd
659 B Marshall St
Ukiah CA 95482

Call Sign: KI6ISE
Marcella J Chandler
860 N Bush St
Ukiah CA 95482

Call Sign: KF6JHV
Timothy J Marsh
951 Low Gap Rd
Ukiah CA 95482

Call Sign: K6QCV
James I Menzmer
1175 Marwen Dr
Ukiah CA 95482

Call Sign: W6LG
Samuel H Kline
1391 N Bush St
Ukiah CA 95482

Call Sign: KF6LVA
Gary W Hudson
589A Low Gap Rd

Call Sign: KF6JHT
Norma J Gibson
3601 McClure Rd

Call Sign: KA6ARX
Phyllis D Parker
81 N Court Rd

Ukiah CA 954826812   Ukiah CA 95482   Ukiah CA 95482

Call Sign: KA6ASP   Call Sign: KG6NXO   Call Sign: KI6IDX
Douglas F Parker   Kelly J Boesel   Claire A Chan
81 N Court Rd   5290 N State St   1150 Orr Springs Rd
Ukiah CA 954826812   Ukiah CA 954829454   Ukiah CA 95482

Call Sign: KE6SPG   Call Sign: KF6QAO   Call Sign: KG6NXM
Joyce E Hill   Christopher R Wichlaz   Jo Anna Marsh
800 N Oak St   1190 N State St 184   1150 Orr Springs Rd
Ukiah CA 954823904   Ukiah CA 954823416   Ukiah CA 954829001

Call Sign: KE6PYC   Call Sign: KB6TIU   Call Sign: KG6GFS
Carlyn J Rohrig   Steve C Alvarado   John D Hooper
1082 N Oak St   3251 N State St 7   5700 Parducci Rd
Ukiah CA 954823956   Ukiah CA 954823060   Ukiah CA 95482

Call Sign: KE6FBO   Call Sign: W6PJO   Call Sign: K6HFS
Albert P McQueary   Robert F Nosek   Robert L Miner
610 N Orchard Ave 49   4801 N State St Sp 42   2500 Park Creek Ln
Ukiah CA 95482   Ukiah CA 95482   Ukiah CA 954829391

Call Sign: WD6AOE   Call Sign: KE6CQL   Call Sign: KJ6DX
David A Johnston   Bryan R Rudow   Steven E Levin
989 N Pine St   3251 N State St Sp 8   1400 Pepperwood Pl
Ukiah CA 95482   Ukiah CA 95418   Ukiah CA 95482

Call Sign: N4WRU   Call Sign: WA6HLB   Call Sign: KI6KDV
Lee C Hall   A Wendell Marsh   Rickey L Wright
570 N School St   2891 Oak Ct Rd   600 Pinoleville Dr A
Ukiah CA 95482   Ukiah CA 95482   Ukiah CA 954827120

Call Sign: KI6IDS   Call Sign: KJ6MMT   Call Sign: KE6HHH
George T Perrone   Tim K Oden   Herb Brockett
4520 N State   8605 Oak St Apt C   401 Pomo Ln
Ukiah CA 95482   Ukiah CA 95482   Ukiah CA 95482

Call Sign: KD6MMD   Call Sign: KG6PBQ   Call Sign: KF6JHO
Tom C Garrison   Dustin Kingwell   Donald G Bone
3900 N State Sp 42   460 Observatory Ave   6980 Potter Vly Rd
Ukiah CA 95482   Ukiah CA 954825642   Ukiah CA 95482

Call Sign: KI6ISW   Call Sign: KI6KZY   Call Sign: KF6JHP
James L Switzer   Belinda M Smith   Donna V Bone
1059 N State St   2750 Old River Rd   6980 Potter Vly Rd

Ukiah CA 95482

Call Sign: WA6OWK
Harry P Vance
2465 Redemeyer Rd
Ukiah CA 95482

Call Sign: KE6GNN
Marc L Fortin
3030 Redemeyer Rd
Ukiah CA 95482

Call Sign: KJ6FKC
Tim Butler
3091 Redemeyer Rd
Ukiah CA 954823527

Call Sign: KJ6VIB
Josiah K Butler
3091 Redemeyer Rd
Ukiah CA 95482

Call Sign: KA7FXC
Harland E Reed
1490 Reisling Ct
Ukiah CA 95482

Call Sign: K6PKG
James T Alexander
1800 Ridge Rd
Ukiah CA 95482

Call Sign: WB6LNM
Virginia E Alexander
1800 Ridge Rd
Ukiah CA 95482

Call Sign: KB6MYA
Vincent H Angell
1891 Ridge Rd
Ukiah CA 95482

Call Sign: KD6ONH
Vincent P Valente
1441 Ridgeview Dr

Ukiah CA 95482

Call Sign: KC6JPS
Mark D Vogel
1812 S Dora
Ukiah CA 95482

Call Sign: KI6ISX
Melissa A Wuoltee
1120 S Dora St
Ukiah CA 95482

Call Sign: KI6MJC
Marcella J Chandler
1188 S Dora St
Ukiah CA 95482

Call Sign: WB6ITQ
Richard C Paige Jr
1336 S Dora St
Ukiah CA 954826513

Call Sign: KA6IAR
William L Bittenbender
350 S Highland
Ukiah CA 95482

Call Sign: KE6SPH
Robert V Knudsen
7751 S Hwy 101
Ukiah CA 954829317

Call Sign: KF6GYI
Genevieve E Knudsen
7751 S Hwy 101
Ukiah CA 95482

Call Sign: KI6RIT
Nick A Wharff
541 S Main St 11
Ukiah CA 95482

Call Sign: KG6PXA
Ukiah Area Radio Club

175 S School St MESA
Rm 107
Ukiah CA 95482

Call Sign: WA6ESM
Ukiah Area Radio Club
175 S School St MESA
Rm 107
Ukiah CA 95482

Call Sign: KD6MMB
Kenneth A Trumble
1510 S State St
Ukiah CA 95482

Call Sign: KB6YBN
Le Roy B Kershaw
3301 S State St
Ukiah CA 954826941

Call Sign: KI6SXA
Michael A Williams
1346 S State St
Ukiah CA 95482

Call Sign: KD6BC
William P Keaveney
761 Sanel Dr
Ukiah CA 95482

Call Sign: KI6BGJ
Loren F Mcgarvey
1480 Sanford Ranch Rd
Ukiah CA 95482

Call Sign: W6UME
Loren F Mcgarvey
1480 Sanford Ranch Rd
Ukiah CA 95482

Call Sign: N6VSG
Orville A Barr Jr
1380 Sequoia Plaza
Ukiah CA 95482

Call Sign: N6BBB
Orville A Barr Jr
1380 Sequoia Plaza
Ukiah CA 95482

Call Sign: KD6CJS
Christopher G Solomon
475 Spanish Canyon Dr
Ukiah CA 95482

Call Sign: KF6LUX
Ronald E Quigley
389 Stutsman Ln
Ukiah CA 95482

Call Sign: KI6URK
Michael Porter
1723 Tanya Ln Apt 3
Ukiah CA 95482

Call Sign: KE6MNX
Arthur C McChesney IV
761 Tokay Ave
Ukiah CA 95482

Call Sign: KD6LSR
William E Crow
2540 Townsend Ln
Ukiah CA 95482

Call Sign: K6SJ
Sandra J Wirth
296 Toyon Rd
Ukiah CA 95482

Call Sign: KQ6DG
Steven C Wirth
296 Toyon Rd
Ukiah CA 95482

Call Sign: KE6FRP
Kim D Remick
8888 Valley View Dr
Ukiah CA 95482

Call Sign: KI6YZT
The World Famous
Chicken Net
760 Village Cir Apt C
Ukiah CA 95482

Call Sign: W6CKN
The World Famous
Chicken Net
760 Village Cir Apt C
Ukiah CA 95482

Call Sign: KI6URM
Cody J Snodgrass
760 Village Cir C
Ukiah CA 95482

Call Sign: K6MEU
Cody J Snodgrass
760 Village Cir C
Ukiah CA 95482

Call Sign: KI6PBH
Ronald G Mcdaniel
407 W Henry
Ukiah CA 95482

Call Sign: KI6BEM
Michael A Heath
1141 W Standley St
Ukiah CA 95482

Call Sign: KJ6MYK
Jason R Silva
305 W Stephenson St
Ukiah CA 95482

Call Sign: KE6IYT
James R Shoberg
782 Waugh Ln
Ukiah CA 95482

Call Sign: KI6HTA
Rex L Eiffert
68 Whitmore Ln

Ukiah CA 954826930

Call Sign: KA6PGT
Jacob Markowitsch
1960 Wildwood Rd
Ukiah CA 95482

Call Sign: KD6VAR
John W Kvasnicka
871 Yosemite Dr
Ukiah CA 95482

Call Sign: KF6QAM
Raymond C Morris
745 A Yosemite Dr & A
Burns
Ukiah CA 954825168

Call Sign: KF6DAC
Weldon E Jones
540 Zinfandel Dr
Ukiah CA 954823239

Call Sign: KA6VKS
Monica L Burney
Ukiah CA 95482

Call Sign: KB6YGE
Chris A Gray
Ukiah CA 95482

Call Sign: KA6OBP
Eugene C Marcheschi
Ukiah CA 95482

Call Sign: KC6UNN
Paul C Snider
Ukiah CA 95482

Call Sign: K0DYS
Paul C Snider
Ukiah CA 95482

Call Sign: KF6ZTB
Patrick M Burnstad

Ukiah CA 954821435

Call Sign: KI6RJH
Guadalupe Chavez
Ukiah CA 954826340

Call Sign: KA6VHT
Christopher S Corniola
Ukiah CA 95482

Call Sign: WA6TZX
Richard D Corniola
Ukiah CA 95482

Call Sign: KD6DM
Gerald F Davis
Ukiah CA 954820415

Call Sign: KI6KBG
Marc D Imerone
Ukiah CA 954821741

Call Sign: KI6LZR
Toshiro C Kida
Ukiah CA 95482

Call Sign: KI6IDT
Alex S Kyle
Ukiah CA 95482

Call Sign: KI6TIB
Elizabeth J Macdougall
Ukiah CA 95482

Call Sign: KG6VGZ
Marjorie A Robinson
Ukiah CA 95482

Call Sign: W6ANI
Marjorie A Robinson
Ukiah CA 95482

Call Sign: KA6UBB
Cynthia L Sassenrath
Ukiah CA 95482

Call Sign: KB6ZST
Carl E Sassenrath
Ukiah CA 954021510

Call Sign: KI6ISY
Cynthia S Snider
Ukiah CA 95482

Call Sign: K1ORA
Cynthia S Snider
Ukiah CA 95482

Call Sign: KJ6VHV
William Todd
Ukiah CA 95482

Call Sign: K6VGZ
Leonard W Winter
Ukiah CA 95482

FCC Amateur Radio Licenses in Viola

Call Sign: KF6JRJ
Dennis H Peters
36688 Viola Meadows Ct
Viola CA 96088

FCC Amateur Radio Licenses in Weaverville

Call Sign: KN6RF
Harris W Mitchell
115 Beaujane Ln
Weaverville CA 96093

Call Sign: WB6DMS
Frank E Adams Sr
306 Center St Box 611
Weaverville CA 96093

Call Sign: KB6EHF
Lillian Galusha
109 E Weaver Rd

Weaverville CA 96093

Call Sign: KF6WLM
William W Talkington
332 Glen Rd
Weaverville CA 96093

Call Sign: KA6ZVR
Bobby R McNeil
127 Short
Weaverville CA 96093

Call Sign: KU6C
Frederic N Rounds
11 Tye Ln
Weaverville CA 96093

Call Sign: ND6T
Donald D Cantrell
621 Washington St
Weaverville CA 96093

Call Sign: KB6YTD
Robert E Jackson
150 Willow St
Weaverville CA 96093

Call Sign: KD6SAJ
Sondra A Jackson
119 Wilson Rd
Weaverville CA 96093

Call Sign: KD6GCR
Joe Baudizzon
Weaverville CA 96093

Call Sign: KD6QBS
Viola M Carpenter
Weaverville CA 96093

Call Sign: K6RVG
Wayne C Lewis
Weaverville CA 96093

Call Sign: KD6GCP

Thelma G Shaw
Weaverville CA 96093

Call Sign: N6WSX
James M Shaw
Weaverville CA 96093

Call Sign: W6ZUD
Lyle S Taylor Sr
Weaverville CA 96093

Call Sign: N6CSP
Robert N Beard
Weaverville CA
960931229

Call Sign: NC6A
Donald H Borden
Weaverville CA 96093

Call Sign: KI6GR
John G Budman
Weaverville CA 96093

Call Sign: KD6RKJ
Tubal Cain
Weaverville CA
960933055

Call Sign: KG6BHZ
Raymon J Campbell
Weaverville CA 96093

Call Sign: KB6EHA
Russell F Carpenter
Weaverville CA 96093

Call Sign: WB6JZN
Edwin D Carpenter
Weaverville CA
960930652

Call Sign: KJ6PEK
George M Coulter
Weaverville CA 96093

Call Sign: KD6GDT
Mark W Duckett
Weaverville CA 96093

Call Sign: KF6JXZ
Melinda L Duckett
Weaverville CA 96093

Call Sign: KF6NKL
Christopher W Duckett
Weaverville CA 96093

Call Sign: KF6WLO
Erik M Flickwir
Weaverville CA 96093

Call Sign: WB6FZH
Gregory C Greenwood
Weaverville CA 96093

Call Sign: KG6TVK
Molly A Greenwood
Weaverville CA
960933232

Call Sign: AE6PS
Richard C Greenwood
Weaverville CA
960933232

Call Sign: WA6ZSZ
John R Herring
Weaverville CA 96093

Call Sign: KI6WAT
Robert E Jackson II
Weaverville CA 96093

Call Sign: KE6MGV
Willard O Jacobson
Weaverville CA 96093

Call Sign: K6UHS
Willard O Jacobson

Weaverville CA 96093

Call Sign: WD6AIA
Robert D Martin
Weaverville CA 96093

Call Sign: KD6GCQ
Teresa C McNeil
Weaverville CA 96093

Call Sign: KI6WAX
Bobby M Mcneil
Weaverville CA 96093

Call Sign: N6BPQ
Kenneth E Melton
Weaverville CA
960932598

Call Sign: KN6RI
Beau Mitchell
Weaverville CA 96093

Call Sign: KJ6PEI
William E Mitchell
Weaverville CA 96093

Call Sign: KI6WBD
Nicholas J Prindiville
Weaverville CA 96093

Call Sign: WB7EIA
Scott H Richey
Weaverville CA 96093

Call Sign: KF6WLN
Roman Ritachka
Weaverville CA 96093

Call Sign: KA6TEE
Raymond J Roske
Weaverville CA
960933208

Call Sign: WJ6R

Richard W Russell
Weaverville CA 96093

Call Sign: AC6GG
John L Shaw
Weaverville CA 96093

Call Sign: KI6WBL
Jeanne R Simmons
Weaverville CA
960931749

Call Sign: KG6WGE
Dale V Taylor
Weaverville CA 96093

Call Sign: K6SDD
Trinity County ARC
Weaverville CA
960932283

Call Sign: KC6EJH
Horacio G Uribe
Weaverville CA 96093

Call Sign: N6VLI
Ronald E Waterhouse
Weaverville CA 96093

Call Sign: WA6BXN
John R Weil Jr
Weaverville CA 96093

Call Sign: N6NNT
Dianne M Wiberg
Weaverville CA 96093

Call Sign: N6NOS
Jeffrey R Wiberg
Weaverville CA 96093

**FCC Amateur Radio
Licenses in Weed**

Call Sign: KD6WYZ

Harold D Ritchey
1976 Angel Valley Rd
Weed CA 96094

Call Sign: KD6DHU
Mary A Burchfield
1984 Angel Valley Rd
Weed CA 96094

Call Sign: KO6DW
Burdon E Burchfield Jr
1984 Angel Valley Rd
Weed CA 96094

Call Sign: KJ6RSU
Dennis M Cisar
6042 Arron Ct
Weed CA 96094

Call Sign: KE6MZS
Elaine W Komrij
9104 Aspen Dr
Weed CA 96094

Call Sign: KG6IXN
James M Tye Jr
8401 Aspen Dr
Weed CA 960949073

Call Sign: KO6ZP
Richard A Mohr
412 Beacon Hill Ln
Weed CA 96094

Call Sign: WB6HRN
Paul L Katter
19500 Big Springs Rd
Weed CA 96094

Call Sign: KA6WUK
Anthony J Moser
184 Broadway Ave
Weed CA 96094

Call Sign: KA6WUL

John C Moser
184 Broadway Ave
Weed CA 96094

Call Sign: KA6WUM
Nancy M Moser
184 Broadway Ave
Weed CA 96094

Call Sign: KB6ZIY
Mark J Moser
184 Broadway Ave
Weed CA 96094

Call Sign: N6SRG
Robert S Moser
184 Broadway Ave
Weed CA 96094

Call Sign: NY6O
Theodore J Moser
184 Broadway Ave
Weed CA 96094

Call Sign: KZ7B
Richard L York
5725 Dogwood Dr
Weed CA 96094

Call Sign: KJ6AHS
David W Chiment
6031 Dogwood Dr
Weed CA 96094

Call Sign: K9RUS
David W Chiment
6031 Dogwood Dr
Weed CA 96094

Call Sign: W6FVV
Louis E Tepfer
Emerald Isle
Weed CA 96094

Call Sign: KD6DHV

John C Christ
3721 Evergreen Ln
Weed CA 96094

Call Sign: K6GPB
Earl D Wilson Jr
536 Florence Dr
Weed CA 960942321

Call Sign: KI6ADB
Cindy C Tappenbeck
1024 Hidden Meadow Dr
Weed CA 96094

Call Sign: K1KAT
Cindy C Tappenbeck
1024 Hidden Meadow Dr
Weed CA 96094

Call Sign: KG6ZDX
James W Tappenbeck
1024 Hidden Meadow Dr
Weed CA 96094

Call Sign: K9TAP
James W Tappenbeck
1024 Hidden Meadow Dr
Weed CA 96094

Call Sign: AB6UE
George S Dibelka
5238 High Meadow Rd
Weed CA 96094

Call Sign: KG6TTA
Patricia C Dawson
1170 Hillside Dr
Weed CA 96094

Call Sign: KA6YZO
Ray D Ferrero
4300 Hilltop Ln
Weed CA 96094

Call Sign: W6SSN

John R Abbott Sr
2101 Hwy 97
Weed CA 96094

Call Sign: KE6QCS
Donald C La Voy
16036 Indian Hill Dr
Weed CA 96094

Call Sign: KO6JM
Kenneth R Palmer
65 Mill St
Weed CA 96094

Call Sign: KE6ICZ
Betty K Leas
1512 Mule Deer Dr
Weed CA 96084

Call Sign: KG6NWH
James M Linsley
11001 N Old Stage Rd
Weed CA 96094

Call Sign: W2YAK
James M Linsley
11001 N Old Stage Rd
Weed CA 96094

Call Sign: KG6ZEC
Wanda J Linsley
11001 N Old Stage Rd
Weed CA 96094

Call Sign: W2GAB
Wanda J Linsley
11001 N Old Stage Rd
Weed CA 96094

Call Sign: KE6OEZ
Patricia A Matthews Ms
2925 Nighthawk Ln
Weed CA 96094

Call Sign: KE6RZY

Jon E West
17432 Otter Ct
Weed CA 96094

Call Sign: K6JO
Thomas J Allen
4031 Rainbow Dr
Weed CA 960949336

Call Sign: N6ITZ
Jeffery M Moser
810 S Weed Blvd
Weed CA 96094

Call Sign: KF6QVU
Robbie J Stobbs
848 S Weed Blvd
Weed CA 96094

Call Sign: AB6RI
Mac W Hilliard
737 S Weed Blvd 17
Weed CA 96094

Call Sign: W6UBJ
Scott Adams
5220 Saddle Ridge Rd
Weed CA 96094

Call Sign: KD6WHP
Roy G Bergfors
1825 Shastina Dr
Weed CA 96094

Call Sign: KC6QXT
Marvin L Zeman
5826 Shastina Pl
Weed CA 96094

Call Sign: KE6MNB
Hadji T Ahrns
5012 Spear Point
Weed CA 96094

Call Sign: KE6JCR

Marvin L Hanson
418 Walnut St
Weed CA 96094

Call Sign: KQ6GQ
Paul L Brigaerts
14210 Wildhorse Rd
Weed CA 96094

Call Sign: KF6GJW
Cheri R Barnes
16627 Woodside Pl
Weed CA 96094

Call Sign: W7OTC
Charles H Barnes
16627 Woodside Pl
Weed CA 96094

Call Sign: KD6LZI
Marla E Banuelos
Weed CA 96094

Call Sign: KD6LNG
Dennis A Cody
Weed CA 96094

Call Sign: KD6DIA
Robert J Kehr
Weed CA 96094

Call Sign: WA6MDQ
Russell S Sterling
Weed CA 96094

Call Sign: KE6JCU
Steve J Anderson
Weed CA 96094

Call Sign: KG6VEU
Robert C Berg
Weed CA 960940490

Call Sign: K7RCB
Robert C Berg

Weed CA 960940490

Call Sign: KE6CHU
Tim G Biffle
Weed CA 960940339

Call Sign: KB7ORV
Gale H Carlson
Weed CA 96094

Call Sign: KF0G
Robert L Coppock
Weed CA 96094

Call Sign: KE6HUK
James D Haines
Weed CA 96094

Call Sign: KD6WP
Charles N Marshall
Weed CA 96094

Call Sign: KO6IS
Arlette A Marshall
Weed CA 96094

Call Sign: KE6UAI
Allan Y Takahashi
Weed CA 96094

FCC Amateur Radio Licenses in Weott

Call Sign: KI6YDH
Thomas E Booth
Weott CA 95571

Call Sign: KG6BFO
Kimberly A Cabrera
Weott CA 95571

Call Sign: KI6TFF
Jacques P E Cadgene
Weott CA 95571

Call Sign: KG6BFP
Gordan G Gotcher
Weott CA 95571

Call Sign: KG6BII
Melvina Gotcher
Weott CA 95571

Call Sign: KF6OUO
David L Harmon
Weott CA 95571

Call Sign: K6TZN
Loudon B McCormack
Weott CA 95571

Call Sign: WA6JTV
Lillian C McCormack
Weott CA 95571

FCC Amateur Radio Licenses in Westport

Call Sign: WB6GGR
Milton R Kerchenko
37033 Omega Dr Box 74
Westport CA 95488

FCC Amateur Radio Licenses in Westwood

Call Sign: KD6FD
Charles A Gonzales
101 Delwood St
Westwood CA 96137

Call Sign: KB6PWS
Ricardo F Valerga
418 Delwood St
Westwood CA 96137

Call Sign: N6FZJ
Donald D Gestner
100 Delwood St 22
Westwood CA 961370221

Call Sign: KD6DOJ
Richard B McBride
305 Fir St
Westwood CA 96137

Call Sign: KA6PQB
Vincent F Mueting
545 Peninsula Dr
Westwood CA 96137

Call Sign: KI6YUS
Robert J Macarthur
639 Pine Canyon Rd
Westwood CA 96137

Call Sign: K6CPI
Walter G Kelley
462 825 Rainbow Dr
Westwood CA 961379445

Call Sign: KB2CIQ
Grace W Kelley
462 825 Rainbow Dr
Westwood CA 96137

Call Sign: N6LWU
Robert L Riggs
10966 Rochester Ave 3A
Westwood CA 96137

Call Sign: KE6ALP
Terry J Ferguson
Westwood CA 96137

Call Sign: WD6BHR
Carol J Stewart
Westwood CA 96137

Call Sign: KI6NWQ
Forest F Duerksen
Westwood CA 96137

Call Sign: KF6OHN
Thomas A Good

Westwood CA 96137

Call Sign: K6TTR
Michael O Leland
Westwood CA 961370414

Call Sign: KF6QOR
Curtis E Quam
Westwood CA 961370517

Call Sign: KC6BYN
Tabrina J Reed
Westwood CA 961370311

FCC Amateur Radio Licenses in Whitehorn

Call Sign: KI6PHG
John W Greiser
12500 Briceland Rd
Whitethorn CA 95589

Call Sign: K6AXL
Jess B Kinser
16427 Briceland Rd
Whitethorn CA 95589

Call Sign: KI6PHM
Walter E Prince
18269 Briceland Thorn Rd
Whitethorn CA 95589

Call Sign: KI6PIF
Lyle C Hill
1176 Lower Pacific Dr
Whitethorn CA 955899139

Call Sign: KI6PHK
Douglas B Lyon
116 Ridgeview Cir
Whitethorn CA 95589

Call Sign: W6HOQ
Douglas B Lyon
116 Ridgeview Cir

Whitethorn CA 95589

Call Sign: KI6PHL
Charles M Mcclure
448 Seafoam Rd
Whitethorn CA 95589

Call Sign: WB6CTV
Russell A Montgomery
20 Seafoam Rd
Whitethorn CA 95589

Call Sign: KI6PJV
Janis G Scheidt
61 Seaview Rd
Whitethorn CA 95589

Call Sign: KF6HRE
Reba E Selk
36 Shaker Rd
Whitethorn CA 95589

Call Sign: KI6PHJ
Joe M Lopes
96 Shaker Rd
Whitethorn CA 95589

Call Sign: KI6PHI
Janet E Lopes
96 Shaker Rd Shelter Cove
Whitethorn CA 95589

Call Sign: KB6LAD
Nancy R Peregrine
77321 Usal Rd
Whitethorn CA 95589

Call Sign: KG6BJC
Jillian E O Conner
77555 Usal Rd
Whitethorn CA 95589

Call Sign: KF6BLR
Jessica L Van Arsdale
77321 Usal Read

Whitethorn CA 95589

Call Sign: KB6LAF
Glenn S Hawthorne
Whitethorn CA 95589

Call Sign: KF6FQI
Jon R Anderson
Whitethorn CA 95589

Call Sign: KI6IUO
Zoe S Chapman
Whitethorn CA 95589

Call Sign: KI6PQW
Denise L Hebard
Whitethorn CA 95589

Call Sign: KI6PHH
John H Jennings
Whitethorn CA 95589

Call Sign: KG6LEH
Cathy R Lentz
Whitethorn CA 95589

Call Sign: W6JTI
Frank H Letton
Whitethorn CA 95589

Call Sign: KB6LAH
Merrill A Lynn
Whitethorn CA 95589

Call Sign: KF6HRH
Ian M Moore
Whitethorn CA 95584

Call Sign: KF6HRG
Wayne F Moore
Whitethorn CA 95589

Call Sign: KF6HUD
Amanda N Moore
Whitethorn CA 95589

Call Sign: KF6HUF
Patricia J Moore
Whitethorn CA 95589

Call Sign: KF6HRD
Daniel L Thomas
Whitethorn CA 95589

Call Sign: KF6IZD
Linda S Yates
Whitethorn CA 95589

FCC Amateur Radio Licenses in Whitmore

Call Sign: W1NV
Donald C Hascall II
31295 Swallowtail Ln
Whitmore CA 96096

Call Sign: KI6IBY
Richard E Watson
28832 Whitmore Rd
Whitmore CA 96096

Call Sign: KE6ALF
Michael F Brink
31091 Whitmore Rd
Whitmore CA 96096

Call Sign: KF6VIS
Terri L Brink
31091 Whitmore Rd
Whitmore CA 96096

Call Sign: N6ECS
Harold C Fisk Jr
Whitmore CA 96096

Call Sign: KR6LA
Harold C Fisk Jr
Whitmore CA 96096

FCC Amateur Radio Licenses in Wildwood

Call Sign: NT6O
John A Riddle
770 Wildwood Rd
Wildwood CA 960760245

Call Sign: KJ6ATY
John A Riddle
Wildwood CA 960760245

Call Sign: AF6WO
John A Riddle
Wildwood CA 960760245

FCC Amateur Radio Licenses in Willits

Call Sign: KF6PGV
Bruce D Carmichael
6850 3rd Gate Rd
Willits CA 95490

Call Sign: KJ6TNY
Dirk J Johnson
97 Alameda Ave
Willits CA 95490

Call Sign: KI6FRW
Linda J Morrison
1413 Archer Pl
Willits CA 954909520

Call Sign: N6RAD
James A Yokum
180 Baechtel Rd
Willits CA 95490

Call Sign: KJ6VHW
Denise L Kreps
1475 Baechtel Rd C4
Willits CA 95490

Call Sign: WA6KLK

Leonard D Gwinn
2960 Blackhawk Rd
Willits CA 95490

Call Sign: K6QXR
Robert E Thompson
4101 Blue Lakes Ter
Willits CA 95490

Call Sign: KD6SBC
Jeanette F De Lisle
202 Bonnie Ln
Willits CA 95490

Call Sign: KD6SBD
Leon A De Lisle
202 Bonnie Ln
Willits CA 95490

Call Sign: KD6LSV
Robert J Lovejoy
24241 Buckeye Pl
Willits CA 95490

Call Sign: KD6FER
Robert F Melluish
1506 Casteel Dr
Willits CA 95490

Call Sign: KD6KPZ
Stephanie Melluish
1506 Casteel Dr
Willits CA 95490

Call Sign: K7WWA
George O Burton
2032 Clover Dr
Willits CA 954908837

Call Sign: W6PKT
Mendocino County Packet
Association
2032 Clover Dr
Willits CA 95490

Call Sign: KJ6IAJ
Rachael M Mosley
2032 Clover Dr
Willits CA 954908837

Call Sign: K6DFM
Daniel K West
2790 Coyote Ln
Willits CA 95490

Call Sign: KD6LSQ
Lois J Bender
2640 Coyote Rd
Willits CA 95490

Call Sign: KE6MWV
Diane L Wilson
380 Creekside Dr
Willits CA 95490

Call Sign: KJ6DJZ
Mei E Horn
300 Creekside Dr Apt 27
Willits CA 95490

Call Sign: KD6IBD
Gary S Kavanagh
24523 Cypress Dr
Willits CA 95490

Call Sign: KE6HHG
Nancy K Kavanagh
24523 Cypress Dr
Willits CA 95490

Call Sign: KD6FEP
John R Thomen
463 Della Ave
Willits CA 95490

Call Sign: KD6IBG
Jeanette D Thomen
463 Della Ave
Willits CA 95490

Call Sign: KE6COJ
Terri A Thomen
463 Della Ave
Willits CA 95490

Call Sign: WA6HPN
Leslie C McClelland
580 Della St
Willits CA 95490

Call Sign: KE6MKT
Ralph R Hein
1521 E Hill Rd
Willits CA 95490

Call Sign: N6RWH
Roy Wormington
1600 E Hill Rd
Willits CA 95490

Call Sign: KE6BPX
Scott G Jones
162 E Mendocino Ave
Willits CA 95490

Call Sign: KJ6IAG
Ruth A Hubbell
580 E Valley St
Willits CA 954905735

Call Sign: KF6UGQ
Cecil E Caldwell Sr
620 E Valley St
Willits CA 95490

Call Sign: KG6AZC
Paul T Futscher
22461 Eastside Rd
Willits CA 954905703

Call Sign: KI6ISP
Samuel M Knapp Jr
21460 Eva Clair St
Willits CA 95490

Call Sign: KE6SPE
George Dudley Jr
118 Fort Bragg Rd
Willits CA 954904105

Call Sign: KB6FFB
Paul B Ubelhart
38 Hillside Dr
Willits CA 954903013

Call Sign: KD6BQM
David J Thomen
206 Madden Ln
Willits CA 954903517

Call Sign: KI6FRT
Janet M Rayner
2645 Goose Rd
Willits CA 954908010

Call Sign: KJ6VIC
Carole J Bergman
78 Hillside Dr
Willits CA 95490

Call Sign: KI6LAB
Daniel D Jones
1 Madrone St
Willits CA 95490

Call Sign: KJ6VHX
Jeffery A Crawford
2645 Gosse Rd
Willits CA 95490

Call Sign: WA6CBJ
Winthrop H Owen
2201 Hilltop Dr
Willits CA 95490

Call Sign: K6KSK
Harry Sanneman
383 Main St 230
Willits CA 95490

Call Sign: KE6KRM
Tracie A Mello
1780 Hawk Pl
Willits CA 95490

Call Sign: KD6BQQ
Timothy M Castleman
16200 Hwy 101 N
Willits CA 95490

Call Sign: KE6JEI
Linda L Pettipiece
1121 Maize Ct
Willits CA 95490

Call Sign: KE6FBL
Arnold S Mello Jr
1780 Hawk Pl
Willits CA 95490

Call Sign: K6WC
John D Brand
16100 Hwy 101 N Sp 21
Willits CA 95490

Call Sign: KB6BME
Don E Smith
27120 Maize Pl
Willits CA 95490

Call Sign: KI6LAD
Leticia Amador
45 Hazel St
Willits CA 95490

Call Sign: WR6C
Carmen L Brand
16100 Hwy 101 N Sp 21
Willits CA 95490

Call Sign: KF6JNU
James G Sanford
1210 Maize Way
Willits CA 954909587

Call Sign: KI6RJG
Jenn S Creekmore-Juenke
45 Hazel St
Willits CA 954904222

Call Sign: NA6I
Irma J Osborne
16100 Hwy 101 N Sp 71
Willits CA 95490

Call Sign: KF6UVG
Rebecca M Sanford
1210 Maize Way
Willits CA 954909587

Call Sign: KE6RTK
Jon O Patton
6501 Hearst Rd
Willits CA 95490

Call Sign: KI6ISU
Manuel J Orozco Jr
21481 Locust St
Willits CA 95490

Call Sign: KI6A
Kenneth E James Sr
1211 Maize Way
Willits CA 95490

Call Sign: KE6SPL
Loraine F Patton
6501 Hearst Rd
Willits CA 954909223

Call Sign: KE6CSK
Franklin H Henry
1200 Loucst St
Willits CA 95490

Call Sign: N6RVX
Bruce A Strachan
30601 Metzler Ridge Rd
Willits CA 95490

Call Sign: N6RVY
Anne E Strachan
30601 Metzler Ridge Rd
Willits CA 95490

Call Sign: N6SLZ
Lois L Giese
156 Mill Creek Ct
Willits CA 95490

Call Sign: KG6PBO
Scott J Guy
134 Mill Creek Dr
Willits CA 954903017

Call Sign: KJ6VHU
Andrew T Hilkey
128 Mill Creek Dr
Willits CA 95490

Call Sign: KJ6VHZ
Louis M Lucier
128 Mill Creek Dr
Willits CA 95490

Call Sign: W6LNA
James H Boschma
16100 N Hwy 101 17
Willits CA 95490

Call Sign: W6AUO
Ben G Eizinger
16100 N Hwy 101 6
Willits CA 954909711

Call Sign: KD6BQL
Tancy N Whitney
19925 N Hwy 101 Sp 14
Willits CA 95490

Call Sign: KA4GJB
Dorsey D Simmons
16100 N Hwy 101 Spc 91
Willits CA 95490

Call Sign: WA6MHX
William D Fleming
266 N Main St
Willits CA 954903111

Call Sign: KJ6IBO
David F Pollin
75 N Main St 104
Willits CA 954903107

Call Sign: K6PRO
Pacific Railcars Operators
Arc
10 North St
Willits CA 954903418

Call Sign: KF6KOA
Kathleen M Whitney
10 North St
Willits CA 954903418

Call Sign: WD6FGX
Roderick D Whitney
10 North St
Willits CA 954903418

Call Sign: KG6PBR
Carolyn A Whitney
10 North St
Willits CA 954903418

Call Sign: K6MOW
Motorcar Operators West
ARC
10 North St
Willits CA 95490

Call Sign: KD6OPJ
Jeffery P Judson
493 North St
Willits CA 95490

Call Sign: KE6MWX
Sara K Hanna
90 Northbrook Way

Willits CA 95490

Call Sign: KE6YKY
Sharon S Hanna
90 Northbrook Way
Willits CA 954903019

Call Sign: WB9NJS
Timothy D Hanna
90 Northbrook Way
Willits CA 954903019

Call Sign: KD6BAP
David K Edgar
27120 Oriole Dr
Willits CA 95490

Call Sign: KE6COB
Ronald D Durbin
2443 Perch Dr
Willits CA 95490

Call Sign: KD6BQK
Lawrence J Wise
2040 Perch Pl
Willits CA 95490

Call Sign: KD6BRW
Denise H Wise
2040 Perch Pl
Willits CA 95490

Call Sign: KE6HHE
Jason L Wise
2040 Perch Pl
Willits CA 95490

Call Sign: KF6UVJ
Roberta M Schulz
375 Pine St
Willits CA 954903330

Call Sign: W6FQX
John E Lemmer
25224 Poppy Dr

Willits CA 954909432

Call Sign: KG6PBS
Betty J Lemmer
25224 Poppy Dr
Willits CA 954909432

Call Sign: KJ6OQN
Mendocino County
Amateur Radio C S
25224 Poppy Dr
Willits CA 95490

Call Sign: NC6MC
Mendocino County
Amateur Radio C S
25224 Poppy Dr
Willits CA 95490

Call Sign: KC6AJR
Richard A Cavigliano
27931 Poppy Dr
Willits CA 954909066

Call Sign: KI6FRV
Annie L Morris
27951 Poppy Dr
Willits CA 954909066

Call Sign: KF6YHK
John S Buckner
28131 Poppy Dr
Willits CA 95490

Call Sign: KG6CTM
Robert W Terry
2111 Poppy Ln
Willits CA 954908518

Call Sign: KI6ISV
Tara K Shannon
2355 Poppy Terr
Willits CA 95490

Call Sign: KE6SPJ

Aubrey G Maynard
3508 Primrose Dr
Willits CA 954908536

Call Sign: KD6AEP
Dorothy J Edmondson
3774 Primrose Dr
Willits CA 95490

Call Sign: N6OUW
William B Edmondson
3774 Primrose Dr
Willits CA 95490

Call Sign: N6OYB
Darlene D Jones
23819 Primrose Dr
Willits CA 95490

Call Sign: KG6CTN
Judi A Berdis
245 Redwood Ave
Willits CA 954903429

Call Sign: WA6MZE
Melvin D Jolley
590 Redwood Ave
Willits CA 95490

Call Sign: KJ6VID
John F Schuster
601 Redwood Ave
Willits CA 95490

Call Sign: N6XHX
Robert F Arnold
24861 Ridge Rd
Willits CA 95490

Call Sign: KE6SPI
Brenda L Klugherz
3201 Ridgewood Rd
Willits CA 95490

Call Sign: KF6HIK

James H Klugherz
3201 Ridgewood Rd
Willits CA 95490

Call Sign: KG6EYL
Roger E Stange
3339 Ridgewood Rd
Willits CA 954909786

Call Sign: KE6CCD
Karl D Amo
5000 Ridgewood Rd
Willits CA 95490

Call Sign: WA6MWD
Kathleen K Hopper
25061 Robin Cir
Willits CA 95490

Call Sign: KJ6IAD
Peter J Johnston
25248 B Robinson Rd
Willits CA 954909490

Call Sign: KD6JAJ
Carolyn A Perez
889 S Main St 238
Willits CA 95490

Call Sign: KD6JAK
Angel U Perez Sr
889 S Main St 238
Willits CA 95490

Call Sign: KE6ULK
Felix W Camp
1750 S Mian 55
Willits CA 95490

Call Sign: W6FXO
Charles W Davison
84 School St
Willits CA 95490

Call Sign: KG6CTJ

Arlene G Davison
84 School St
Willits CA 954903442

Call Sign: KF6LVC
Jose A Aparicio
18701 Shafer Ranch Rd
Willits CA 954909629

Call Sign: KF6QAR
Teri L Aparicio
18701 Shafer Ranch Rd
Willits CA 954909629

Call Sign: KE6SPK
Noah G Mervine
19659 Shafer Ranch Rd
Willits CA 954909631

Call Sign: KE6YKX
Evan C Senter
201 Sherwood Rd
Willits CA 954909501

Call Sign: N6TCS
Sharon C Statler
25050 Sherwood Rd
Willits CA 94550

Call Sign: WA6JSW
Delmar A Statler
25050 Sherwood Rd
Willits CA 94550

Call Sign: KE6ZID
Jay E Haegele
26771 Sherwood Rd
Willits CA 954909568

Call Sign: K6AFL
Jay E Haegele
26771 Sherwood Rd
Willits CA 954909568

Call Sign: KD6YOG

Dorothy L Roediger
274 State St
Willits CA 95490

Call Sign: KD6YOH
Gene C Roediger
274 State St
Willits CA 95490

Call Sign: N6RVW
Thomas J Wormington
24261 Tulip Ave
Willits CA 95490

Call Sign: W6EIP
Jack W Coe
2025 Valley Rd
Willits CA 95490

Call Sign: KF6FEB
Ralph Collett
949 W Standley St
Willits CA 954824226

Call Sign: KQ6KN
James L Cloud
10301 West Rd
Willits CA 954709754

Call Sign: KI6URR
Sean S Spicer
3310 Williams Ranch Rd
Willits CA 95490

Call Sign: KI6FRU
Charles Harden
24008 Willow Pl
Willits CA 954909487

Call Sign: KI6IDL
Josefina Guevara
24091 Willow Pl
Willits CA 95490

Call Sign: KW6AR

Percy L Cartwright
Willits CA 95490

Call Sign: KB6YNU
Ronald A Cote
Willits CA 95490

Call Sign: W6JCG
William M Perac
Willits CA 95490

Call Sign: K6DEN
Evelyn F Roediger
Willits CA 95490

Call Sign: KD6LSX
Doris E Stayer
Willits CA 95490

Call Sign: KJ6HZV
Robert J Anderson
Willits CA 954902254

Call Sign: W6RJA
Robert J Anderson
Willits CA 954902254

Call Sign: KJ6VIH
Thomas A Brundige
Willits CA 95490

Call Sign: KI6URG
Leo C Buc
Willits CA 95490

Call Sign: KF6HHB
Pete A Caragher
Willits CA 954900805

Call Sign: KI6IUS
Anne R Crowder
Willits CA 954901413

Call Sign: KI6IDV
Roy Jones

Willits CA 95490

Call Sign: KJ6HZW
Bernard B Kamoroff
Willits CA 954901240

Call Sign: KB6HYC
Daniel M McManus
Willits CA 95490

Call Sign: KB6EYG
Kyle E Pinson
Willits CA 95490

Call Sign: KJ6VHS
Kyle E Pinson
Willits CA 95490

Call Sign: KI6IVB
Douglas Prado
Willits CA 954901413

Call Sign: W6JP
Oscar H Roediger Jr
Willits CA 95490

Call Sign: W6WDG
Robert E Simonson
Willits CA 95490

Call Sign: KD6BQO
Charles E Stayer Jr
Willits CA 95490

Call Sign: KF6ZTA
Gregg V Stebbins
Willits CA 954901407

Call Sign: KG6SZD
Jeffrey P Thompson
Willits CA 95490

Call Sign: KJ6VHT
Terry L Wilcox
Willits CA 95490

Call Sign: KI6RIU
Theresa Wilcox
Willits CA 954900151

Call Sign: W6MMM
Willits Amateur Radio
Society
Willits CA 95490

FCC Amateur Radio Licenses in Willow Creek

Call Sign: KA6BID
Gregory E Lane
80 Poplar Ln
Willow Creek CA
955731526

Call Sign: KF6AAJ
Hadley G Thomas
691 Titlow Hill Rd Box
855
Willow Creek CA
955730855

Call Sign: WB6NBE
Eugene C Harpe
Willow Creek CA
955730317

Call Sign: KE6IAS
Wesley A Holmberg
Willow Creek CA 95573

Call Sign: W5OM
Howard M Krausse
Willow Creek CA 95573

Call Sign: KC8SUW
Anne E Potts
Willow Creek CA 95573

Call Sign: N6ZKA
Kevin L Walker

Willow Creek CA 95573

Call Sign: N6TWH
Daniel A York
Willow Creek CA
955730984

FCC Amateur Radio Licenses in Yorkville

Call Sign: N6IRJ
Susan Z Rutherford
Yorkville CA 95494

Call Sign: WB6PER
Jim Rutherford
Yorkville CA 95494

FCC Amateur Radio Licenses in Yreka

Call Sign: KF6IRE
Logan T Mathos
250 Anderson Rd
Yreka CA 96097

Call Sign: KE6GXM
Patricia L Golly
316 Anderson Rd
Yreka CA 96097

Call Sign: KI6VZM
Marcus G Issoglio
910 Arlene Ct
Yreka CA 96097

Call Sign: KJ6OAY
Ray R Smith
915 Arlene Ct
Yreka CA 96097

Call Sign: KE6IIH
Keith R Brandaw
6416 Bowen Centers Rd
Yreka CA 96097

Call Sign: W6HXZ
Edwin D Babbitt
1106 Cedar St
Yreka CA 96097

Call Sign: KE6FHO
John A Bessent
1060 Deer Creek Way 6
Yreka CA 96097

Call Sign: WA6OMS
Raymond O Murch
1501 Dove Ln
Yreka CA 96097

Call Sign: KF6IRC
Richard O Kimball
1540 Dove Ln
Yreka CA 96097

Call Sign: KF6IRD
Jamie K Kimball
1540 Dove Ln
Yreka CA 96097

Call Sign: W6JVF
James N Freemyers
130 E Blake
Yreka CA 96097

Call Sign: K6NGN
James T Golly
118 E Lennox St
Yreka CA 96097

Call Sign: KE6MZL
Steven B Drageset
2606 Eastman Ln
Yreka CA 96097

Call Sign: KJ6MZW
Jerod B Knox
725 Hearn St
Yreka CA 96097

Call Sign: AC6A
Clarence H Freeman
705 Hill St
Yreka CA 960972310

Call Sign: W6PYU
Warren L Weaver
400 Hiram Page Rd 19
Yreka CA 96097

Call Sign: KB6XX
William T White
400 Hiram Page Rd Sp 59
Yreka CA 960979505

Call Sign: W6OTL
De Witt C Holfinger
400 Hiram Page Sp 23
Yreka CA 960979504

Call Sign: KG6ZED
Sandra E Lindley
237 Humbug
Yreka CA 96097

Call Sign: K6QOX
Stacey G Elam
Humbug Creek Rd
Yreka CA 96097

Call Sign: N6OEO
June M De Buhr
171 Humbug Rd
Yreka CA 96097

Call Sign: WB6FEL
Milton D De Buhr
171 Humbug Rd
Yreka CA 96097

Call Sign: KD6EVH
Robert M Crawford
1625 Hwy 263
Yreka CA 96097

Call Sign: KD6VXB
Gerald R Crawford
1625 Hwy 263
Yreka CA 96097

Call Sign: KE6SXO
Harry C Willis
308 Jackson St
Yreka CA 96097

Call Sign: W6AKT
William T Belt
800 Jasper Pl Apt 41
Yreka CA 96097

Call Sign: KF6PIN
Tim P Artellan
103 N Lange Way
Yreka CA 96097

Call Sign: KE6SXQ
Lee E Messenger
207 N Oregon
Yreka CA 96097

Call Sign: WA6MSC
Gordon E Loomis
514 N Oregon
Yreka CA 96097

Call Sign: KE6YJH
Siskiyou County Amateur
Radio Association
514 N Oregon
Yreka CA 96097

Call Sign: K6SIS
Siskiyou County Amateur
Radio Association
514 N Oregon
Yreka CA 96097

Call Sign: WL7LX
Matt P Holmes

804 N View Dr
Yreka CA 96097

2520 Oak Valley Dr
Yreka CA 96097

4811 Schulmeyer Rd
Yreka CA 96097

Call Sign: KF6ERK
Theodore E Cummins
743 North St
Yreka CA 96097

Call Sign: W5QZW
Nolan S Maloney
2520 Oak Valley Dr
Yreka CA 96097

Call Sign: K6CEI
Robert L Hickerson
5309 Schulmeyer Rd
Yreka CA 96097

Call Sign: KE6DNF
Harold O Peery
815 North St
Yreka CA 96097

Call Sign: KE6JCN
Richard L Stuck
616 Oakwood Ln
Yreka CA 96097

Call Sign: NB6W
James R Scott
711 South St
Yreka CA 96097

Call Sign: N6BQS
Ronald P Dorris
1101 North St
Yreka CA 96097

Call Sign: W6GEF
Lauren H Clark
1005 Quarry Cir
Yreka CA 960979432

Call Sign: KF6HYE
Jerry P Hardy
4202 State Hwy 263
Yreka CA 96097

Call Sign: KE6ZRY
William D Kesner
812 Northridge Ct
Yreka CA 96097

Call Sign: KG6JSB
William R Wise III
201 Rose Ln Apt B
Yreka CA 96097

Call Sign: KB6USP
Orion J Dix
802 Sutter
Yreka CA 96097

Call Sign: KA7NPI
Thomas P Pelsor
1201 Northridge Dr
Yreka CA 96097

Call Sign: W6DFL
William R Maginnis
1230 Rt 263
Yreka CA 96097

Call Sign: KC6EBX
Ira R Anthony Jr
810 Terrace Ct
Yreka CA 960972143

Call Sign: NT6N
Thomas P Pelsor
1201 Northridge Dr
Yreka CA 96097

Call Sign: KJ6PZY
David W Weiler
816 S Oregon St
Yreka CA 96097

Call Sign: KI6NB
Jan H Blomquist
1000 Terrace Dr
Yreka CA 96097

Call Sign: KE6DES
James L Jacobsen
903 Oak St
Yreka CA 96097

Call Sign: W2JLR
David W Weiler
816 S Oregon St
Yreka CA 96097

Call Sign: KE6JCO
Francis G Palmer
1001 Terrace Dr
Yreka CA 96097

Call Sign: N6RHI
Michael D Maloney
2520 Oak Valley Dr
Yreka CA 96097

Call Sign: WA6HVC
John W Batts
814 S Oregon St
Yreka CA 960973306

Call Sign: WB6WZO
Ronald B Washington
2412 W Hwy 3
Yreka CA 96097

Call Sign: KI6LPW
Nolan S Maloney

Call Sign: KF6QBH
Bernie F Paul

Call Sign: KF6DPM
Lynn A Peterson

704 W Lennox
Yreka CA 96097

Call Sign: KF6BAH
William L Gardner
704 W Lennox St
Yreka CA 96097

Call Sign: KF6DPN
Jonathan W Gardner
704 W Lennox St
Yreka CA 960972350

Call Sign: N6SYN
Peter Warshaw
208 Wetzel Way
Yreka CA 96097

Call Sign: KD6YIO
William E Leigh
5430 Woodland Dr
Yreka CA 96097

Call Sign: KC6WTG
Ronald C Carver
Yreka CA 96097

Call Sign: N6BIO
Normond L Girard
Yreka CA 96097

Call Sign: K6WTG
Ronald C Carver
Yreka CA 96097

Call Sign: KG6MQT
Sandra S Elam
Yreka CA 96097

Call Sign: KJ6UYR
Peter J Fennell
Yreka CA 96097

Call Sign: KI6MQX
John R Hasemeyer

Yreka CA 96097

Call Sign: KI6RTL
Kash E Hasemeyer
Yreka CA 96097

Call Sign: KJ6CHQ
Joshua A Kiser
Yreka CA 96097

Call Sign: K6ZZA
Bill P Sowle
Yreka CA 960970448

Call Sign: K6ZZA
Alice Sowle
Yreka CA 96097

Call Sign: KI6OVK
Alice F Sowle
Yreka CA 96097

Call Sign: N6TIL
Kevin J Stensether
Yreka CA 96097

Call Sign: KD6GAH
Vurl L Trytten
Yreka CA 96097

Call Sign: K6VRL
Vurl L Trytten
Yreka CA 96097

Call Sign: KG6ZEF
Jacob S Vance
Yreka CA 96097

Call Sign: WD6FTU
William R Wise Jr
Yreka CA 96097

Call Sign: KB6W
William R Wise Jr
Yreka CA 96097

FCC Amateur Radio Licenses in Zenia

Call Sign: W6NNA
Edward F Burgess
Star Rt 1 Box 37
Zenia CA 95495

Call Sign: K6TWR
Howard E Benninghoven
Route 1 Box 38
Zenia CA 95595

Call Sign: KJ6KZJ
Brian L Craig
Zenia CA 95595

Call Sign: K6FTY
Brian L Craig
Zenia CA 95595